LASHED BY A TEMPEST

The Story of Kate Farmer Morgan

Ghost of the Hotel del Coronado

Elizabeth McGovern

HER FRIENDS CALL HER "THE DEL"

There is a formidable Victorian hotel clad in thick white planking and exterior-facing verandas. She arrived in 1888 and sits towering over the Southern California Coast. She wears a variety of bright red hats: some conical, some rectangular in form, some oblong, and some adorned with cupolas and small white dormers that peer in all directions. Her flags sit atop the highest points, snapping in a never-ending dance with the wind. She stands beside her benevolent friend, the Pacific Ocean, who pays her eternal homage through his rhythmic bows, as he eagerly reaches out for a chance to touch her. Inside her walls, she holds the stories of days gone by: Presidents who stayed in her beds, royalties who banqueted her halls, a celebration of Lindbergh's first solo flight, entertainers and socialites who complimented her beauty with equally ornate dress.

Along with all of this magic, she carries a secret. A secret that is held in the very confines of her wooden soul. A scene in which the very beams of her magnificent constitution have not yet been fortunate to shake.

Author: Elizabeth McGovern

Publisher: Elizabeth McGovern

Editor: Alicia Guide

Lashed by a Tempest: The story of *Kate Farmer Morgan, Ghost of the Hotel del Coronado* / Elizabeth McGovern

Based on the true story of Kate Farmer Morgan | Includes bibliographical references.

Historical Non-Fiction, 19th Century, Crime, Biography, Suicide, Murder, Unsolved Mystery, Paranormal.

ISBN 979-8-9929809-2-9 (Print)

First Edition

Book Cover Design: by Getcovers

elizabethmcgovern.author@gmail.com

https://elizabethmcgovernbooks.com

Author's Note

Lashed by a Tempest, the story of Kate Farmer Morgan, was written using a combination of historical documents, news and other media available to me at the time of this writing. While I have used my best efforts in capturing all of the truths related to this story, I make no representation or warranties to the accuracy or completeness of the contents.

In addition, the process I used in writing this book interweaves portions of news articles with my own words in order to provide a clean flow to the story. In those instances, there will be no quotation marks used. It is not my intention to take personal credit for their work. It is done with the utmost respect for their elegantly-crafted writing and to enrich the reader's experience. The source locations for the articles can be found in the bibliography section at the back of this book.

Warning: This book contains stories related to suicide. Readers who have experienced suicidal thoughts or know someone who has attempted suicide may find the content disturbing. If you are in crisis, please call the National Suicide Prevention Lifeline at 988.

CONTENTS

Part I

The Scene

Deputy Coroner Stetson

On March 4, 1892, Mr. Collins, the president of the California National Bank, had been confined to his room on the third floor of the Hotel Brewster on charges of embezzlement of $200,000 of the bank's funds. He was held on $50,000 bail, which he was unable to furnish. Collins had been confined to his hotel room for more than a week awaiting his preliminary hearing that was scheduled for the following Wednesday but that morning things changed. The United States district attorney ordered Marshal Gard to bring Collins back to Los Angeles. Marshal Gard was reluctant to deliver the news immediately and decided to give Collins the news after he had lunch. During his lunch, Collins was in good spirits, shaking hands and chatting with friends inviting some to his room, but his spirits changed when he was informed to pack; he must return to Los Angeles on the 2:40 p.m. train.

Mr. Collins called for his friend Ed O'Brien, a cashier of the California National Bank, to convince Marshal Gard to postpone the departure and then telephone Harry and George, a banker and cashier respectively, and tell them to hurry up and complete the bonds.

After Ed left Gard, Judge Wilson stopped in to have a word with him. Suddenly, Wilson and Gard heard a shot. They immediately ran to Collins' room but didn't find him. When they flung open his bathroom door, Collins was on the floor, blood flowing from his mouth and a smoking revolver in his hand.

The news spread quickly and within five minutes the Brewster's rotunda was filled with a crowd of anxious and concerned men.

When Deputy Coroner Stetson and Dr. Fred Baker arrived, they pushed their way through the men to get to the third floor and investigate.

Stetson looked down at the body of Collins and could not believe what he saw. Here was a man who not long ago had control of millions of dollars and held respect from everyone in the community and now he was laying in a pool of self-inflicted blood.

H.J. Stetson was a young 25-year-old man who came to San Diego from Modesto some five years earlier. He was new to his job, having received his appointment to deputy coroner just a week prior, and it took little time for him to be thrust into the world of unnatural deaths.

In less than a week after Collin's death, Stetson was called again to another death that took place at the foot of Sixth Street, near the shore end of a walk leading to an outhouse. No one saw the shooting, but they heard the shot and found the man lying on his back. Directly under him was a long-barreled, old-fashioned 32-caliber revolver. The man was George Golden, a native of Ireland, and a shot in his mouth was the cause of his death.

When Stetson went through Golden's pockets, he found a small diary with the following passage written:

"Wells Fargo clerk is the cause of this. He told me to put my money in the bank that failed. He said it was the place they had done business with, November 11, 1891. M.L. Rawson, the lawyer, has got my account. Mr. Peters of the Manvel will tell you all. San Diego is a good place to stay away from, nothing but swindlers of any use in this cursed place. I served in the Navy during the war and was at the taking of Richmond. I was in the Mendota (USS Mendota was a steamer built for the Union Navy). I lost $1,300 in that bank one hour before it closed. -G. Golden"

A third call came, less than a week later. Stetson was called to examine the death of Judge J.A. Dillar in another apparent suicide. At 11:30 that morning in the canyon near the corner of Ninth and Cedar streets, it appeared Dillar had also placed a revolver in his mouth and took his life. He used a 41-caliber British Bulldog revolver. Judge Dillar was a 45-year-old man who came to San Diego from Wellington, Kansas six years earlier. He had a wife and three children. He came with a large sum of money, some being his mother's, and invested in properties during the boom, but during the following six years, the properties depreciated and he lost nearly all of his money. Before he took his life, he left a letter to his mother explaining his financial condition. Deputy Stetson examined the judge's body and removed items from his pockets as evidence before his body was removed to the undertaker.

With each death, Stetson had to impanel a jury and hold an inquest. Witnesses were called, evidence was examined and the proceedings were recorded. For each case, the jury would make their determination on the cause of death. Death certificates would be issued and Stetson would submit his bill to the city of San Diego. A coroner was paid a set sum of around $8 per case in the late nineteenth century.

By early May, three witnesses brought accusations against Deputy Coroner Stetson to the district attorney. The witnesses reported that they were positive they saw gold pieces in a buckskin purse which Deputy Coroner Stetson had collected from the pocket of the deceased Judge Dillar. The value of the gold pieces, which were not reported in the dead man's effects, equaled about $25.

Stetson was surprised when he was arrested, but in a half-cocky way treated the matter lightly. He believed he would have no difficulty proving his innocence.

When Stetson was called to his preliminary hearing on the thirteenth of May, J.A. Davis was the first to testify to what he witnessed. He observed Stetson take from one pocket two silver dollars, a 25-cent piece, a nickel, a bunch of keys, and a pistol cartridge. From another pocket he took a buckskin purse containing a $20 gold piece, a $5 gold piece and a slip of paper. He was positive as to the amount and that it was gold. He did not see Stetson put the purse back in the pocket. The same testimony was said by two other witnesses, Dow and Richardson, and all three were positive they saw gold in the purse when Stetson opened it.

Mr. Dorsey, an agent for the deceased, testified that Stetson had turned over to him a purse that contained $2.95 and asked him for a receipt of the cash amount for which Dorsey provided. Dorsey said Stetson then instructed him to return the purse so Stetson could hold it as evidence. J.A. Davis countered that testimony, though. Davis said he heard Dorsey telling Stetson that if he had any more money in his possession belonging to the deceased, he had better turn it over, as there was likely to be trouble over the matter.

On Stetson's defense, Chief of Police Brenning testified that he saw Stetson with the purse in his hand but only saw two silver pieces. Then Stetson took the stand. He explained that during his examination of the body, he found in one pocket $2.95 in change and other articles previously enumerated. In another pocket, he found a purse containing a Wells Fargo receipt, some postage stamps, and other papers. He put the Wells Fargo receipt, stamps and other papers in his own pocket and put the change in the purse.

Judge Sloane spent nearly two hours speaking to all on the case and concluded that Stetson's reputation as an honorable man outweighed the likelihood of doing such a dastardly and cowardly thing as to steal gold from a dead man's body; he discharged Stetson from the charges.

Deputy Coroner Stetson breathed a sigh of relief but his reputation was back in question when the embezzlement charges returned again on June 17. The grand jury had reviewed the case and a bench warrant was sent for his arrest. Sheriff Folk served an indictment issued by Judge Puterbaugh. Stetson's $1,500 bail was furnished by P.M. Johnson of Johnson & Co Undertakers, and W.J. Davis, an auction house owner, and Stetson were released on bond.

Within a week of his release, Stetson was called once again to another body found on a beach. A group of women, who were enjoying a picnic party that afternoon, were out gathering wildflowers about a mile south of Ocean Beach. When they looked over the edge of their 30-foot-high bluff, they saw a body entangled in seaweed. Startled, they called for the gentlemen who were there with them. The men took a look using a powerful marine glass and made out the details of what they saw. It appeared to be the body of a headless woman. The feet were twisted in such a manner as to indicate that the ankles were broken. The body was entirely naked with the exception of one stocking, which was down around one foot. The flesh was entirely gone. In the left breast, they plainly saw a knife wound.

When Stetson and Constable Tom Weller arrived, they had a look and realized there was nothing they could do without a rope, so they arranged to return the next morning to secure the body and take it to the undertaker.

That following morning, they brought ropes, which they used to lower themselves down to the body. The body had been decomposing rapidly and the remains were very offensive. Stetson and Weller tied the remains to a plank and with one end of the rope, they made their way back to the top. With the other end, they hauled up the body. The body was so decomposed, the horrific sight and smell made them sick.

Stetson recorded as much as he felt possible. Her feet were small with high insteps and the general contour of the headless body indicated that of a woman. The breasts and flesh had fallen completely away from the chest, obliterating the knife wound that was plainly discernible at the time the body was found. There was no trace of clothing anywhere in the vicinity and as there was no possible chance to identify the body that afternoon, it was buried at the top of the cliff and marked by a plain wooden slab bearing the inscription "Found drowned. Unknown."

Stetson returned two days later and brought an impaneled jury to the bluff to conduct an inquest. He was joined by Dr. Mertzmann, Justice Sloane, a stenographer and several others who volunteered to come as well.

While the ocean breeze assisted in reducing the fumes, the sickly smell was still nauseating once the body was exhumed. Dr. Mertzmann proceeded to examine the body. He pronounced the remains were that of a man about five foot, seven inches in height. The sock found on the body was identified by Mrs. Curtis as one worn by her husband. The jury concluded it was Benjamin Curtis, and the cause of death unknown but presumably from drowning.

On the ninth of July, Stetson was back in the courtroom. His attorney J.S. Callen made motions related to flaws in the grand jury. He told the judge that Mr. C.E. Heath was not a proper juror because of his inability to find the indictment raised without showing partiality and prejudice. He said Fred W. Swope was not a proper juror because he was a deputy sheriff of the county. He claimed that seven of the jurors were neither drawn from the jury box nor selected by the sheriff of this county and therefore they were "pretend jurors." The judge denied his motions for dismissal and proceeded with the trial anyway.

In the courtroom that day, the final testimony on Stetson's embezzlement case was heard. Little Robbie Dillar, the son of the late judge, testified he saw his father place gold pieces in his purse on the morning he died, but said the purse in evidence was not the same purse he saw his father use. With that testimony, Deputy Coroner Stetson was acquitted of the crime of embezzlement. Stetson left the courtroom content with the judgement but the idea that there were individuals in that town trying to ruin his reputation and career left him unsettled.

In less than a week after the trial, Stetson was back on another assignment. He was called out to La Mesa on a fatality there. Henry Lester, a 17-year-old boy, had been crushed by some falling timbers. Henry was working with his father to tear down a house for Mrs. Tripp, who had hired the two. Henry and his father had managed to get 14 square feet of the flooring propped up on the edge of the wagon when the father left to get some tools from the house. While in the house, Mr. Lester heard a crash and ran back to see his son pinned and bleeding under the heavy flooring. When neighbors came to help lift the flooring off the boy, it was too late.

The Lester family had been followed by a series of strange fates. Mr. Lester and his wife and two sons emigrated from England. They first settled in Kansas when shortly after their arrival their younger son fell from a tree and broke his neck. They moved to New Mexico where the wife was literally frightened to death by local Native Americans. The father then took his son Henry and moved to Los Angeles, where he bought a small ranch by a river south of the city. After settling on the ranch, the dike in the river broke and a flood washed the ranch away. They then lived a nomadic life, wandering from place to place. The boy Henry was heir to $40,000 left to him by an English relative and to be paid on his attaining his majority (21 years old). From that, a small annuity was paid, which they subsisted on comfortably.

When Stetson arrived, the father was frantic with grief. Barefooted, Mr. Lester was pacing up and down in front of the cabin in which the body of his son was lying, refusing to allow anyone to enter. He raved and threatened to take his own life until the officers finally took possession of all of his firearms. Once Stetson was able to look over Lester's son he concluded the boy had died from a crushed skull and a broken neck. The neighbors around the home asked Stetson if an inquest would really be necessary since it was obviously an accident. Stetson agreed and had the boy's body brought to the city of San Diego in preparation for a funeral.

At the end of July, Deputy Stetson received a telephone message that a young girl had been shot and killed in Jamacha, just east of Spring Valley and fifteen miles southeast of San Diego. Stetson immediately drove to the scene.

W.S. Clark, the girl's father, was working on a move with his wife and nine children from the Stonewall Mine east of Lake Cuyamaca to Jamacha, a 40-mile distance. They had brought the four oldest children with them, along with some of their furniture, on their first trip. They went back to Stonewall mine for more of their things, leaving the four children there in Jamacha. Soon after they left, the oldest boy took an old double-barreled shotgun and accompanied by the other three, went out to shoot doves. After firing one of the barrels, the hammer flew off of the gun. He sat down to make repairs and his sister helped by holding the muzzle in her lap. While the boy was pounding on the lock, the left barrel discharged, lodging the contents into his sister's thigh. The boy ran for help and brought back several neighbors, but his sister had lost so much blood she was weak and soon died.

When Stetson arrived, he determined the young girl had died from shock and that an inquest was not necessary. He had her body removed and sent to the undertaker in preparation for a burial.

Things quieted down for Stetson until mid-October when a man and his wife were found slain at their home in Otay. At the central station, Stetson received a telephone message related to the double murder and he left at once. Stetson was followed by the Deputy District Attorney Frank Goodbody, who brought with him a *San Diego Union and Daily Bee* reporter.

On their way, they passed Deputy Constable Tom Smallcomb who was driving a two-horse farm wagon. On the bed of hay were three Native Americans securely bound. Two were crouched in a sitting position. The third man was stretched at full length on the hay and had a severely battered head swathed in bandages and covered by a coat. Smallcomb stated that the man lying there was the murderer and his name was Indian Joe. Indian Joe was about five foot eight inches tall, roughly 175 pounds, with a solid, muscular frame and a face with prominent cheekbones tapering to a pointed chin that held a tuft of beard tinged with gray. He had to have been in severe pain but he did not show it. Not a word uttered, his small snake-like eyes took in everything by furtive glances. Smallcomb was taking the three men to the county jail.

It took Stetson a while to reach the "Big Mesa," which was eight miles east of Otay. They passed orchards and vineyards of pastoral beauty. The serene quietness was only broken by the sounds of laughter from the nearby grape pickers. They had to request a local postmaster to help guide them to their final location. A small cottage seen across the broad, level mesa, near the eastern edge. That was the residence of Mr. and Mrs. John J. Geiser.

John Geiser was aged 66 and his wife 72 and both had moved there a few months ago from Nebraska. They had purchased a five-acre tract, erected the small cottage and began improvements with the expectation of living there through their senior years.

In the front of their cottage, on the freshly graveled walk, lay the bodies of Mr. and Mrs. Geiser. Mrs. Geiser was partly doubled, her head resting on her arm, her feet near the door, her silver hair clotted with blood. Mr. Geiser's feet lay close to Mrs. Geiser's head; his head had a gash in the front, while the back had been pounded to a pulp. Brain matter was found close to the walk. The weapons lay nearby, one a greasewood club two inches in diameter and the other a 2x4 covered in blood.

Indian Joe had been a laborer in that vicinity for several years. He was contracted to build a cistern at the Geiser's property. The news reporter covering the story reported that the citizens of Otay missed their opportunity to have lynched the murderers. Now the murderers would be held in custody for trial.

Stetson completed the inquest into the Geiser couple's death but his work would not end there. He would be called regularly in the ongoing murder trial of Indian Joe that would run through the end of that year and into the next.

Two more untimely deaths occurred that November and those would conclude Stetson's investigations for the year. An unknown man of Mexican descent had apparently died by suicide on the Alpine Road, three-quarters of a mile east of Lakeside. The other was a woman found dead on the beach steps of the Hotel del Coronado.

Drenched in Black

It was a foggy and drizzly morning that Tuesday, November 29. David Cone, an electrician for the Hotel del Coronado, was making his rounds along the oceanside walkway, trimming the arc lamps that illuminated the exterior. Each lamp sat atop a pole that rose more than 15 feet and was equipped with short metal pegs, which David used to climb and adjust. When he approached the lamp located near the northwest corner of the hotel, something caught his eye. Among a landscape of diffused beige colors of sand, white painted rails and the soft browns of the shell walk, was a splash of black. Thinking it was a clump of seaweed that washed up from the terrible storm the night before, he focused his eyes on it and caught the glimpse of a pale, delicate hand. David quickly ran to have a closer look. There on the steps leading to the beach was a dead woman with a rusty revolver laying near her right hand. A sense of urgency took over, and he rushed to notify the chief clerk.

While on his way, David ran into Frank, the gardener. Quickly David told him what he had just found and they both ran back to see the body. Frank immediately became concerned that the hotel guests might see the body, too. While Frank ran to the garden shed to grab a tarpaulin, David doubled back to notify the chief clerk.

Frank carefully laid the cover over the body and stayed to watch over her under the gloominess of that gray morning. The faint sounds of rain were softly tapping on the newly laid tarp when a loud sound of crashing waves jolted his body. The hair rose on his arms and he became acutely aware of what lies before him.

When Chief Clerk Gomer arrived, he peeked under the tarp. He knew who she was but remained quiet. "Could you please stay with the body? I need to wire the coroner," Gomer asked.

Frank stammered a hesitant, "Yes."

Deputy Coroner Stetson was at his office when he received the telegram from Gomer with the news of the woman. He quickly told the Western Union messenger to notify Johnson's Undertakers to meet him at the Hotel del Coronado. With that, Stetson grabbed a coat, hat and bag and headed to the wharf to catch the ferry.

When Stetson boarded the ferry, he was joined by a *San Diego Union* news reporter. The ferry ran on a schedule every day between San Diego and Coronado, but for Stetson the ferry driver didn't linger to wait on more passengers; it immediately disembarked. The bay water was placid that morning and the ferry rode smoothly along. The remnants of the storm from the night before were on display as the water's surface was dotted with small, round splashes. The ferry took roughly 10 minutes to arrive at the Coronado side of the bay. The men transferred over to the Orange Street Electric Trolley, which ran for another 10 minutes until it reached its final stop near the Hotel del Coronado.

Once they entered the hotel's rotunda, they were met by Chief Clerk Gomer. "Hello, I'm Deputy Coroner Stetson," as he reached his hand out to Gomer.

This was the first time they had met each other and it may have surprised Gomer that Stetson was such a young man. Gomer introduced himself and asked them to follow as he began to escort them down the stairwell located across from the check-in desk. On the floor below was a wide corridor lined with various shops that ended at the hotel's saloon. The room was softly lit by the morning's gray rays. The large windows displayed a mesmerizing view of the Pacific Ocean. To the left was a bar made of rich and dark ornately carved wood. A mirror-covered wall behind it lit up a myriad of blue and gold glass liquor bottles. The men continued to follow Gomer as they skirted around large, delicately carved posts and small, round tables that were scattered about the room. He opened a door and led them out onto the shell walk. They followed him northward alongside the hotel's western face, and just past the end of the hotel, on a set of concrete steps leading down to the beach, was a tarp-covered body.

A small number of hotel guests had already started gathering there in curiosity. Frank carefully removed the tarp and Deputy Coroner Stetson began to assess what he saw. She was still seated on the steps with her upper torso slumping slightly over to her right side. Her right arm lay along the steps and a rusting gun sat one step below her hand. He picked up the gun with two fingers, looking for anything unusual to note. He placed it in his bag and jotted notes of its type and location. He checked the dress pockets and pulled out a purse. He nervously glanced up at the inquisitive crowd, who were all watching his every move. He popped the purse open to have a look and then carefully placed it in his bag. He lifted the woman's arm and moved it a little forward and back. Grabbing the corner of the tarp, he drew it back over her body.

Stetson headed back to the bar to get away from the crowd and find a spot that would be warm and dry and Gomer followed.

Stetson looked at Gomer and started throwing questions at him: "Who is she? How long had she been at the hotel? Who was her family and where were they now?"

Gomer started spilling all that he knew. "Well, she came to the hotel on Thanksgiving Day. She said her name was Lottie Anderson Bernard from Detroit. I don't know her or her family. She claimed she was waiting for her brother, who would be joining her, but the man never showed! She didn't have any luggage because she said her brother had the claim tickets. The bellboy and the housekeeper said she had been sick ever since she arrived. I asked the housekeeper to get her to see a physician but she wouldn't do it. She said her brother was a doctor. Then yesterday she fell into the bath drenching her head and hair and she called the bellboy to help dry her hair! I went up to ..."

But he was cut off. Not by Stetson who was just listening to all of Gomer's rants. No, instead it was the reporter who asked, "Do you think she was attempting suicide in the bath?"

Gomer answered, "It could be possible! Her hair was drenched to the roots! The bellboy helped rub her head because she said she was too weak to do it herself!"

"I just received a telegram this morning from a bank in Hamburg, Iowa to authorize a draw of cash on her behalf," Gomer added.

"She also had money in her purse so she was not short of money!" Stetson added.

The reporter was about to ask another question but Stetson cut him off. "Was that money coming directly from her family?"

Gomer replied, "No, just yesterday she asked me to request funds from a man named G.L. Allen from Hamburg, Iowa."

"Is Mr. Allen related to her?" Stetson asked.

"I don't know," Gomer replied.

"Wire them back and tell them of her death and ask them to notify us to make arrangements for her body. Be sure they copy the coroner's office with the information," Stetson ordered.

Stetson looked out of the windows and realized Johnson Undertakers had just arrived and he went out to have a few words with them. When he returned he gave another order to Gomer. "I would like to see her room now."

When Lottie's room door opened, Stetson immediately noticed the room was relatively clean. The bed was nicely made. He looked at the fireplace mantle and saw a woman's black hat there leaning against the wall. A large bottle was on the other end and he picked it up, sniffed and placed it back down noticing a small pen knife that was lying beside the bottle. *Nothing interesting*, he thought. He squatted down at the fireplace. A thick block of light gray ash lay there. *Looks like a large pile of papers were burned.* He poked the ash in an attempt to see if he could find pieces that he could read but instead it collapsed into a small cloud of gray dust that immediately clung to his pants. *Burned beyond recognition*, he thought as he stood back up. He bent over and attempted to brush the gray dust off, only getting it on his hands too. Near the room's door was a table with paper and envelopes and a satchel sitting on the floor beside it. He opened the satchel and looked at its contents. He reached in, pushing a few small bottles around. He pulled out a piece of paper and saw it was an invitation to the Hotel del Coronado. He continued rummaging and pulled out a scrap of paper that was curled to the shape of a small bottle of some sort with a note written on it. *Nothing much here*, and he returned the small note and invitation back into the satchel. He looked at the envelopes and papers on the desk and picked them up, reading each one, and then placing them inside the satchel. He returned to the fireplace and collected those things. He looked in the closet where he saw a night dress hanging but left it there. He jotted notes and then clasped the notebook shut and placed it in his bag.

As Stetson and Gomer were returning to the rotunda he explained, "I'm going to be holding the inquest tomorrow morning and I need you, the bellboy and anyone else who had any interactions with the woman to be there."

"Yes, I'll be sure to be there and bring them with me," Gomer answered.

With that, Stetson grabbed his bag and evidence and headed out to return to San Diego. He wasn't finished yet. He had much more to do. He needed to secure a jury, arrange for an acting coroner to conduct the inquest, get a physician to examine the body, and entertain anyone else who might shed more light on the suicide and get it done before the end of the day.

THE INQUEST

The San Diego reporter had remained behind to gather more information about the unfortunate woman. When he returned to San Diego, he crafted a story with a certain level of empathy which was rarely seen from reporters of that day. He worked diligently to complete his story in time to make publication for the following morning.

"BY HER OWN HAND"

"Night before last an attractive, prepossessing and highly educated young woman came down from her room at Hotel del Coronado, and between 9 and 10 o'clock stepping out upon the veranda facing the ocean, which was roaring at her very feet, lashed by the tempest that is sweeping over the whole coast. The lady was quietly and elegantly dressed in black and wore only a lace shawl over her head. Nothing more was seen of her until at 8:20 yesterday morning, when the assistant electrician of the hotel, passing by the shell walk at the end of the western terrace, saw the lady lying on the steps leading to the beach. She was dead, and an American Bulldog revolver was lying within two inches of her outstretched right hand. A ragged wound showed on the right temple, but the rain had washed away all stains of blood. Her body was soaking wet, stiff, and cold. Deputy Coroner Stetson was notified, and he had the body removed to Johnson & Co's undertaking rooms in this city before many of the guests of the hotel were stirring.

The young woman came to the hotel on Thanksgiving Day, and registered as 'Mrs. Lottie A Bernard, Detroit.' She was reserved and ladylike. Her clothing was fine, but she had no baggage except a small handbag. She kept her room most of the time, and was visited often by the housekeeper, who learned that she was afflicted with cancer of the stomach. She said she was 24 years old, and spoke often of her physical condition, and was noticeably despondent, sometimes seeming to verge on melancholia, as when on one occasion she told the housekeeper that she was also troubled with heart disease and despaired of recovering her health.

There are signs pointing to an attempt on her part to commit suicide on Monday afternoon by means of drowning in her bath. She told the housekeeper that she proposed to take a warm bath for two hours or more and said it would help her. The matron remonstrated, saying it would weaken her, but the lady persisted, and the bath was prepared. At the end of an hour, however, she appeared and sent for the bell boy to rub her head. It was then noticed that her hair was drenched to the roots, an unusual incident, and that her manner was nervous and unstrung.

Undoubtedly the lamentable suicide was the despairing act of one suffering from incurable disease, perhaps induced from depression of spirits caused by utter loneliness. It is understood that she was expecting a brother to arrive at the hotel, and she was anxiously awaiting his coming. Monday morning, she inquired of a bell boy if he had arrived, and receiving the usual discouraging answer, she said, 'Oh, no one comes to me anymore!' She then nerved herself to the final act, burning all her letters and papers, except an envelope addressed to 'Mrs. Lottie Anderson, Bernard,' and on which she had casually scribbled as if in reverse, her own name. 'Coronado,' 'Lillian Russell,' and 'I don't know any such man.' The dreary day perhaps added to her despondency, and at night she went out to the heart of the storm, within fifteen feet of the ocean's edge and took her life.

In her purse was found something over $20, and she seemed in no stress for money, having telegraphed to a Mr. Allen at Hamburg, Ia., and received his answer that she could draw on him for $50 on sight. Her bill at Coronado was not presented, as she had not been there a week.

A telegram was sent to Mr. Allen, to notify her relatives there and in Detroit, and the authorities will await their instructions as to the disposal of the remains. Deputy Coroner Stetson also wired Coroner Kellar, at Escondido, and receiving no response will empanel a jury this morning and hold an inquest."

-*San Diego Union and Daily Bee*, Vol XXVII, Num 8751, 30 November 1892.

The news had been read by many in San Diego that morning, including those who attended the inquest. One witness pointed out that the only way he knew her name was through the news that was published that morning. Is it possible the details from that story have had any effect on what witnesses recalled? A witness's memory can be distorted and less accurate when they learn of new information related to an event. It is referred to as the "misinformation effect" and often, today, can disqualify a juror or witness. That was not known in the late nineteenth century and one detail related to Kate's health will appear in some of their testimonies.

A coroner's inquest in the nineteenth century is not much different than it is today. The inquest is an investigation to determine cause of death in cases that are unnatural, unexplained or suspicious. It is a fact-finding process done in a court with a jury. It is not a criminal proceeding but only done for the purpose of establishing cause of death.

Deputy Coroner Stetson made arrangements for W.A. Sloane to be the acting coroner for the inquest. They had worked together all year and Stetson trusted Sloane, especially after Sloane had defended his honor in the embezzlement trial. Mr. Sloane was not only a San Diego justice of the peace but also an attorney-at-law, and he resided at 2222 C. Street.

Nine jurors were selected: E.A. Stevens, who was living at the Llewelyn Building, T.J. McCord, who was employed by Howard & Lyons at the Gilbert Building, a rancher named Frank Kemmer, William Cooper, who was a plasterer by trade, A.T. Randall, who was a local resident, J.S. Dowd, who worked at Star Stables as a liveryman, J.M. Spenser, who was an elderly retired man, L. Dampf, who worked in art goods, and Milton Lamb, a retired sailor.

The transcriber was W.W. Whitson and he made some mistakes that morning. Frank Heath's address was 1560 not 1516. Harry West's was 1925 not 2519 and B.F. Mertzmann's name ends with two Ns. Small, simple mistakes, but considering he took their testimony by shorthand, that might be to blame.

B.F. Mertzmann was also known as Frank Mertzmann and he was a homeopathic physician and surgeon. He was one of 90 local doctors that could be found in the San Diego city directory. He was also a co-partner with James Waide of Mertzmann and Waide Hay and Grain Company. His home was located at 1034 Fifth St., putting him relatively close to Johnson & Co. Undertakers at 907 Sixth St. He assisted Stetson with other examinations during that year and was once again called for this case.

Mertzmann testified that he was asked to examine the body that morning, right before the inquest, and the examination was completed 30 minutes before his testimony. His testimony certainly backed that statement. He focused his exam on the bullet entry to the right side of the head and the direction of slightly upward. He took a guess on the gauge of the ball that went in and then agreed it would match the gun in evidence. He concluded she died of hemorrhage of the brain.

He did not testify whether she had powder burns on the head or hand which would prove she shot herself and how close the gun was at discharge. He did not provide any other physical observations related to her body. Was the examination done before or after embalming? He did not present any of this and he wasn't asked either. He gave very minimal testimony.

There were three local San Diego City townspeople who also testified as witnesses. They were Martine Chick, who testified he sold her the gun, W.P. Walters, who was in the gun shop when she bought the gun, and Frank Heath of the Ship's Chandlery, where the woman asked if he sold gun cartridges. It was very convenient for Stetson to have found these three witnesses. Without their testimony there was no means to prove the gun was hers. San Diego was a small city in 1892 and the population was actually declining at that time, but there were still a lot of people who lived there. The first news published on the suicide wasn't until the morning of the inquest. Up until then, the news had travelled by word of mouth. How did these three townspeople realize the woman taken to the morgue the day before was a woman they did business with on Monday? When did they decide to place their eyes on her body even before the news was published on her death?

Martine Chick had been a gun shop owner for many years in San Diego. There was one other gun shop in downtown San Diego, The Leading Gun Store, with which he competed. Martine lived at 1663 Sixth Street.

Martine remembered selling a gun and cartridges that Monday to a woman who dressed a lot like the woman at the undertakers. He didn't remember her face well enough to be positive it was her but he was keen on the time she came to purchase it. He said she came in around 3 p.m. Monday. He also remembered the exact gun he sold to be a 44-caliber American Bulldog revolver and that he sold her two bits of cartridges. Martine admitted the gun was the same exact type as the one lying on the evidence table but wouldn't commit to it being the exact same gun sold.

A juror asked if he loaded the gun for her. Martine replied, with no, that he only turned the cartridge cover back to demonstrate how to load it. Martine recalled she was buying the gun as a Christmas present for a friend and he boxed the gun and she wrapped it up and that was how she took it away. He didn't recall any conversations or anything unusual about her. His testimony was short and simple.

W.P. Walters, a cabinet maker and furniture dealer at 657 5th St., and a nearby business neighbor to Chick's Gun Shop, happened to be in Chick's shop during her purchase.

Walters testified he recalled seeing her between 3 to 4 p.m. on Monday in the gun shop. He gave a great number of specific details on the whole process of her purchase. She entered the shop and walked slowly. She went directly to the gun counter. She wanted an inexpensive gun. She wanted cartridges. She handled the gun and asked how to load it. Martine showed her by placing a cartridge in and then removing it. She took it in her hand and tried to fire it but had a hard time. She wanted to know if it was hard to fire. Martine took the gun back from her and showed her by pulling the trigger, click, click, click. She tried again and achieved a click. Mr. Walters had far more detailed information about her purchase than Martine had. He also told the same story about the gun being boxed and wrapped.

After she had finished the purchase and stepped out from the gun shop, Mr. Walters remembered saying to a nearby man that she was going to hurt herself. The man also agreed.

Mr. Walters couldn't identify her by face, either. He said he never saw her, except from behind, but he did have a vivid memory about a black sealskin sacque or coat that she wore. A coat he remembered to be longer than the fashion of the day.

When she stepped away from Chick's gun shop, Mr. Walters asked a gentleman on the covered wooden walkway if he saw where she went. The gentleman said he believed she went into the Combination (A building containing various shops similar to today's mall but at a much smaller scale). It was located in the same block and on the same side of the street as Chick's gun shop. Mr. Walter's testified that he stood there watching for her and then observing her leave the Combination and cross the street to Schiller and Murtha's (a dry goods store in the same block.) Mr. Walters was patiently tracing her every move in what some would consider creepy in nature.

It was observed that Martine's testimony didn't include any gun safety tips for the young lady, either. He had to have noted her lack of gun handling experience. Couldn't he have at least told her not to fill all six chambers with cartridges so the pin was not resting on a live round? That is how accidental discharges occur! But Martine and Walters' testimonies both stated the gun had been boxed and wrapped as a gift and there should have been no more concerns that she would handle the gun after that. It begs the question as to why anyone would be worried she could hurt herself.

In California at that time, it was illegal to carry a concealed weapon and even more so if it were loaded. The fact that they both said it was boxed and wrapped would clear them of any responsibility for allowing the woman to purchase and leave with a loaded concealed gun in her pocket. That would have led to all sorts of questions from the jury. However, it would make sense why Walters said she was going to hurt herself. It would make perfect sense for him to follow where she was heading. Maybe he wondered if she was about to use it on someone. Maybe he wasn't a creep after all, but merely a concerned citizen.

Frank Heath worked as a clerk at the Chandlery store. Both Frank and his brother James worked there. Frank testified that after seeing her at the undertaker, he was certain he had seen her before. The time was between 4 and 5 p.m. on Monday. Frank recalled that she came into the store and asked if he carried revolver cartridges. He said she spoke so softly he could hardly hear her and she had to repeat the question four or five times before he understood her. He told her he did not carry cartridges and told her she could find that at Chick's Gun Shop. He said he pointed out to her where to find the shop, which was right across the street.

Frank testified she never mentioned how many cartridges or the size she wanted. She didn't go into those details. Instead, he recalled how nervous and excited she was and that he clearly identified her by her appearance and not by the clothes she wore. He said she looked very bad in her general appearance and that she walked slowly, as if she felt sick. He did not know who she was and where she went after that.

Frank Heath also didn't say she was carrying a package, one containing a gun wrapped up, which she had just bought at Chick's. He didn't mention that and he wasn't asked, either. That was because his testimony was done before Martine and Mr. Walters' testimony. The coroner and jury were not aware she should be carrying a package with a gun yet. It is very possible her nervous behavior might have been related to carrying a concealed, and probably loaded, weapon in her dress pockets. Her demeanor may have been the result of trying not to draw attention to herself. It seems curious why she believed two bits of cartridges (about 10 rounds) might not be enough and why she hoped to get more.

The Combination, Ship's Chandlery at 624 Fifth St, W.P. Walters' Furniture store at 657 Fifth St., Chick's gun shop at 641 Fifth St., and Schiller and Murtha's at 600 Fifth St, were all on the same block of Fifth Street between G and H Streets. They were all located five blocks north of the Ferry landing and were on the Fifth Street electric trolley line.

David Cone, F.W. Koeppen, T.J. Fisher, Harry West and A.S. Gomer were all employees of the Hotel del Coronado and some interacted with the woman in some manner during her short five-day stay.

In the search for records on David Cone, he could not be found in either census or city directories. Nothing was found in the San Diego papers of that time, either. Attempts to try alternative names such as Coen, Cohn or Cohen produced no results, either. No matter, this was how he presented himself at the inquest; his name was David Cone, electrician.

F.W. (Frank) Koeppen was the superintendent of gardens for the Coronado Beach Company. E.S. Babcock was its President and Babcock was also the General Manager of the Hotel Del Coronado. Most contractors and businesses used by the hotel were either owned or operated by Mr. Babcock.

David Cone and Frank Koeppen appear to be innocent bystanders. Both had little or no interaction with hotel guests. There was nothing unusual about their testimony. The electrician found the body and the gardener covered her up. Their reaction would match a reaction by anyone finding a body. Their details of the body matched the coroner perfectly: key evidence. They also said they had never seen her before: additional evidence. In the five days the woman was at the hotel wearing the same black dress, she was either not interesting enough to leave a lasting impression, or she simply didn't walk around the garden or beach area during those five days, maybe both.

T.J. Fisher said in his testimony that his occupation was real estate and his place of business was the hotel drugstore. T.J. said he saw the woman first on Saturday, when she came into the drug store and walked up and down the floor two or three times. She seemed to be suffering. He says she was looking for something to relieve her suffering and he referred her to Mr. Fosdick, the manager of the store. T.J. reported that Mr. Fosdick had advised her to see a physician but she told him she had a brother who was a physician and she was expecting him there.

T.J. said he didn't see her again until Monday. On Monday afternoon, she returned and walked up and down the floor again, still looking like she was suffering. Then he said to her that it seemed too bad she had to go into town in that stormy weather while suffering from neuralgia. She told him she was compelled to go. She forgot her baggage checks and had to go over and identify her trunks personally. When she left the store, it was the last time he saw her alive. Then yesterday he saw her dead body lying on the beach steps around 8:30 a.m. He said he didn't know her by name. He learned her name only through the newspaper that morning. T.J did not know the time of her death or anyone else who might know, either. T.J. was asked if he had heard the shot and he said no. Acting Coroner Sloane spoke up to explain they probably didn't hear the shot because it was near the ocean and the surf tended to prevent people from hearing. T.J.

agreed with him. T.J. also said he only knew of her malady based on her own words to him.

T.J. stated that he had little knowledge about Lottie other than the two times she dropped into the drugstore. He didn't know her name, or any specific details about her other than that. He also said his occupation was "real estate," but he had just gained that occupation on the first of November when he won a five-year contract to rent the hotel's pharmacy. Before that, he was the hotel's head bartender and had managed the bar and billiard rooms at the hotel since it opened in 1888.

Although T.J. made no mention of his past management of the saloon and bar in his testimony, he also didn't mention his wife Della Fisher was the Hotel del Coronado's "housekeeper." It is important to distinguish what the hotel housekeeper role was at the Hotel del Coronado in 1892. The housekeeper role was a management role over the hotel's chambermaids and other cleaning staff. T.J.'s wife was the hotel's "housekeeper" and she held that role for many years.

Della was not called to testify at the inquest, either. It raises the question as to why. In the news published that day and the following days, it shows the "housekeeper" had built a very close relationship with Lottie. Much of what was learned related to Lottie's health and her personal details were coming from the "housekeeper." Unfortunately, though, most of what was written as stories told by the "housekeeper" were actually coming from others who were passing on the information. It also begs the question as to why T.J. Fisher was testifying that he didn't know very much about Lottie.

Harry West worked at the Hotel del Coronado and answered that he lived at his parents' home at 1925 I Street (transcribed as 2519) between sixteenth and seventeenth. Considering his late hours and the limited means of transportation between Coronado and San Diego, he, too, might have been staying at the hotel. In the 1892 city directory, Harry was listed as an employee of Philips & Bone, a dry goods store. It was his previous employment before he was hired at the hotel.

When Sloane asked Harry if he knew her name he said, "No, sir." When Sloane asked how long she had been at the hotel, Harry answered since November 23. Sloane asked if that date was gathered from others or whether that was his own recollection. Harry answered that he saw it on the register. An unusual answer after stating he didn't know her name that was also written on that register.

West testified that he also observed her neuralgia and that she was very sick from day one. She spent the majority of her time in bed. He saw her lying in her bed moaning and waking up moaning; she told him she expected her brother, a doctor, to arrive to take care of her.

When West was asked if she sent him for medicines or anything else, West replied, "Not by me. Let's see, today is the 30th. On the 26th, she sent me down to the drug store for an empty pint bottle and a sponge, and that is the only thing she sent me for. She sent me to the bar twice."

"What for?" Mr. Sloane asked.

West explained, "Liquors. She sent me once for a glass of wine, and once for a whiskey cocktail. That was the day before yesterday."

Harry said she also requested a bath, which he prepared on that Monday morning. and she expected it to last a few hours. He provided her with a pitcher of ice water. Then she called him close to noon, asking for help to rub her hair. He says she explained to him what happened. She was so weak that when she stood by the tub, she fell in. He said he had rubbed her hair and got it dry and after this, she asked him to get her a whiskey cocktail.

The last time Harry said he saw her was that Monday evening at half past six. He saw her on the second-floor veranda. They asked Harry where her room was, relative to where her body was found. He explained her room was on the north side, and the body was found on the opposite side, but he pointed out to the Acting Coroner Sloane that he did not actually see the body that Tuesday morning.

Harry made a few mistakes related to dates. Her arrival date was wrong. She arrived on the 24th not the 23rd, but nobody caught that. He also answered "Yes" to seeing her last on Sunday, but the jury corrected his answer to Monday evening. Harry was probably nervous, though. He was not only in front of the justice of the peace and coroner's jury, but also the chief clerk of the hotel, Mr. A.S. Gomer.

Mr. Gomer also resided at the hotel. He can also be found in the 1894 San Diego City Directory as A.S. Gomer, Room Clerk for the Hotel del Coronado. It can be noted that in the 1880 Census, there is a record of Alonzo S. Gomer, who was born around 1856, living in Morris, New Jersey as a hotel resident. Later, after 1892, he is found working as a hotel clerk in New Orleans, and then in 1910, he is back in Morris, New Jersey working as a hotel clerk.

Mr. Gomer gave the most detailed stories about the suicide victim. It seemed very peculiar that a chief clerk, who was responsible for all the front desk employees and guaranteeing the best experience for a large number of hotel guests, had such finite details on this one young lady by the name of Lottie. He gave more details than Harry the bellboy, including details Harry had left out. He spoke for the housekeeper, Della. He spoke for another clerk who checked her in. He spoke for the house physician who was away the day the body was found. He spoke for the bank president who telegraphed approval for the funds. A lot of what is known about the last days of the unfortunate woman was painted by Mr. Gomer.

A.S. Gomer started off with the obligatory occupation as chief clerk and his residence, which was the hotel. He was new to his position saying he had been working there for only six or seven weeks. The coroner asked if he had seen the corpse and could he identify the remains? Mr. Gomer replied, yes, she was the one who had stopped there at the hotel.

After Mr. Gomer identified the body as a person he had seen, Mr. Sloane asked, "And what is the name?"

Mr. Gomer replied, "Well the only means, of course, that I have of knowing her name, is the manner in which she registered."

Sloane asked, "What name did she go by?"

Gomer responded, "Mrs. Lottie A. Bernard, Detroit."

Sloane asked, "Is that the way she registered?"

"She did not register herself. I was not in the office at the time of her arrival, but the young man there registered for her, at her request. That is the name she gave him," explained Gomer.

Acting Coroner Sloane was merely trying to establish the deceased's name for the record. Mr. Gomer, on the other hand, appeared to be avoiding any responsibility for validating it.

The next question posed by Sloane was a subjective one. "What do you know of her condition and circumstances during her stay at the hotel?"

"Well, all I know is that the young man spoke to me of her arrival when I came to the office that evening. Said there was a rather peculiar person that came in this afternoon, and I asked him to point her out to me, and between 7 and 8 o'clock she came along and he pointed her out. There was nothing said until the next morning, she came to me, asking my advice as to how she could get her baggage, which she claimed had been checked to San Diego, and the checks she said her brother had kept with him, and her brother had been called away from Orange, to either Los Angeles or Frisco, she in fact did not know where."

"From Orange?" asked Sloane.

"Yes, sir," replied Gomer.

"Did she speak of having come here to this place from Orange?" Sloane asked.

"That is the way her story began, Orange, she said Orange; her brother was obliged to leave her, to remain there, or go to Frisco, she didn't know which, and that she came on alone from Orange, and that her brother would be along that afternoon. That was the day after her arrival, and every day she inquired if her brother had arrived. She claimed that her brother was Doctor Anderson, and that the initials were M.C., I am not sure about that," said Gomer.

Sloane was now interested in learning more about her brother. He asked, "Did she state anything as to where he was, or as to where he had gone?"

"She didn't seem to know where he was," Gomer explained.

Sloane asked another subjective question: "What do you know of her circumstances financially, whether she was under financial embarrassment?"

Gomer told a rather long story to this question and not much was related to her financial situation. His testimony went as follows: "After the boy came to the office Monday, and asked for whiskey, I thought it necessary for someone to see her. The housekeeper had been trying to induce her to call the house physician; rather, I insisted that the housekeeper should persuade her to call the house physician, and see just what her condition was, and the housekeeper was unsuccessful; she kept telling the housekeeper that her brother was a physician, and that it was not necessary to call a physician, but after this boy, who just testified, came to the office and asked for whiskey, and said the lady had fell in the tub and wet her hair, I went up to her room myself, and suggested first, that we call the house physician. She was in bed then covered up, and she was totally opposed to calling the physician. It was a very gloomy, dreary sort of day, and she was on the east side of the house without any fire, and I suggested that she have a fire, and be made comfortable. She said no, she was very comfortable, as good as she could expect. She further told me that the doctors had given her up, that she had cancer of the stomach, and that her case was hopeless, but she told us in such an off-hand way that it did not appear suspicious to me, and I endeavored to find out something about her identity. On the table in her room were some letters. I could not find out the contents of them without picking them up, and of course that was out of order. The only thing I saw on the table were some envelopes, addressed to herself, and finally, after I found she was so much opposed to having the physician, I just put the question to her, if she had got her baggage over, and then I asked her if she was supplied with funds; that in her condition she must necessarily need some funds, and she said yes. Then I said to her, wouldn't it be a good plan to telegraph your brother. She said, 'I do not know where to find my brother, I do not know whether he is in Los Angeles, or Orange, or in Frisco.' Then I said, 'Is there no one else you could telegraph to for funds?'

and she suggested the name of G.L. Allen, Hamburg, Iowa, and at her suggestion, I wrote a telegram, and sent it to Hamburg, and left her then, in the room, that was about one o'clock, or half past twelve possibly, on Monday. And then the last time I saw her after that, the next time, and last, was that evening, about somewhere between seven and eight o'clock, she called at the office..."

Mr. Gomer's answer was cut off by Mr. Sloane who had another question, "Now what day was this?"

Mr. Gomer replied, "This was on Monday, she called at the office and inquired if there were any letters or telegrams for her. I said no, nothing, and went about doing something, and that was the last I saw of her until yesterday morning, this man done came to me and reported there was a corpse out on the ocean side of the house, and I immediately went out there, and of course discovered that it was this woman."

Mr. Gomer's story had revealed extraordinary details. He also revealed that his idea of Lottie was that she was not like their usual guests. She was "peculiar." It revealed that her order of whisky was the first thing on his mind that prompted him to see her personally. He revealed he and the housekeeper talked about her regularly. He also revealed that he had looked upon her belongings, and his story said it happened during his discussion with her that Monday. He revealed that he had inappropriately asked her if she had a supply of funds days before her bill would be due. He revealed that she was lying in bed under the covers sometime past noon, or close to 1 p.m., and although nobody seemed to find that unusual, the room had already been serviced that morning; so why did the bed look untouched on Tuesday morning? If the room had been cleaned Tuesday morning before the coroner looked at it, then why was there still ash in the grate of the fireplace?

Mr. Gomer appeared to use his testimonial time to establish his idea of the woman's character and that the suicide had been a problem that he had been dealing with ever since she checked in. In all this time, he still hadn't really shown proof that she was financially strained. Instead, what he did achieve was enough distraction to pique the curiosity of the coroner and jury. They started asking about the envelopes, papers, and whether there were addresses he could see on them.

Finally, Sloane asked Gomer if he received any reply to the telegram he sent to G.L. Allen.

Gomer answered, "Yes, yesterday morning as soon as the office opened, a telegram came from Hamburg, Iowa, signed by some bank, but I neglected to bring that telegram with me and forgot the name of the bank – saying that they would honor her draft for $25. Show this to the bank. Then I immediately telegraphed to the same party that this person had suicided on the hotel grounds."

Finally, they discovered she had means and connections to cover her stay. Finally, they could set aside any questions they might have had about her identity. The approval of funds was in the name of Lottie Bernard after all. It must also be noted that Gomer testifies that the draft was for $25. The reporter had ascertained the day before that the draft was for $50 which is how he wrote it in his news story. Did Gomer conveniently forget that telegram?

Lottie's bill would not be due until Thursday, though. If the hotel decided to ask her to pay for what was owed on that Monday, it would be for four nights. The Hotel del Coronado had newspaper advertisements for room rates at three dollars a day or fifteen a week at that time. That would mean Lottie owed, at worst, $12 plus incidentals (her drinks etc.). Lottie had enough in her purse to cover those charges when Gomer visited her that morning. After his visit, she went into San Diego, she purchased a gun for around $3.50 and bought two bits (.25 cents) worth of cartridges. She paid for another round-trip ticket back to the hotel, which ran at least .25 cents, although it often cost as much as .60 cents. When her body was found the next morning, she still had $16.50 in her purse.

It doesn't seem reasonable for her to admit to needing funds and it doesn't seem reasonable for her to ask Gomer to request funds on her behalf. She was fully capable of making that request herself at the Western Union office in the hotel, but this was the story given by Mr. Gomer.

Mr. Gomer wasn't finished with his testimony. He felt a need to throw in one more piece of information, one more detail. Nobody asked him, but he felt a need to tell. Mr. Gomer said, "It seems that some time Monday afternoon–in relation to the papers, the memorandum–she rang her bell, and the bell was answered by the boy, she asked for a box of matches, but he said if she only wanted a few, he had a few in his pocket. She made the remark that she wished to burn some papers, so that may account for the disappearance of anything of the kind."

That unprompted piece of information Mr. Gomer decided to throw out there would start another round of questions from the acting coroner and jury. They asked if she had a fireplace in her room. They asked again about the envelopes and what addresses he could see on them. They asked if he had any idea on the immediate circumstances of her death. They asked him more about her brother and his name, but Mr. Gomer only knew his name was Doctor Anderson and he was a practicing physician in Indianapolis (later the news would write he was from Minneapolis). They asked him if he had notified the house physician, to which he replied that he could not reach him because he was off hunting. They asked if he had any idea how long she was dead and he said no.

Mr. Gomer seems to push a narrative that the woman was acting in a suspicious manner. She was not living by the laws set for women's behavior of that time. She was a "peculiar" and "sick" woman who was ordering bar drinks, alone, with no other man responsible for her. Even after he had received funds in the name of "Lottie," he still believed she was deceptively hiding her real identity and burning important papers. Indeed, Gomer's testimony went above and beyond the level of information needed to determine how the unfortunate woman had died. Mr. Gomer revealed something else. He revealed his fear. In the little time he had her at the hotel, she became a problem for him, a problem with which he was compelled to deal with.

Coroner's Testimony

Deputy Coroner Stetson was the last of the 10 who testified at the inquest. Sloane asked Stetson what his response was to the message that there was a dead person at the hotel. Stetson replied, "I went over and found the body covered, found the lady lying there covered with a tarpaulin. The undertakers came over on the next boat, and she was placed in the receiving box and brought to this city and taken to Johnson & Company's."

"Did you form any judgement as to how long she might have been dead?" Sloane asked.

Stetson replied, "She laid as though she might have been dead at least six hours – six or seven." He confirmed she was stiff and cold.

Stetson did not state the exact time of death and he did not provide the time he made that observation, either. We only know that at some point on the morning of Tuesday he believed her to be six or seven hours dead. Neither Acting Coroner Sloane nor the jury asked him to provide any further details of the exact time of death, either.

Stetson arrived about 30 minutes before the undertakers (equal to a round trip by the ferry) and testimony was given by Gomer that they removed the body around 9:30 or 10 that morning. That would mean that Stetson had examined the body sometime around 9 that morning.

Forensics have well documented that from the eighth to twelfth hour after death, the body becomes so stiff and rigid that it is nearly impossible to bend limbs. Stetson remarked that he judged the woman had died about six to seven hours based on "how she laid."

That would put the time of death sometime on Tuesday morning around 2 to 3 a.m.

Sloane asked Stetson if he did any examination of her effects in her room.

He replied, "Yes, sir, I found the things that are right there. I found that valise, and on the table I found this envelope she had addressed."

Sloane interrupted him and asked him to read it out loud.

Stetson began to read out loud all the different pieces of paper and envelopes that were laying on the evidence table. "Denman Thompson, the Old Homestead and Frank is written here four times, Lottie Anderson Bernard and Mrs. Lottie Bernard and Lottie Anderson Bernard, Detroit. Then on this paper I found, I merely heard of that man, I do not know him. Here is an invitation to the Hotel del Coronado, signed by Louise Leslie Carter, and Lillian Russell."

Sloane asked what the name on the handkerchief was. Stetson replied, "L-t-tle, I think it is, I cannot quite make it out, but the last name is Anderson. She had a purse on her person that contained $16.50, and there was a little ring in the purse, a plain ring, and the key to her valise."

Sloane asked, "Nothing else?"

Stetson replied, "Nothing else, just some.."

He was interrupted again by Sloane, "That is the purse, is it?"

Stetson was feeling uncomfortable with the narrowing question related to the purse, but he trusted Sloane had a reason for it. Stetson replied, "Yes, sir; that is the purse."

Sloane asked, "What else was in there?"

Stetson answered, "Just some handkerchiefs."

Sloane asked, "Nothing that would throw any identity upon where she was from?"

Stetson replied, "Not a thing. In the grate of the room, it looked as though quite a package of papers that had been burned, it was all in ashes, you might say. Whether she made them for a fire or what they might have been you could not tell, but they had all been burned."

Sloane asked him if he found any night clothes.

Stetson answered, "Just one night dress was hanging in the closet. The bed had not been touched at night. It was all made up; the hat lay on the mantle, a bottle, and a penknife. There was considerable medicine in there, a bottle of camphor and a bottle of alcohol."

Sloane picked up a large bottle and said, "This large bottle here?"

Stetson responded, "That is brandy, I think, or alcohol," Then he continued on, "..and some quinine pills. Then there is a little piece of paper. I found a piece of paper that had been wrapped around a bottle of some kind. It says if it does not relieve you, you better send for a doctor. It was just signed 'druggist,' but it did not say where it was from."

Sloane paused while the recorder feverishly finished his scribblings. Sloane then asked Stetson if he had received any information from the clerk at the hotel or anyone else.

Stetson replied, "Yes, I received word. I received a telegram in the morning to come over to Coronado immediately."

Sloane adjusted the question, "I mean with reference to parties to whom you were to telegraph in reference to her case?"

Stetson replied, "Yes, Mr. .." and Stetson paused. He couldn't recall Gomer's name.

Sloane speaks up, "What was the name, do you remember?"

Stetson continues, "The gentleman who just left the stand here, the clerk there (points to Gomer). He telegraphed I think it was Iowa, to the bank, and to those people to whom she had been writing, I do not know the name, he did the telegraphing. I asked him at the same time to just include for them to telegraph to the coroner, and he said he would, but there has been no reply."

Surprised, Sloane asked, "You have heard nothing whatsoever?"

"Not a thing, no, sir," Stetson replied.

Sloane was finding this information rather incredible. "No trace of her friends?"

Stetson shook his head, "No, sir."

A juror spoke up and asked, "Have you been to the baggage office, to find out whether she had any there or not?"

Confused, Stetson replied, "No, I have not been to the baggage, but she had no checks or anything put away, to know."

"She said her brother had the checks, but you do not know anything about whether she had baggage?" Sloane asked with utter disbelief.

Stetson responded, "No, sir, I do not know anything about it, I have not been."

Sloane turned to Mr. Marks. Mr. Marks was another deputy with the coroner's office. "Have you made any inquiry at all about it to any of the baggage men?"

Mr. Marks replied, "No."

Sloane paused and mulled over all that he had heard from everyone's testimony. Maybe he realized this wasn't a murder trial but only an inquest for determining the cause of death. He turned to the nine jurors. "I believe, gentlemen, we have got all the testimony we can get. Unless there is some further inquiry you can suggest, I will submit the case to you. You can take the case and prepare your verdict. Here is a blank. You can fill it out in accordance with the facts."

The jury took the form to a side room and began to fill it out. Cause of death: "Suicide."

When they chose that decision, it was clear they didn't put much thought into it. It was as if they read the room and the room begged them to agree that she took her own life. That was the verdict they delivered. For those who dug up that inquest more than a century later, there were some obvious glaring details the jury overlooked or chose to dismiss.

A woman lacking gun-handling experience chose that as the tool for ending her existence. She used a gun that she had trouble firing. Rather than end her life immediately after she purchased the gun, she went through the trouble to return to the hotel. She decided that rather than taking her life in the warmth of her hotel room, she would do it outside during a terrible storm. She chose to go out in that drenching rain without the sealskin coat she wore earlier in that day. Instead, she covered her head with a simple lace shawl. She decided to make her way to the opposite side of the hotel, a good long walk from her third-floor hotel room to do the deed. A weak woman, as the hotel staff clearly established, chose to put her stamina to the test in order to end her life. She went into the pouring rain, then headed to a location where the wind whipped the ocean foam into the air and upon her face. Then, in that moment of blindness, she finished the act. She burned all those papers but left out the envelopes with her name on them, not to mention that she waited until nearly 2 a.m., and in all that time, she didn't even lie down once on her hotel bed.

Justice Sloane and the jurors' minds must have been made up and they dismissed the obvious oddities of the suicide. They didn't consider asking questions about the revolver, which was the key evidence that prompted their decision. They didn't raise questions as to the cartridges. Were any cartridges left in the gun? Where were the rest she purchased that day? Nowhere did anyone bring up powder burns. None of this garnished enough attention to raise suspicions that this might not necessarily be a suicide. Instead, they seemed more interested in the trunks left at the D Street station.

It is important to also note that there were studies that were made in the late nineteenth century related to suicide. It was rare for women to commit the act as they were considered very optimistic. Suicide by gun was considered a violent death to which women were not prone. When women chose to take their life, they usually did so by lethal drugs. In addition, women made up just a fraction of the total suicidal deaths counted during the late nineteenth century.

The inquest was done quickly. It was completed the very next day after the body was found. Was it because Deputy Coroner Stetson was preoccupied with Indian Joe's trail or was it because the unfortunate woman had no immediate family there to hold anyone accountable? Once the death was established as a suicide, it ended any justification for additional investigation. It ended quickly and the remains were left for the undertaker to handle. He would look for her immediate family to receive instructions. With the inquest completed, Stetson could proceed to submit his bill for payment, too.

The transcriber used shorthand to collect the testimony at the inquest. He proceeded to have it typed up. What was unusual was that at the bottom of the typed transcript was a handwritten statement. **"I hereby certify that the forgoing transcript contains full, true and correct statement of the proceedings had and testimony given in the within mentioned inquisition, and that the said transcript was mislaid while in my possession which is the reason for its not having been heretofore filed. (signed) W.W. Witson, Reporter"**

How long was it mislaid? When was it filed? Could Stetson submit his bill to the city without a properly filed inquest transcript?

Deputy Coroner Stetson, Justice Sloane, San Diego Chief of Police Brenning, and the Hotel del Coronado and its staff needed that event to be finished so their lives could move on. That was not how it went, though. During the following days they would discover she had not checked in under her real name. The undertaker would be stuck with a body nobody wished to claim. They could not simply bury her in a potter's grave. This was a woman who had a room at one of the nation's finest hotels. They didn't know if she came from a wealthy family or not. At least one person familiar with her, G.L. Allen, could hold them accountable. If they did not handle this correctly, it could put the hotel in legal jeopardy.

The newspapers did not have that kind of responsibility or concern. They liked stories like this. Lottie's death was a sensation, and the mysterious reason for her suicide was appealing. When they discovered she may not even be "Lottie," but a woman using that name as an alias, they had a treasure trove of mystery to spin in their daily articles.

NEWS THAT FOLLOWED

Over the following 10 days, the investigative reporting brought out a lot more details related to this case. It also brought out a lot of speculation and over time, a blurry line grew between fact and fiction.

On Thursday, December 1, the *San Diego Union* reported another physician had examined the body and provided additional details and opinions on the deceased. In his personal opinion, she did not have cancer. One of his reasons was her age; she was far too young to be afflicted with stomach cancer. She was healthy looking and if she was at the point of hopelessness, she would have been wasted away. He injected an opinion that if she were pregnant she would have similar symptoms to stomach cancer: great pain in the stomach, sourness and occasional vomiting. He then pointed out that her complexion, which was sallow, could indicate she may have attempted a miscarriage using medicine and that could also produce pain. He said he could not prove any of this unless he were to do a full post-mortem exam but he did notice she had given birth to a child at some point in her past. He then stated that a woman in the last stages of cancer couldn't have gone out on a three-hour horseback ride.

The news of a horseback ride came from a man named Charles Stevens of Star Stables. He had told reporters that she came to their business early in her stay to rent a horse, although he did not know exactly what day it was. Her horse was misbehaving and Stevens came to rescue her before the horse ran off with her. They rode for three hours around downtown San Diego and they even stopped at Marston's, a dry goods store, where she bought a pair of gloves. At the end of their ride, he escorted her back to her hotel where he gave her his card. He said if she ever wished to ride again, he would make sure it was a gentler horse.

Nobody questioned the story of Charles Stevens. Why would he go so far as to escort her across the bay to the Hotel del Coronado? That was not an easy feat. There were no gloves or his calling card in her effects, either.

A clerk at the Hotel Brewster also stepped forward with a story to the *San Diego Union*. The clerk stated that when she arrived on Thanksgiving Day she dropped in, asking if Mr. and Mrs. Anderson had checked in. He told her no and she responded that they must have gone to the Hotel del Coronado and she would go there to find them. Now everyone believed she not only was expecting her doctor brother, but also his wife.

It had been two days since the hotel sent a wire to Hamburg, Iowa, and yet, there still was no word from either the bank president or Mr. G.L. Allen. With this news blasted in all of the major newspapers, they were highly surprised nobody had come forward yet. Not even her brother Dr. Anderson.

On Friday, December 2, news was published by the *San Diego Union* that the deceased was seen on the train coming to San Diego on Thanksgiving Day. The reporter reported that the news came from a man named Joseph E. Jones of Boston. He was on the same train with the woman as he rode to San Diego from Denver. She was riding with a well-dressed man. Jones didn't notice them until the car reached the coast, where he then overheard them having a verbal fight, which escalated so much that it gained attention from others in the car. Their fight went on at intervals until she started begging for forgiveness. The man was too upset, though, and he left her. Jones believed it was at Orange that the man left. Jones says he didn't think any more about it until he saw her at the Hotel del Coronado and immediately recognized her as the same woman.

Coincidentally, two days before the woman was found dead, the *San Diego Union and Daily Bee* published a small mention about Jones in the Sunday, November 27 newspaper. It had written:

"CORONADO NOTES - James A. Jones is another contented sojourner hailing from the Hub at the Hotel del Coronado. Mr. Jones is a member of the large importing firm of Arnold, Cheney and Co. of New York, and was for years the resident partner at Aden, in Arabia, in the heart of the coffee plantation region."

The details relating to Arnold, Cheney and Co. are verifiably true. That company was a huge importer of ivory for the piano industry and those imports came directly through their overseas Aden office. He appears to be a legitimate person.

The news story reporting Jones' train trip used the name Joseph and not James, though. Maybe that was because it was told by a bellboy and not Mr. Jones. The "unidentified" bellboy also stated that Jones did not come forward with the story to avoid being called into the coroner's inquest.

How was Mr. Jones certain the deceased was the same woman, though? When did he put his eyes on the woman after she died? Which bellboy gave the "Jones" story? The article didn't say. However, the story points out that she gave the bellboy a dollar for trifling service, which he was reluctant to take from such a sick woman. The only bellboy who spoke of her neuralgia, and the only bellboy that tended to Lottie, was Harry West.

That article continued that Lottie said her brother could be found at either the Palace, San Francisco, or the Nadeau or Westminster, Los Angeles. The news came from Mr. Gomer. He also said she spoke with great familiarity of those hotels and that Lottie spoke of her parents living in Detroit and that G.L. Allen was in charge of her funds; she hesitated to give Allen's name until she was pressed for it. Mr. Gomer also said that Lottie could name every article within her trunks, and that she had one trunk with a peculiar French lock.

The reporter continued to note that there has still been no response from telegrams sent to G.L. Allen.

It is understandable that the reporters were digging for new details on the deceased. What is surprising is that James Jones did not want it known that he witnessed the unfortunate woman on that train. He purposely avoided the story being known to anyone in order to avoid being questioned at an inquest. Now his story was printed in every major newspaper across the country. So much for his attempt to avoid attention and involvement. It would also be found that going forward after this day, there would be no more news coming from the hotel staff. Did James Jones send a blunt message to Mr. Babcock after he discovered his name was printed in every major newspaper?

On Saturday, December 3, the *San Diego Union* reported a telegram was received by Chief of Police Brenning of San Diego. A Miss May Wyllie of Detroit asked for a full description of the deceased's body. She asked if she had short hair, a black corset, and a large black hat with a gold buckle. Deputy Coroner Stetson replied with a full description. The dead girl had a black corset and black hat but no gold buckle and her hair was of medium length.

Since sending telegrams on Tuesday (four days earlier), there was still no response from James P. Beach, president of Farmers' and Merchants' Bank, regarding the identity of either the deceased's husband or G.L. Allen.

The *San Diego Union* also wrote that an examination was made of three trunks at the D-Street Station. They arrived from Omaha via Denver about Thanksgiving Day. The key found in the deceased's effects partially fit one of the trunk locks but they were not permitted to open it without proper authorization by the division baggage agent. It said they would secure that today.

On Sunday, December 4, breaking news came out from the Detroit, Michigan newspapers. They wrote the identity of Lottie Bernard was that of Lizzie Wyllie. Lizzie's mother, Elizabeth Wyllie, of 102 National Avenue, received the dispatch, which identified the dead girl as her daughter, from relatives in San Diego. The news wrote that the clothes matched that of Lizzie when she left there five or six weeks ago. The deceased's two moles matched. The ring on the finger and the other ring found in her pockets matched. It goes on to say that Lizzie and her sister May worked for Winn & Hammond's book bindery and they both were discharged because Lizzie was too intimate with John Longfield, who was also discharged. Before

Lizzie disappeared, she said she was going away to look for work and might go as far as California. The Detroit police were positive they left together. They wrote that John Longfield was a married man. Lizzie's mother stated her relatives in San Diego had not seen Lizzie since she was a little girl. She has relatives in Pasadena who had seen Lizzie more recently and they had telegraphed for them to go down to San Diego and take care of the remains. Then Lizzie's mother asked for a tin-type (photo) of the dead girl to be sent to her.

The *San Diego Union* reported that Sunday, December 4, that a telegram was finally received from J.P. Beach, president of Farmers and Merchants Bank. It was dated Saturday, December 3 and sent to Johnson & Co. Undertakers from Hamburg, Iowa. J.P. wrote:

"Neither Allen nor myself know of the relatives of Mrs. Bernard. Her husband was supposed to be in Wichita, Kan."

A *San Diego Union* reporter attempted to put a theory together with the new details on Mr. Bernard, while maintaining Lizzie Wyllie was the suicide. He wrote, **"The erring girl and Longfield must have been traveling under the Bernard name and then stopped in Hamburg, Iowa, first. They made relations with Allen and that enabled the girl to call on Allen for money. Longfield then must have shared that he was going to Wichita. The couple traveled from Denver and they quarreled, with the result being that the man deserted the girl at Orange; that theory must be correct. The girl invented the story of her brother to account for being present in San Diego without baggage or money."**

The Los Angeles Herald wrote a detailed description of the suicide in an article published on Monday, December 5. **"Her height was 5 ½ feet; complexion fair but sallow; she had medium length black hair; two small moles on left cheek; broad features, high cheekbones; brown eyes; weight, 150 pounds; age, about 26; good teeth; plain gold ring on third finger of left hand; ring of pure gold, with four pearls and a blue stone in center; black corsets; large black hat."**

Meanwhile, the *San Diego Union* reported that the body was still unclaimed. The cousin of Lizzie in Pasadena hadn't arrived, but they believed she would arrive that afternoon. Meanwhile, a number of curious people dropped in to look at the dead girl, mostly ladies.

They also wrote that another telegram was received from J.P. Beach of Farmers' and Merchants' Bank in response to a request for a description of the dead woman's alleged husband. J.P. wrote he had never met the man but that he thought his name was John W. Bernard.

On Tuesday, December 6, exactly one week after finding the body on the beach steps, the *San Diego Union* reported that they were certain Lottie Bernard was Lizzie, but the niece in Pasadena has yet to materialize to identify and take care of the remains. They believed maybe she had moved since she wrote Detroit last, and that is why telegrams had failed to reach her. Johnson & Co. Undertakers also sent a telegram to John W. Bernard in Wichita, informing him of his wife's suicide, but the man had not seen fit to respond. It was believed to be a cold bluff that this man even existed.

The article continued with an interesting story about Lizzie. They said she lived with her mother, a widow, and a brother and a sister, May. Even after Lizzie and John Longfield were discharged, they were still going together. The handkerchiefs marked "Lottie Anderson" may be related to Lizzie's married sister who lived in Grand Rapids, Michigan, and whose last name was Anderson. Just after Lizzie was discharged, she made a long visit with her sister in Grand Rapids. After Lizzie returned to her mother, she said she was going downtown on an errand from which she never returned. John Longfield dropped by on the Saturday before Lizzie's disappearance to bid them all farewell. He told them he was going south and would probably reach Southern California before he returned. They believed Lizzie followed him. When Lizzie left she was penniless. The article concluded that Longfield was known in Detroit as a sport and a rounder of not the best reputation, even for one of his class.

On Wednesday December 7, the *San Diego Union* reported that Johnson Undertaking sent by mail to Elizabeth Wyllie, Lizzie's mother, a tin-type photo of the deceased. He also wired Elizabeth a detailed description of the deceased. The girl's ears were not pierced. She also carried a large Canadian penny for a pocket piece. The handkerchief clearly has "Louisa Anderson" embroidered on it, and the undertaker asked to verify that Lizzie's aunt was Louisa. With that confirmation, they could feel more confident the deceased was Lizzie.

The *San Diego Union* also shared a news article written in Hamburg, Iowa that was dated the Tuesday, December 6.

"It is not believed here that Mrs. L. Anderson Bernard, who killed herself in Coronado, was Lizzie Wyllie of Detroit. It has been learned that there was recently in this place a man named L.A. Bernard, a professional gambler, and he is believed to have been the suicide's husband. Bernard left Hamburg November 7 for Topeka. He said his wife was sick in California and he intended to bring her back to Iowa. He tried to borrow money for that purpose but failed. No word has since been received from him. G.L. Allen of this place, to whom the woman telegraphed for money, was a schoolmate of Bernard's in Illinois, and never met Mrs. Bernard. Simply out of charity he sent her $25. Therefore, it is strongly believed here that the Detroit identification is a mistake."

The *San Diego Union* wrote that a San Diego man came forward and said he knew Allen and that he was a cattleman, of some wealth, a sport and a lady killer. The reporter concluded that Mr. Allen must be more deeply interested than to the extent of the $25, and that he had invented everything about Bernard as a blind. He was either a consummate liar and had dealings with Lizzie Wyllie, which he was trying to conceal, or the girl lying on the slab was Mrs. L.A. Bernard, the wife of a gambler.

The next day, Thursday, December 8, the *San Diego Union* news reported that Lizzie's mother had sent a telegraph saying Lizzie's ears were pierced and she wore silver earrings. The deceased, whose ears were not pierced, could not be Lizzie Wyllie.

The reporter then added some personal questions to the article. He wrote, "When L.A. Bernard was in Hamburg needing money, why didn't Allen hand it to him then? If the suicide is Bernard's wife, then Allen's promptness in remitting money to her was for other reasons he wishes not to be known. Allen has delayed and appears to avoid any response to telegrams and there is also no news coming from the Hamburg city marshal's office either, leaving high suspicions of lies and deceit."

A letter was received by Deputy Coroner Stetson on that Thursday, December 8 from Miss Florence S. Howard. She wrote that she would like a description of the suicide because she strongly believed the woman who died by suicide was Josie Brown, the same woman that had stayed with them last summer for nine weeks. Josie Brown, 24, was also from Detroit, and had a sister named Mrs. Anderson. Also, a man named Dr. Brown from Minneapolis came around the hotel claiming to be Josie's brother.

The *San Diego Union* also reported that the trunks at the D Street station were still unclaimed.

It appears that San Diego was unaware that the *Los Angeles Times* had also published breaking news on the suicide on that same day of Thursday the 8th of December. The article states that a domestic by the name of Kate Logan, who worked at the residence of contractor Grant, was believed to have been the woman who died at the Hotel del Coronado. The domestic left Los Angeles with just a gripsack and a shawl. She said she would be back in time for Thanksgiving dinner the next day but instead went missing.

In the late nineteenth century, women who worked in a household or residence as a chambermaid, house cleaner or cook were referred to as a "domestic" much like we refer to someone as a nurse or a landscaper.

The *Los Angeles Times* continued to say that she came to Los Angeles from Omaha about two months earlier. She said her husband was a gambler but didn't know what became of him. She went to agencies and secured work, first at R. M. Widney's, then T.H. Hughes. Shortly before her disappearance, she got employment with Mrs. Grant at 917 South Hill Street. The day before she went missing, she was anxious to get some papers signed and appeared worried about something, but no one seemed to know why. She wore the same ring and had the same black underclothes. She also had two moles on the left side of her face. She told several people her name was Lizzie but she liked Kittie better, and so she adopted that. Mrs. Logan bore an excellent reputation. She stayed strict to her work, never went out at night, and as far as they could tell, never had any men around her. The Los Angeles reporter concluded with a speculation that maybe she was employed in San Francisco, which accounts for her knowledge of hotels in that city.

The next day, the *San Diego Union* published their own story and corrected what was written by the *Los Angeles Times*. They reported Friday the ninth that the domestic's true name was Mrs. Bernard, but that she was going about changing her name to Josie Brown, then to Kate Logan. But when she appeared at the Hotel del Coronado, she registered under her real name, Bernard.

The *Los Angeles Herald* also wanted to correct the *Los Angeles Times'* story. They wrote on Friday the ninth that the domestic was not the woman who died by suicide at the Hotel del Coronado. They reported that the trunks of the domestic Kate Morgan were taken to the police station and a cabinet-sized photo of her was found in the trunk. They wrote, "The photograph does not denote the appearance of a woman accustomed to stopping at first-class hotels as a guest or wearing lace shawls; neither does it show her to be pretty, and the features certainly are not those of a highly educated woman."

The *Los Angeles Herald* article included a detailed list of Kate's trunk contents held at the Los Angeles police station. They wrote, "A tin box was found marked 'Louise Anderson.' In the tin box were several photographs. One was that of a man aged about 50 years, with a full beard, tinged with gray. On the reverse side of the photograph the name was scratched out, but the written word 'Visalia' was left. Another picture of a man aged about 35 years, black mustache, black hair, thick skull, and who looked something like a sporting character. There were photographs of two boys, aged about 9 and 10 years: the photograph of a girl of about 2 years, and still another of a baby. In a piece of paper was a lock of pretty blonde hair. On the paper was written, in rather coarse characters, 'Elizabeth A. Morgan's hair.' On two other photographs the names had been carefully erased. A certificate of marriage was also found, uniting Thomas E. Morgan and Kate K. Farmer, on December 30, 1885, in Hamburg, Iowa. The ceremony was performed by the Rev. W.E. Howe. A letter was found in the box recommending Mrs. Morgan as an honorable and trustworthy woman and signed by W.J. Farmer, Hanford, Cal. There were also found the cards of several ladies, together with their addresses. These were Mrs. J.H. McDonough, San Rafael, Mrs. M.R. Abbott. Fifth and Mission, San Francisco; Mrs. Ottinger. 602 Stock Exchange, San Francisco. A cabinet size photograph of Mrs. Morgan, found among the others, shows her to be a woman of about 28 years of age, black eyes, large ears, rather large, open face and somewhat coarse features; her mouth is rather large and lips thick. The photograph contained no marks and had evidently been taken recently."

The *Los Angeles Herald* also reported that the Chief of Police Glass sent a telegraph to Mr. Farmer in Hanford, California and he received a response back from the Hanford sheriff that Farmer lived a few miles out in the country, and that the dispatch had been forwarded to him. Chief Glass also telegraphed to Chief Brenning at San Diego asking as to the disposition of the remains of the unfortunate woman. The answer was to the effect that the corpse was still at the morgue awaiting identification and instructions.

On Saturday, December 10, the *San Diego Union* reported that it was no longer a mystery; Kate Morgan was the identity of woman who had died by suicide. They wrote that even though the *Los Angeles Herald* didn't believe she was the woman who had died by suicide, the name on the handkerchiefs matched the name on the tin box in the trunks. The *Los Angeles Herald* also didn't believe the photo would match a beautiful woman who would stay in a high-end hotel, but all of the other evidence was too strong not to admit it was Kate Morgan. The police had traced Mrs. Morgan's route. She went from Chicago to Omaha to Cheyenne to Ogden to Sacramento and to Hanford, where she remained a short time, and then to Los Angeles.

Deputy Coroner Stetson telegraphed Mr. Farmer (Saturday the tenth), asking for instructions to the disposal of the body.

The *Los Angeles Herald* reported that same Saturday the tenth that they were still not convinced that Kate Morgan was the woman from the Coronado suicide. Kate Morgan matched the woman who was in Orange last year as Josie Brown. The paper questioned whether Josie Brown knew Mrs. Bernard. They could not understand how a domestic with a trunk at the Grant's home would also have two more trunks waiting in San Diego. How was she supplied with so many trunks?

The following day, Sunday, December 11, the *San Diego Union* reported that Coroner Stetson received a letter from a man named A.D. Swarts. He said he knew Kate and her family ever since 1869 when he lived in Hamburg, Iowa. Joe Chandler in Riverton was the grandfather. Tom O. Morgan was a wealthy uncle to her husband. She had a number of rich relatives. Mr. Swarts said he moved to California last November.

The *San Diego Union* reported that "they acknowledge the mystery as to why she did the act is still unknown but her identity is solved. None of her other relatives have uttered a word. There is still no word back from her Uncle Farmer in Tulare County either."

The *San Diego Union* also reported that the trunks that had been at the D Street station since Thanksgiving were no longer there. They had been claimed by the owners.

On Monday, December 12, Stetson sent telegrams to Joe Chandler and Tom O. Morgan asking for instructions to bury the body. He received a response that same day from Joe Chandler, Kate Morgan's grandfather. Joe wrote: **"Bury the body and send me the statement. – J.W. Chandler."** After receiving those instructions, the undertaker immediately arranged for her burial for the next day.

On Tuesday, December 13, a funeral was held at 10 in the morning at the parlors of Johnson & Co. Undertakers. Rev. H. B. Restarick officiated the service. Several members of the Brotherhood of St. Andrew were present and some ladies of the Episcopal Church spoke. When the service ended, the body was placed in a hearse for conveyance to Mount Hope Cemetery, though nobody followed.

The next day, the *Los Angeles Times* published a letter that had been received by the Chief of Police Glass from W.T. Farmer. It also explained that the telegraph sent to Mr. Farmer on December 9 notifying him of his niece had ended up being sent to him by regular mail, which caused him to have a delay in receiving it. He promptly sent a letter back to the Los Angeles chief of police. It was dated Monday, December 12, the day before Kate was buried.

"To Mr. J.M. Glass, Los Angeles   Hanford, Cal.,
December 12, 1892

Dear Sir, your message was received yesterday. I am more than surprised to hear of the tragedy if it was Kate Morgan you can rest assured that it was no case of suicide for the reason that she had no cause for committing such an act. When she left me I told her if she needed anything to send to me and I would assist her. Her people are well to do. Her husband Thomas Morgan has been traveling in the interest of some manufacturing company. His home is Hamburg Iowa, I have known them for a good many years. She wrote to me soon after her arrival in Los Angeles that she had secured a situation at a Mr. Whitney's, a banker, on the West side. She had when she left here quite a sum of money, one large, flat-top trunk, two leather satchels and a lady's gold watch. She said she was going to deposit her money in a national bank for safekeeping. Her relatives are Henry Brumback and Thomas Morgan, Hamburg, Iowa, Joe W. Chandler, her grandfather, and John Samuels, Riverton Iowa. I cannot help but think there is some mistake about it being Kate Morgan. She was troubled with rheumatism while here and went to Los Angeles

on account of its fine climate, with the intention of living there if she liked it. You say you have positive evidence that it is her. What is it? She has a second cousin living in this county. She certainly would have written to someone if she had contemplated the awful act.

Yours most respectfully – W.T. Farmer"

It was too late, though. Her body was already buried, and the police had hoped the story of the woman found dead at the Hotel del Coronado was finished. Instead, Mr. Farmer raised concerns to her identity. Friday, December 16, three days after Kate was buried, P. M. Johnson of Johnson's Undertaking made a special trip to Los Angeles. Mr. Johnson, was there to verify that the photo they had taken from the trunk matched the body of the suicide. Mr. Johnson confirmed they were one in the same. With that, the Los Angeles news published that all doubts had been removed. With that confirmation, Chief of Police Glass shipped the woman's effects to her grandfather in Iowa.

Coincidentally, on that same day of Friday the 16th of December, the Hamburg, Iowa news printed an article stating the following: **"This town was much surprised on learning that the woman who committed suicide a few weeks ago at San Diego, Cal., and was supposed to have been a Detroit lady, proved to be Mrs. Kate Morgan of this place. Mrs. Morgan had not been living with her husband for several months."**

It would seem the news of the woman was finished and no more would be printed on the matter. However, a letter came into the office of the *San Diego Union* a week later and they chose to publish it. In the December 24 paper they wrote:

"The connection of G.L. Allen's name with that of Mrs. Kate Morgan, alias Lottie Bernard, the Coronado suicide, was unjust to him, and conveyed a wrong impression. Mr. Allen is an unassuming and honorable gentleman, and that through charity he sent the unfortunate woman $25, not knowing her personally, but being acquainted with her husband, who was

his schoolmate. **The highest references are named with which to prove Mr. Allen's standing. The San Diego man who says that Mr. Allen is a sport and a lady killer, is a coward and is afraid to make the statement over his own signature. – Peter Wikoff, Hamburg Iowa"**

The letter sent on Allen's behalf fell on deaf ears. Nobody cared any more about the connection of George and the unfortunate woman. The investigation had ended. It ended when the police chose to determine the identity of the woman based on items in a domestic's trunk. A photo that was determined to be a physical match to both the Grant's domestic worker and the suicide victim; and two documents that were also in that trunk: a marriage certificate of Kate K. Farmer to Thomas Edwin Morgan, and a letter of recommendation from Kate's Uncle W.T. Farmer.

It was highly unusual that they did not pursue a next of kin to identify the body. When they thought the suicide was a Lizzie Wyllie of Detroit, they waited patiently for a member of the Wyllie family to identify her. When it was discovered instead that it was the Grant family's domestic, they allowed the photo and marriage certificate to be enough. They knew she had an uncle who lived in Hanford, northwest of Los Angeles. They knew A.D. Swartz had been a friend of her family for many years. He lived right there in Los Angeles and was a short train ride away from going to identify her. They could have chosen to demand that her husband, Thomas Morgan, come forward and not only identify the remains of his wife but take responsibility for her burial, too. There was no excuse not to ask any of them to come forward and prove it was her.

Their determination on the identity was extremely shoddy, even for the late nineteenth century. The California police and investigators were quite good, even back then, when they were put to task investigating a murder. But Kate's death was not determined to be a murder. The investigation was not conducted by police investigators, at least not at the beginning. It was conducted by the undertaker, the coroner and the newspapers.

Part II

Her Beginnings

FREMONT COUNTY

In the Midwest lay a community of people: proud people who took great risks to leave the comforts of their eastern homes to build a new life in the untamed west. They came when there were no lawmen, no lawmen who could protect their interests and no lawmen who could get in the way of them, either. Settlers from all walks of life came using the trails carved by the Native Americans. They came and set their claims and filed their names in the property offices. They fenced their lands and sowed their grounds. They built homes, barns and a community of people who, through their collective experiences, looked out for each other, a community that yielded to the stronger hand.

This story starts in one of those communities, in an area known as McKissick's Grove, in the township of Madison in Fremont County, Iowa.

Madison was and still is a farming and ranching community. It encompasses an area of about eight miles east to west and four miles north to south. Its southern border lies at the Iowa and Missouri state line. Its western border sits alongside the Nishnabotna River. About a mile west of the river is the small town of Hamburg. Hamburg sits less than a mile north of the Iowa State line and just south of the Loess Hills. The Loess Hills are steep bluffs that rise in a spine-like fashion and run 200 miles northward along the western border of Iowa. The bluffs are covered in thick, bluestem grass, soapweed yuccas, and Pasque flowers that color the hills purple during the springtime. Brush and trees hunker in the rain-carved crags, where they take refuge from the sweeping winds that apply the very dust the hills were born from. At their peaks are awe inspiring 360-degree views of Iowa, Nebraska, Missouri and on an exceptionally clear day, even Kansas. Much of Fremont County falls to the east of those hills, where they maintain a level of protection from the ground-ripping tornados their western neighbors endure. The bluffs also separated the community from the large swarms of mosquitoes and yellow flies that abound along the Missouri River.

There were several towns a half day's drive away. Just across the Missouri River is the town of Nebraska City and a little further west is Lincoln. To the north is Council Bluffs, which sits on the eastern side of the Missouri River with Omaha along the western shore. South of Hamburg past the Missouri state line is Atchison, followed by St. Joseph and Kansas City. All of these were thriving hubs of growth and resources supplying the people of Fremont County very well. Most travelled by horse, coach or wagon, but by the late nineteenth century, an ample number of rails were laid and trains would soon be the dominant means of travel.

Religion was strong and the community built numerous churches of various denominations, but conditions were not the same in the west. The power religion had on a community was overshadowed by the men who held roles of power: men who made their own rules over their communities, men who did not bear the same accountability as their neighbors to the east.

Kate was born in 1866, a year that followed the end of the Civil War. The community was still reeling from the effects of that war. Quantrill's Raiders had just been released from a prison in Independence, Missouri the year of Kate's birth. The James and Younger brothers were riding and wreaking havoc in the lands not too far south of Hamburg. Their Dalton cousins would soon be turning hard of heart and would keep the U.S. Marshals on their toes. Wyatt Earp was riding on the land southwest of there, between Dodge City and Wichita, Kansas. This was the climate of those days.

Kate was born into a man's world. Men made the rules. Men controlled the money and property and business and industry. Women were there to be the men's wives, housekeepers, or prostitutes of pleasure. They were women who reflected their man's status by adornment, showed obedience by appearing chaste and pure, and bred the men's sons. The sons who would partner with their fathers to manage the land, businesses, and industry. The sons who would inherit their father's wealth and carry on their legacy.

Not all women were confined to the home. Many were teachers. Others pushed against societal norms by taking up roles in science or medicine or writing books or publishing articles. The nineteenth century was evolving for women as they pushed against those barriers. There was not so much in the southwest corner of Iowa, though, not in the world with which Kate was familiar. Kate may not have conceived of being anything other than a farmer's wife, not in those early years, not until she left and experienced the differences that were found outside of her present reality. Until then, she would spend her youth in Madison of Fremont County and in the home of her grandparents Joe and Matilda Chandler.

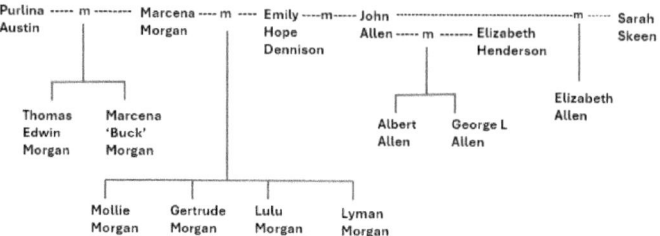

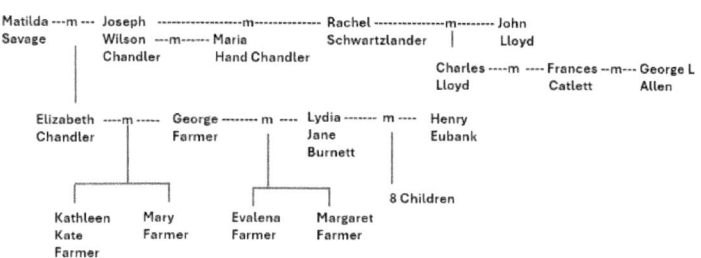

JOE AND MATILDA

When a telegram was sent to Kate's grandfather in Riverton, Iowa, notifying him that the body of his granddaughter was in San Diego, and asking him what he wanted to do with her remains, his response came immediately: "Bury the body and send me the statement."

He did not choose to have her returned and buried alongside her mother or sister at the Mount Olive Cemetery. He did not wish her to be returned and buried beside her son Thomas at the Utterback Cemetery, either. It was clear he had no intention of requesting her body be returned and he had no interest in where her body would lay for eternity.

Joseph Wilson Chandler, or Grandpa Joe as Kate would know him by, was not just a grandfather to Kate. He and her grandmother Matilda were essentially her parents. They took Kate in when she was only two. It was never a part of a plan of theirs but rather a response to a tragic circumstance. When Kate moved in with them, most of their children were already married and on their own. Even the last one, Emery, had moved out by the time Kate was four. Joe and Matilda could not rest in their later years. They had the responsibility of childcare again. For some grandparents this would be a welcome treat no matter what the circumstance was. For Kate, at least, one might not have found this an ideal situation.

Her grandparents were not originally from Iowa. Both came from Ohio, Illinois and Wisconsin before they settled there. Joe's father, Tom Chandler, was one of nine siblings whose parents were a second-generation Quaker family. They were raised in Ashland, Ohio at a time when it was merely raw land. They watched it grow to a township filled with gristmills, blacksmiths, tannery, wagon and wheelwright shops, sawmills, cabinet shops, and dry goods suppliers.

When Joe was old enough to have memories, he found himself surrounded by a large Chandler presence. He grew to manhood among many aunts, uncles and cousins. He built friendships with the children of Ashland and one in particular was a young woman named Maria Hand. She was the same age as Joe and she and her family were close to the Chandlers. Joe had been growing fond of Maria and maybe she knew that, but when she was 17, another man was showing her interest, too. He was much older and more established and he happened to be Joe's uncle, too. Uncle Shadrack Chandler took Maria to be his wife on January 15, 1837.

In those early years, Joe had been gaining experience in the carpentry and building trade. A number of the Chandler men were skilled in the trade and Joe had great potential in his future among this community, but that all changed. Maybe his father Tom recognized his son's feelings for Maria and what trouble that would cause for his brother Shadrack. Maria was already pregnant and due to have her first child later that year. Tom decided to leave Ashland and take his family west to Illinois, a distance that would make family visits very difficult. Joe was 19 when his father made that decision and although Joe was old enough to make his own choices, he chose to follow.

Tom and Mary's children were all mature enough to ease the burdens of that long trip. The oldest daughter, Mary, was 22, followed by Joe, then Thomas Jr, who was 14. The last two, Eleanor, 13, and Jacob, 10, completed their family of five. Although the rest of the Chandler relatives heard about their plans and the future possibilities in Fulton County, Illinois, no one considered joining them.

The 4-week trip involved 440 miles of overland travel, most using large schooners pulled by oxen. They traveled alongside others who were also from Ohio, and there would be a sense of camaraderie and mutual teamwork to achieve a successful trip.

Tom Chandler may have had high expectations about this new destination. Just like the days he witnessed when he first arrived in Ohio, he envisioned the bustling atmosphere of a community coming together to build a new town. There was an abundance of coal in the nearby hills, which meant warm meals and warm winters and a level of wealth for the town. Tom must have been certain the choice was a good one.

When they arrived, they made a crude home in the Cass section of the county and Tom and Joe used their skills to build a house that would best suit the large family. It wasn't long before the oldest sister Mary was taken as a wife. Asa Savage was a 30-year-old man from Rutland, Ohio. His 25-year-old sister Matilda had joined him on the move to Fulton.

Matilda was a grown woman but she was still single. She relied on her brother Asa and like most women, she handled the chores of cooking and housekeeping. When Asa married Mary, Matilda's contributions were no longer necessary. Still, Matilda required her brother's support, so Matilda remained with them, and in that time Mary bore Asa two sons.

In those early years in Fulton, Joe remained single and he appeared in no hurry to take a wife. Maybe Asa or Mary applied pressure on him to consider Matilda. They may have feared she would remain single if they didn't intervene and find her a suitable husband. It is impossible to know why it took Joe so long, but he finally asked Matilda to be his wife and they married that November of 1843.

Matilda was five years older than Joe, and at first it might have looked like a marriage of convenience, but in less than a year she was pregnant; the following November she bore him twins. They named them Elizabeth and Erastus. Just two months after her twins were born, Matilda found herself pregnant again. When September came, she gave birth to a baby girl they named Harriet. She had her hands full juggling three infants under the age of one and it took a toll because shortly after she bore Harriet, her baby Erastus passed away.

Following the tragedy of her baby's death, every one of the Chandler and Savage family members decided to move. They chose to go north to Wisconsin. Joe's parents, Tom and Mary, and his younger siblings, as well as Asa and Mary and their children, all left the area, all except Joe, who made the decision that his family would stay. Matilda may not have found that decision a welcome one. She would experience an uncomfortable level of isolation while recovering from childbirth and the emotional loss of her baby.

Life in Fulton County was a lonely one for Matilda and the children. It was unusual for a family to live so far from other family members in those days. When her baby Harriet reached her first birthday, Matilda was pregnant again and in no time she had another son they named Thomas. It wasn't until three years after Thomas' birth, when Matilda was pregnant again, that Joe finally decided to move to Wisconsin and join the rest of the family.

Joe's younger brother Tom Jr. had just married a woman named Almira and he had moved to the town of Cassville, Wisconsin. Cassville was Joe and Matilda's destination, too. Joe and Matilda's children were still young; Elizabeth was now 5, Harriet was 4 and Thomas was 3. Matilda was already showing her pregnancy when they embarked on their journey.

River travel, when possible, was considered the preferred means of travel in those days. If rivers were unavailable, then overland was the next alternative. Trains were not a choice as they were still in development at that time. For a trip up the Mississippi, it would take 190 miles and 3 days to reach Dubuque and then another 40 miles to reach Cassville.

Cassville was conveniently located on the eastern shore of the Mississippi, an ideal place for any town to receive supplies and comforts for a community. On the western shore were uninhabitable lowlands of marsh, but just a few miles north, on the river's western shore, the land rose high enough to support the small hamlet of Guttenberg. There was a large German presence not only in Guttenberg but around much of the region.

When Joe arrived in the summer of 1850, the Chandler and Savage families had been settled in Grant County, Wisconsin for at least six years and a lot had been happening during that time. Joe's younger sister Ellen was now engaged to get married. Her fiancé, Oliver Goodell, lived 15 miles southeast of there in the town of Potosi. Their wedding was planned for later that summer. Mary and Asa were living 8 miles east, in the village of Beetown. Another 7 miles east of Beetown was the village of Hurricane, where their parents Tom and Mary were living. Joe's youngest brother Jacob was still living at home with the parents but he was engaged to marry a young woman by the name of Miranda Morel the following spring.

Matilda bore her last child, a son they named Emery, the month after Ellen's wedding. After Emery's birth, they prepared for their first Wisconsin winter.

That first winter wasn't any colder than winter in Illinois or Ohio, but when their mother Mary took her last breath on the eighteenth of January. The bitter Wisconsin winter probably offered no reasonable options to reach the town of Hurricane to attend her funeral. After Mary was buried, Jacob remained with his father Tom Sr. for a short time. When spring arrived, Jacob married Miranda and took her to Beetown to live closer to his brother-in-law Asa and his sister Mary. Jacob and Asa had grown to be quite close in those days and their close bond would last throughout their lifetime.

Their father Tom Sr. was alone after Jacob married and moved to Beetown. He didn't stay alone for long. Just four months after his wife Mary passed, Tom Sr. married again. His decision appears to be supported by the family and their wedding took place in Beetown. Tom Sr. was 60 years old and his new wife, Polly, was a 51-year-old widow. All of her children were grown and on their own except one, an 11-year-old boy named Nathan who joined the household after Polly married Tom.

The next five years passed by and in all that time Joe and Matilda maintained a very modest life. The 1860 census revealed that Joe's property was listed at $300 in value. His two closest neighbors, a carpenter whose home was valued at $600, and a Bavarian family with a home worth $4,000, reveal the level of modesty Joe and Matilda were living. A tailor and grocer who lived a few houses further down the street had homes valued at twice that of Joe's. The vast majority of the neighbors surrounding Joe were listed as either Bavarian or Prussian and either Joe was content with modest living or he was competing with a community that might have been looking out for their own.

It was during this time that Asa and Mary Savage decided to leave Grant County for Richland County, Wisconsin, located much further north. Jacob and Marinda Chandler chose to follow them. At this same time, Tom Jr. and Almira were considering a move, too. He was 35 years of age and was probably looking for something better, a lifestyle he may not have believed possible in Cassville. Their destination was the southwestern region of Iowa.

Joe could have considered a move, too, and joined any one of them, especially his little brother who had been living close by ever since they arrived. That is not what Joe did, though. Joe chose to stay. His choice would once again leave his family isolated from the rest. The families would live distances that would make it very difficult to maintain close relationships. It was unusual in that era, an era where life itself was difficult enough and family support was often crucial.

Matilda was not as vulnerable as she was in Fulton County, Illinois. She was still vulnerable, though. Most women were vulnerable in their state of dependence. Close family relationships eased that burden. Matilda might have become accustomed to the isolation, though. She probably found solace in her children. Her daughter Elizabeth was now 16 and she was also a teacher at the local school. Harriet was 14 and showed a good measure of maturity. Both of her daughters must have been a tremendous help to Matilda. Her sons, Tom, who was 13 years old and Emery, who was 10, were at an age to learn carpentry and construction from their father.

Tom and Almira said their goodbyes and embarked on their 350-mile trip west. They drove by wagon train. Long journeys of this nature were rarely made alone. For those who believed they could save money and attempt the trip alone, the risk was extremely high.

There was little means to recover a fallen ox or horse. Many lost their belongings when their wagons got stuck in the mud of a washed-out stream. Oftentimes, they would fall prey to trail robbers or receive attacks from a local tribe who bore extreme resentments to settlers. Anyone attempting to travel alone would become easy prey. For Tom and Almira, they would travel in numbers with a level of safety and manage to reach their destination in the summer of 1860. They settled on land in Madison, Fremont County, Iowa. They took up a farm located in McKissick's Grove and the two settled in to prepare for their third child due that December.

Joe and Matilda didn't remain in Cassville for very long. When the Civil War broke out the following year, Joe decided to join his little brother Tom Jr. in McKissick's Grove. Joe had traveled overland before, but this time he would not be making the trip with his father Tom. Polly's son Nathan had just mustered into the army and they chose to stay.

Joe had a few choices to reach his younger brother. Although there was a railroad, the Mississippi and Missouri RR, that ran across Iowa from Davenport near the Mississippi River to Council Bluffs, it was a freight train that was not equipped with passenger cars. One option Joe had was by river, which was always considered less troublesome compared to overland, but for Joe, riding south on the Mississippi to St. Louis, and then doubling back on the Missouri, would make for an extremely long trip. Joe chose to travel like his little brother. He would go overland by schooner driven by a team of oxen.

When Joe and Matilda arrived with their four children, Tom and Almira provided them with space in their home. Tom Jr. had purchased a small piece of property in McKissick's Grove where he had a reasonably-sized home built. McKissick's Grove was home to several other settlers that were prominent in that day. Cornelius McKissick lived not far from Tom Jr. He was one of three brothers the grove was named after. It was also the home of the wealthy English family. Tom O. Morgan was also found there. He had just married and though his wealth was in its initial stages it would not take him long to amass wealth that would rival his neighbors. Mr.

Tom Farmer also lived in the grove. He had been there since before Iowa was a state. He, too, carried a level of wealth. All these men were part of the original settlers who came and developed the area long before it grew into a community. It didn't take Tom Jr. long to understand the power each of these men held.

For Joe and Matilda, staying with Tom and Almira was meant to be a temporary situation. Joe did not have much money, though. The house they sold in Wisconsin had little, if any, equity and much was spent on their trip. They stayed with Tom and Almira for a little over a year and if it weren't for the Homestead Act, Joe might have had a lot of difficulty getting a head start for his family. He made a claim for 160 acres of land with no upfront cost other than the filing fee. He received the land for just a promise to have it improved within five years.

It was at a time of great turmoil. They were not far from the Missouri and Nebraska borders where they received daily news of property destruction and death. It was during a time when the character of men was on full display. Maybe the Civil War had its hand in that, but that was not consolable for the residents of McKissick's Grove. They stayed consistently on alert. Maybe Joe believed it would be different further west, further from the southern states and further from the Civil War disputes.

When Joe made the claim and built a home for his family, he took a gamble. Unlike the past, when as a builder and carpenter he had confidence in the money he could earn, he was now embarking on farming, a lifestyle with which he was only vaguely familiar.

George Washington Farmer

George Washington Farmer came from a pioneering family. He was the son of Tom Farmer, a highly respected man of Fremont County, and was often referred to as Colonel Tom Farmer (a title of complement rather than military grade). Tom Farmer also dabbled in politics and, when challenged, had written extensive letters defending his stance. He was also referred to as Tom Farmer Esquire and listed himself as an ex-mayor in the 1870 census. News articles reveal that he was also a money broker and held a remarkable amount of acreage in Madison, Fremont County, all of which was just a small sampling of his fortuitous life.

Before Tom Farmer gained this level of comfort and lifestyle, he first lived south in Missouri. He was one of many settlers that participated in the 1836 land claims of Platte County after the US acquired land from the Sac and Fox tribes. What was supposed to have been an organized claim process turned into a land grab, mostly by Missourians, who already knew what the most favorable parcels of land were. Tom was from Kentucky, though. He made his claim to a parcel and did OK with his wife Mary and three small children. They remained there while their children grew in number from 3 to 7, George being the fifth.

When Tom discovered the conditions were far better to the north, he decided to relocate there. Although it was only 50 miles farther north, it had a better climate and soil and less pests, including yellow flies, which were so bad down in the Missouri bottom that many had lost livestock from their incessant attacks. So, Tom moved the family up to McKissick's Grove, an area aptly named by the McKissick's brothers.

One of those brothers, Cornelius, had already been there for a few years, and it took Tom Farmer little time to build a farm equal to his. It wasn't enough for Tom to simply maintain a profitable farm; he looked for ways to improve the area and its future, too. He built a stagecoach station where the road leading from St. Joseph to Council Bluffs passed through and later added a post office. These things brought him profits and attracted new settlers and the region experienced a boom of growth.

At the end of Tom Farmer's first eight years, the agriculture census revealed he had improved 70 acres of his 200-acre property. He possessed a large amount of farm equipment, held 30 heads of cattle, 28 heads of sheep, 50 heads of swine, and two working oxen. He had seven horses: some for riding and others to haul wagons. In his barn were six milking cows and an operation to produce butter and cheese. In his stores, he held 600 bushels of corn and 100 bushels of oats. The hills and farms in and around McKissick's Grove were farms like this and were growing at a very rapid pace.

Tom's wife Mary had 11 children by then, and five were boys. The three senior boys were: Billy, who was 19 years old, John, who was 17, and George, who was 11. The two youngest boys were James, 6, and Winfield, 4. Though Tom had three productive sons, he also had farmhands. The presence of those farmhands would be normal, as would the presence of their children. Tom's wealth was growing and George grew to age under these privileged circumstances.

Tom and Mary had quite a large family with 14 children, and whatever they did to dodge the infant mortality plaguing nineteenth century children must have included luck, because they never seemed to have lost any children.

Over the next 10 years, most of their children were either adults or were near that age. Billy was the first to leave. He headed off to California to seek a fortune. John married Martha Utterback, the daughter of another wealthy family of the area. George went south to Atchison County, Missouri where his little sister Celia and her husband J.T. Davis lived. George worked there as a clerk in J.T.'s mercantile business. They didn't stay very long there. The tumultuous atmosphere between the pro slavery and abolitionists was too much for them so J.T.'s father-in-law, Tom Farmer, offered J.T. an opportunity to build onto the Stagecoach Station for his mercantile business. It was an ideal location, considering all the traffic that went between Missouri and Council Bluffs. With that, J.T. and his family moved back to Fremont and George followed.

When J.T. had completed the building of his mercantile business at the stage station, the Civil War was raging. For those living in the southwest corner of Iowa, the war held everyone's attention as skirmishes often spilled over the Iowa border and into McKissick's Grove. It was a time of great uncertainty for George and J.T. and many of the men in the county who were being added to the rolls of men subject for military duty.

In the following summer, the U.S. passed the Homestead Act and the area received a flood of settlers. That didn't bode well for these earlier pioneers who paid a price for their land and earned a certain level of respect as landowners. They feared the act would dilute their holdings and power. The new homesteaders would struggle against the suppression these early pioneers would place on them.

The day their son George asked for Elizabeth Chandler's hand in marriage, they might have been aware she was the daughter of a homesteader. They may have also been aware that she was a teacher, too, a kindred spirit in community improvement, and that might have given them some reassurance.

The day Joe and Matilda learned of Elizabeth's intentions of marriage, it might have given them a pause. Their other daughter Harriet had also announced her engagement to marry George Baker. Elizabeth and Harriet worked alongside their mother to milk cows, produce butter and cheese, tend to the chickens and whatever else Joe might ask from them to maintain the farm operation. They did all this while also being responsible for other household duties. In rural areas, it wasn't just cooking and cleaning that were part of the women's duties; they also made and maintained the clothes and linens and even made the mattresses which they filled with straw and refreshed on a yearly basis. Matilda would have to make some serious adjustments to continue her work without the help from these two young ladies.

In August of 1863, the first of the Chandler children married. The Farmer family held a great deal of respect in the community and Elizabeth and George's marriage would be a well-attended event.

Harriet and George Baker were set to marry two months later. George Baker's father was the Reverend Jacob Baker, a local Methodist minister, who had lived in the town of Sidney for several years. George had his own sizable piece of property located not far from Joe. George Baker was an honorable man. He was 13 years older than Harriet, but this was not unusual and on October 15, George Baker took Harriet to be his wife.

The loss of these two daughters had an impact on Matilda. If Joe didn't hire additional farmhands, she would be alone in the burdens of milking, butter making and chicken care. She would still be responsible for meals and clothes and the house, too. Joe would rely heavily on his two sons Thomas, 15, and Emery, 12, as he navigated the management of the farm.

In little time, the two newlywed sisters began to bear children. Harriet had her first baby and named her Estella. Soon afterward, Elizabeth had her first baby and named her Mary. When Elizabeth and Harriet were pregnant again, Harriet's baby Estella passed away. After Harriet gave birth to her second child, Edward, Elizabeth lost her first baby Mary. When Elizabeth gave birth to her second child, the baby arrived just after the end of the Civil War. Elizabeth named her Kathleen Kate Farmer.

Life for the Baker family was wrapped in religion. George Baker was the son of a minister and the community that surrounded them were God-fearing folk. This was not necessarily the same for Elizabeth and George Farmer. George's father Tom was a strong man and a force with which to be reckoned. There was a news story about an incident that occurred at the time when baby Kate was only five months old. A situation occurred on the nearby McMillen Farm.

James McMillen had several horses stolen from his barn. When the neighbors heard about this, a group of men decided they would chase after the horse thieves and bring them back for justice. Tom Farmer was among them.

The group of vigilantes rode south and then across the state line into Nodaway County, Missouri. On the dirt road they were traveling, they came upon a man they believed knew where the thieves were. They pressed him to give them the location but the man would not talk. The vigilantes decided to use force. They hung the man a little and then let him down, but the man simply did not talk. They eventually left him, whether alive or dead we will never know, and rode a little further. Shortly afterward, they found two men and the stolen horses tied nearby. The thieves were identified as William Neff, a Missourian, and John Crosby from Illinois. They tied the men up and brought them and the horses back to McKissick's Grove.

When they arrived back at McMillen's farm, the vigilantes took a vote amongst themselves about whether to put the thieves to death. They all agreed. They chose the mode of execution by firing squad. Tom Farmer collected the thieves' valuables and promised to send them to their next of kin. Edwin Wellington was in charge of the execution, although he had some difficulty getting volunteers to join the firing squad. Once he had enough men willing to participate, John Crosby stepped bravely forward and was shot first. His body crumpled to the ground. Then William Neff stepped forward, bravely standing beside his dead friend and he was shot. They decided to bury the two bodies right there at the spot of their execution on the McMillen Farm.

The execution was not a legal one. The men were executed without a trial. The group that caught them and brought them back to McMillen's farm were well aware that they participated in an illegal act, but the law in 1867 of Fremont County was not yet well established. The neighbors kept quiet and did not get involved; instead, they would continue to pay respect to these men for many years to come.

A TIME OF LOSS

It is unknown what tragedy befell Kate's mother, Elizabeth Chandler Farmer. In the fall of 1868, just a few months before Kate's second birthday, Elizabeth passed away. The loss would turn things upside down for Kate, George, Joe and Matilda. What is unclear, and perhaps telling of the ever-evolving relationship Joe and Matilda had with their son-in-law George, and probably the rest of his Farmer family, is that Joe and Matilda brought Kate home with them.

It didn't appear that George, who was a saddler at the time, lacked the means of finding care for Kate. He was from a large family. His father Tom was a prominent and powerful man who had connections with many important people in the county. George had four brothers and eight sisters, any of which could have offered help and maybe they had, but history shows Kate ended up with her grandparents.

Over the next few years, Kate remained with her grandparents, and by 1870, Joe's farm grew. It consisted of 160 acres of improved land. It contained a good sum of farm implements: four horses, four mules, 17 milk cows, 52 heads of cattle, and 60 heads of swine. The barns stored 100 bushels of wheat, 100 bushels of corn and 470 bushels of oats. Emery was 19 years old at the time, working alongside his father Joe, and there were a few farmhands hired for help. Matilda held all her usual chores on the farm, while also looking after her granddaughter, Kate, who would be turning 4 years old by the end of that year.

It happened that during the past year, Kate's father George had been courting another woman by the name of Lydia Burnett. She was only 18 and had moved to Fremont from Tennessee with her parents. She was one of seven children when they arrived. George had been living an unencumbered life, with Joe and Matilda caring for his daughter. We do not know when they got the word, but Joe and Matilda would have eventually figured it out. That November, George and Lydia were married.

The order of events after the marriage would leave unanswered questions. Had any of them spent time considering Kate's future? Was there an agreement after Elizabeth passed that Joe and Matilda would care for Kate until she became an adult? If Joe and Matilda were only providing care until George could care for her, then wouldn't they press him to do so now? If instead Joe and Matilda had grown attached to Kate, and didn't want to give her up, George could still make a demand for her as the rightful father. We will never know exactly why, but history proves that Kate remained with her grandparents and in a short time, George would become a father again.

Usually farming communities were known for being highly religious and would have held George accountable for walking away from his fatherly responsibilities, but this was the Midwest and it was more on the cusp of the wild west. The laws and powers that existed here overshadowed the power religion had over its community. Instead, George was given the role of postmaster of Hamburg, a position typically given to a resident of high standards. It is also documented that George's postmaster salary was $730 annually; that might not seem like much, but most of the other postmasters listed were paid less than $100. Only a few were listed close to or more than George's salary. To put it in perspective, the average farm laborer in Iowa at that time was paid $20-$21 per month, or about $250 annually. George was doing very well, very well, indeed.

A year after their marriage, George and Lydia had their first child and named her Evaline. Kate was 5 and of an age to remember. Did Kate ever have a chance to meet her father or half-sister? Stories passed down by Evaline in later years never mentioned or acknowledged she had a half-sister. Did she not know about Kate, either?

Harriet and George Baker's farm was not too far from Joe and Matilda's farm. The Baker's farm was much larger, too. They all lived in proximity to the prominent families which Kate had also been exposed to all her life. She attended school and church and events right alongside their children.

In 1867, Joe's son Tom Chandler was married. He was a 20-year-old man when he married Lizzie. They moved into a modest house in the town of Hamburg. Joe's farm operation would have to work around the loss of this son. His youngest son Emery remained with him and provided year-round help, but now Joe would have to rely heavily on paid farmhands. Joe was tight with his money, though. In the agriculture census for that year, Joe reported the salary for farm labor was equal to 6 months. His fellow neighbors were reporting 12 months of paid labor.

After a year or so, Tom and Lizzie moved to a farm of their own and Emery left his father's operation to join them. Joe may not have agreed with his son's choice, but there was nothing he could do. Joe gave room and board to two new farmhands: John Staley, who was only 15 years old, could only work part time while attending school, and Loren Hamilton, who worked full time at the age of 18. Kate was still very young and would be turning 4 years old at the end of that year.

Harriet and George Baker's farm had two farm hands living on their land, too: John Woodland, 25, from New York, and John Mass, 17, from Iowa. George and Harriet's two boys were still very young: Edward, now 4, and Charles, who was 3 months old.

Harriet bore her third son, Chesney, in the fall of 1871. Three boys were a blessing for any family, especially on a farm. They held great hopes for their future but that all changed. In 1873, Harriet lost her husband George. When he passed, she was alone on that large farm. She had three very young boys and another was due in four months.

Understandably, Joe and Matilda were under a lot of emotional turmoil. They would be consoling and supporting their daughter

Harriet while also dealing with the news that George and Lydia Farmer were soon to have a second child. That would be an unwelcome reminder of the circumstances they had with raising George's daughter Kate. Now their daughter Harriet was going through this tragic loss, 5 months pregnant and caring for three young boys.

Harriet would have little time to mourn, as she would need to take the necessary steps to hold on to her late husband's estate. Widowed women did not automatically gain ownership of the home and properties of their marriage. It was an era where men preferred men to control money and properties of worth.

In May, George and Lydia had their second baby girl and in July, Harriet had a baby boy.

Harriet must have received support from her father-in-law. She gained possession of the farm and she chose not to sell it. Instead, she remained and continued the enterprise her late husband had left behind. A rare thing, indeed, for any single woman of the Victorian-era, and a glimpse into Harriet's character and fortitude. Kate would have certainly been influenced and inspired by the tenacity of her Aunt Harriet and the rewards her hard work obtained.

That same year, Joe's son Emery took a wife. The young woman was Mary Catlett, who was the oldest of six and from another of the area's earliest pioneer families. Mary's mother was still bearing children when Emery and Mary joined in marriage. Kate was 7 years old when she attended their wedding. For Joe and Matilda, this would be the last of their children to marry.

In May of the following year, Kate's grandfather, Tom Farmer, passed away. Colonel Thomas Farmer Esquire was one of the community's most prominent and powerful citizens, the one who erected one of the first stagecoach stations, brought one of the first post offices to the area and was elected mayor for a time. Tom left behind a darker past, too: his participation in the illegal executions of horse thieves. The citizens respected Tom and the legacy he left behind. That was not all Tom left behind, though. He was also leaving a substantial estate to his wife and sons.

It is uncertain whether Joe, Matilda or Kate attended Tom's funeral. George and Lydia would certainly be attending. Tom Farmer was buried at the Farmer Cemetery (known today as the Mount Olive Cemetery), a cemetery on land he had donated years before for this use.

Not long after Tom was buried, George and Lydia decided to move away. Maybe Lydia's parent's decision to move at that same time had prompted George and Lydia to do the same. Her parents left for Atchison, Missouri, but that was not where George and Lydia decided to go. They had Texas in mind.

George couldn't have made the decision lightly, either. This move required him to walk away from his substantial postmaster salary. It was an unusual decision, but he may have feared losing the job anyway, without the power and reputation his father had held. In any event, George took Lydia and his girls and left. They rode by train and then overland by schooner, until they reached central Texas.

Joe and Matilda would no longer be subjected to the gossip and rumors of George and Lydia. That might have given them a certain sense of relief. But the reality remained that their granddaughter Kate had truly been abandoned by her father and that would leave a sour note, not only for them but for Kate and her future, too.

Orphaned

There is a shroud of mystery over George Farmer's fate. Sometime after he and Lydia left Fremont, he passed away. There is no grave maker to be found, or death certificate to prove when or where he passed, only court documents related to the deceased estate of George and the stories that were passed down. Those stories explain that shortly after George Farmer arrived in Texas, he passed away. His wife Lydia then married Henry T. Eubank, sheriff of McCulloch County, Texas.

Census records reveal Lydia and Henry were married sometime in 1877 and she became pregnant with their first child in 1878. Some stories written by Lydia's descendants suggest that George passed away in March of 1876. Regardless, his body must lay somewhere in the deserts of Texas and the news of his death didn't reach Hamburg until 1877.

When news of George Farmer's death became known, Joe and Matilda might not have thought too much about the tragic news. They never really had any expectations that he would step up to be a proper father for Kate. Kate was nearly 11 years of age and she would have learned of the news, too. Her feelings might have been far different than theirs, though.

Around this same time, Joe's father Tom and his wife Polly moved from Wisconsin to Fremont County. They brought Polly's son Nathan with them. This would be the first time Kate would become familiar with her great grandfather and he might have enriched her with a deeper sense of family. For Joe, his father would always be a reminder of the sacrifice he made to move with his family from Ohio and away from Maria Hand. However, during the same year Joe's father Tom moved to Fremont, Joe discovered that Maria Hand and his Uncle Shadrack were planning a move west to Brown, Kansas. They were also bringing their 30-year-old daughter Ella with them. It is uncertain what the motivation was, but Joe's son Tom and his wife Lizzie made plans to move to Brown, Kansas. too.

In a rare and unusual circumstance, Shadrack Chandler fell ill during their move to Brown, Kansas. He ultimately passed away and Maria and Ella had to have him buried in Indiana before they continued on with their trip.

Joe would soon face Maria again, but this time his uncle would not be in the way. If feelings still existed between Joe and Maria, he would have to keep them to himself. He would have to conduct himself as a gentleman around her, especially around his wife Matilda.

In the cold month of January 1878, Kate's grandmother, Mary Farmer, passed away. On the very day of her death, Dr. D.W. Swiggart filed in court to be an administrator of her estate. A large surety bond of $12,000 was set with signatures from three townsmen: Beckstead, McCracken and McMillan (the same McMillan whose farm carried the bodies of the horse thieves).

At that time, Mary and some of her children had been maintaining the estate of her late husband Tom. The farm was sizable and of great worth and upon Mary's death, all was placed in escrow. Dr. Swiggart would be required to search for a will, and, if one existed, do what was necessary to distribute the inheritance to the heirs. William "Billy" Farmer was the oldest son and would be an heir apparent if a will could not be found. He had been living in Hanford, California for quite some time, though.

It is impossible to know if Kate attended the funeral of her grandmother Mary Farmer. It would have been the proper thing for her to do to pay her respects. Although George was no longer living, the history between Kate's grandparents and the Farmer family would not be so easily repaired.

In August of 1879, a year and a half after Mary Farmer's funeral, Matilda passed away at the age of 63. It would be one of the most significant events Kate would ever endure. Matilda had been a mother to Kate ever since she could remember. Matilda made sacrifices in the provisions for her future. She clothed her, fed her and kept her out of harm's way. She instilled in her the importance of religion and education. Kate must have experienced a level of loneliness on that fateful day. She may have also had apprehensions and fears about her future alone with her Grandpa Joe.

In less than a week after Matilda was buried, Joe filed in court "Letters of Guardianship" over Kate. The letters requested that considering G.W. Farmer was deceased, and Kate was entitled to a certain estate of his, Joseph W. Chandler applied for and requested appointment as guardian of the person and estate of Kate K. Farmer minor, with full power to demand, sue for, and take possession of, all money and estate belonging to his ward, and in general to do all other acts which may be required of him by law. Cornelius McKissick was one of the two signatories as sureties of the $500 bond.

For the nearly 11 years Kate had lived under the roof of her grandparents, they had never pursued any means of establishing themselves as her "legal" guardians. Joe didn't seem to need any inheritance Kate might be entitled to, either. He had a sizable farm at that time. He had 160 acres of improved land. He had two horses, two mules, and two milk cows. He bought and sold 65 heads of cattle and had seven calves that were born that year. He held 88 heads of swine and 50 or more chickens, for which he had a sizable number of eggs he sold. His barns held 7,000 bushels of corn and 600 bushels of barley.

Instead, it might have become understood that Kate could be entitled to some portion of the Farmer Estate, an estate that had been under escrow since Mary Farmer's death well over a year earlier. Kate was a minor and courts at that time would not distribute money or property directly to minors. Instead, it would either go to the minor's guardian or be held in an account until the minor was at the age of their majority. Fathers were always considered a minor's guardian. If a father were not alive, the mother would be required to file for guardianship. Mothers were not considered in this role automatically. That may seem odd in today's terms but in that day the law preferred men to handle money and anything of worth. Everything revolving around finances and properties were in the hands of men at the court, men in the property offices, men in the seats of decision making, and they preferred it that way.

In Kate's case, both parents were deceased and it would be up to her grandparents to establish guardianship. Joe appeared to have waited until after Matilda's death to file for guardianship and he would be the sole adult receiving the distribution if one was made. At this time, it was unknown how much inheritance Kate could be entitled to. The Mary Farmer estate was still in escrow. Why Joe chose just days after Matilda passed to file could be telling. Either it had become coincidentally known that Kate would be receiving an inheritance; the 14-year-old Kate displayed her will of independence against Joe, and he filed for legal measures to control her; or possibly both.

Nearly a year after Joe set up Guardianship over Kate, it was determined that Kate would be receiving a portion of Mary Farmer's estate. The exact sum is undetermined but was at least $146. At this same time Nancy Brumback's husband Henry made a play to control the estate of George Farmer and any inheritance or distribution required. Nancy was the sister of Kate's father, George Farmer. That June, Nancy's husband Henry Brumback, was appointed by the circuit court of the county to be administrator of the estate of George W. Farmer, deceased; Henry Brumback's goals were to oversee the distribution and administer all of George's goods, chattels, moneys, rights and credits, according to law.

Perhaps Joe was not aware that a special administrator could be assigned specifically to the distribution of George's portion of the Farmer estate. Maybe he presumed the administration of Farmer's estate was all in the hands of Dr. Swiggart. If Joe was holding Kate's inheritance as a tool to control her, that tool was now in Uncle Henry's hands. Henry could set provisions that the monies would be held in escrow until the minor, Kate, reached her majority, which at that time was 21 years of age. He could also administer the money to Kate's Guardian Joe and hold Joe accountable to provide yearly reports that the money is kept in an account till Kate reached the age of her majority.

Shortly after Henry became administrator, Joe sold his farm in McKissick's Grove and moved to Riverton. There he changed from the role of farmer to grain dealer. This move took him a few miles north, away from his daughter Harriet's farm in Madison, and farther away from all who lived in McKissick's Grove, including the Brumback family.

Joe's move would have an impact on Kate, too. It would take her away from the school she had been accustomed to attending. It may have played a part in what happened next. Kate moved out of Grandpa Joe's and took up residence with her Aunt Harriet. It is uncertain whether this was the result of difficulties between Joe and Kate, or simply a means for Kate to remain in the same school system. Maybe it was both.

It was certainly not the first time Kate had spent time at her aunt's home. Her property was relatively close to the home where she grew up. Kate's cousin Edward was the same age as her, the two younger cousins, Charles and Chesney, were 10 and 9, respectively, and it is no wonder how these four spent their time together.

The 1880 Riverton census listed two others living in Joe's home: one boarder by the name of James Lovelady, who was listed as a 21-year-old physician, the other his 13-year-old granddaughter, Kate. In the Madison census, Harriet listed her three sons and Kate Farmer, too. Had Joe given the census taker his granddaughter Kate's name because he was her official guardian, whether she was literally living there or not?

During the past eight years, Harriet had held on to that large farm left by her late husband George. The baby boy she was carrying when her husband George had passed only lived a year before he had passed, too. Harriet did ok, though; she raised her three boys on that farm and the 1880 agriculture census showed how Harriet was doing by then. She had a farm consisting of 360 acres. She showed no record of horses or mules or any wages paid, though. She did own some livestock. She had 20 swine, two milk cows, for which she sold butter, and 80 chickens, which were used for the sale of eggs. Her close neighbor, Tom O. Morgan had a farm and ranch consisting of 440 improved acres with numerous cattle, and his land was valued three times that of Harriet's. Harriet wasn't in any competition with her neighbors. She was doing well enough and was content to have a comfortable home and life for her boys and her niece Kate.

In January of 1881, Kate's great-grandfather, Tom Chandler, passed away. He lived to the remarkable age of 91. As cold as an Iowan winter usually was, the family would do whatever they could to attend the passing of this father, grandfather and great grandfather.

It is impossible to say if Joe's son Tom and his family came up from Brown, Kansas, though. Snow often impeded train travel. The same went for Maria Chandler. Aside from the same restrictions of train travel from Kansas during snow, she would be consoling her daughter Ella, who had just lost her firstborn son earlier that month. It was also possible that Ella's husband was deathly ill. Ella's husband Ernest Rohl was a German immigrant who had lived in Brown, Kansas for years with his mother and father and other siblings before he married Ella just a few months after she arrived. Ella's mother Maria was given a room in their home upon their marriage. Two and a half weeks after Tom Chandler was buried, Ernest passed away. Ella was fortunate that Ernest had written provisions for her in his will. She was allowed the home and belongings. Maria was also safe with a place to remain, but it wasn't long after Tom's burial that she received an offer of marriage from Joe. That summer. Joe and Maria married in the home of Ella Rohl and Joe brought Maria back with him to his home in Riverton.

THE MORGANS

The Morgan family was large and most were living in Fremont County for at least 20 years before Kate's husband Thomas Edwin Morgan had arrived 12 years earlier. When Thomas arrived with the rest of the Morgan family, it merely increased the dominance of the Morgans in the region.

Thomas was born and raised in Old Berlin, Sangamon County, Illinois, just 10 or so miles west of Springfield. His father Marcena was born there, too, and his grandparents and great grandparents all lived the greater part of their lives there.

Marcena was one of five children born to Evan and Elizabeth Morgan. Ann was the oldest, Jane followed after Marcena, and two younger brothers, Lyman and Tom Orr. When Evan passed away, their mother Elizabeth married again. Her second husband was Martin Skidmore and together they had two girls, Sarah and Nancy.

Elizabeth and Martin left Illinois in the summer of 1846 and they took most of their children with them. They left on a long arduous journey west. All except their oldest son, Marcena. He was 21 and decided to stay with his Morgan grandparents, who offered him a room in their home.

Marcena remained for several years on their 80-acre farm in Old Berlin until his grandfather decided to move several miles northwest to Schuyler County. Marcena decided not to follow but instead chose to move to an area east of Springfield.

It was there that Marcena met Purlina. She was a 23-year-old woman and the daughter of Benjamin Robert Austin, a well-known man in the area. Benjamin was a surveyor who had assisted in the original street plan and survey of a new town to be called Decatur. The town was approved by the state and over the following years, Benjamin held the office of justice of peace there. Marcena knew if he were to win Purlina's hand he would have to live up to the expectations of the Austin family.

Marcena took Purlina as his wife in the summer of 1855. In that year's census he was recorded living in Shelby, Illinois. Purlina's sister Margaret and her husband John Day were neighbors listed on the line just before Marcena's household in that census. They remained there in Shelby and it wasn't long before Purlina bore Marcena a child they named Elizabeth. When the baby girl reached the age of two, she contracted scarlet fever and after four hot August days lost the fight. Purlina mourned her baby for more than a year, during which time Marcena decided to move the family back to Old Berlin. Purlina's brother Edmond joined and gave them a much-needed pair of hands.

In those early days in Old Berlin, Purlina found herself pregnant again. She bore her second child on the third of December and named him Thomas Edwin. Her spirits were lifted once again with this new child and when Thomas was old enough to walk she found herself pregnant again. Her third and last child came in August and they named him after his father Marcena, although it wouldn't take them long to nickname him Buck.

The civil climate was experiencing change at this time. They lived near the epicenter of the unrest: a mere half day's ride to the office of a lawyer named Abraham Lincoln. Not long after President Lincoln was sworn in, war broke out.

Marcena spent the next years with a level of uncertainty when he was placed on the list of men subject to military duty. Fortunately, he was never called to duty. Instead, Marcena continued to work and expand his farm. His brother-in-law Edmond, who had spent nearly five years on Marcena's farm, returned home to Decatur.

The war brought a rapid pace in the development of railroads and the farmers reaped from those benefits. By 1865, Marcena's property had grown greatly. The farm and agriculture records show his land, farm and equipment were worth two times as much as the neighboring farms. During those years, they enjoyed the wealth of their farm. The community was as close as any family. They celebrated their new births and they tended to each other's loss. They attended church together and sent their children to school together. They shared the labor to build new barns, homes and harvests, and it would always be followed by food, music and dance. It was not always sunny and bright and perfect. Some drank too much. Some dared the laws of morality. Some partook in divorce. It was perceived that if a community was strong enough, the wrongs could be diminished and a life of perfect harmony was possible, so long as they all worked together towards that goal.

Just before her 38th birthday and their 15th wedding anniversary, Purlina passed away. What was unusual was that the attending physician was unable to determine the cause of her death. When the news of Purlina's death hit the Austin family, they sent Marcena's sister-in-law, Margaret, to help him. Margaret brought her three young children with her. Margaret had been raising her children alone during the past four years. She was not a widow or divorcee, but rather a wife in limbo. Her husband John Day joined the Army before her youngest was born and was sent west to the Montana Territory to help handle the Indian situation. She received only one letter from him for which he wrote "if I come out of the battle which will take place the next day, I will return home." It had been four years since she received that letter and the Army was of no help. They had no record of her husband's death or any other information to determine his whereabouts. Without proof of death, she was left to wait for his return. After Margaret arrived, Marcena's house was full. Besides Marcena and Margaret, there were Margaret's three children, Eliza, 7, Kate, 6, and Elizabeth, 4, along with Marcena's two boys Tom, 9, and Buck, 7, and the two farmhands, Henry Myers and James Simms.

Marcena had time to figure out his future. He had the help of Margaret to care for his boys and the house. He would be in mourning over Purlina, with whom he had spent the past 15 years.

That is not what he did, though. Shortly after Purlina's death and Margaret's arrival, he asked his neighbor Emily for marriage.

Emily was a widow herself and lived at a nearby farm. She was also the stepmother to her late husband John Allen's two children from his two previous marriages and although Emily was married to John for 5 years, she never bore him any children.

When Margaret discovered Marcena's proposal, she packed and returned to her Austin family in Decatur with the news.

In that era, it was often expected that an appropriate time of grief should be paid. That usually was one year. Marcena was nearly 50 years of age and Emily was 26 when they married. Emily became Marcena's wife one year and two days after her husband had passed. That was two days after an acceptable mourning period, but for Marcena it had only been 10 and a half months, and that might have caused some commotion. When Emily moved in with Marcena, her stepson George was already a grown man at the age of 21. George remained on his late father's farm and his younger sister Elizabeth chose to remain there, too.

Marcena had lived in the Springfield region for nearly 50 years. It was all he had ever known. Yet shortly after he married Emily, he decided to move. Marcena and Emily had their first child that January, exactly 12 months after they married. They named her Mollie. That spring, Marcena took the family west to Madison, Fremont County, Iowa where his mother, stepfather and siblings had been living for more than 20 years.

Madison wasn't a traditional town but rather a region where vast farming and ranching took place. Madison may not have had any traditional downtown but it contained schools, churches and cemeteries. Those living there would have to travel to nearby towns such as Hamburg, Riverton or Sidney to obtain staples and everything else they may need and McKissick's Grove was where the Morgan family had been living since 1847.

During the time the Morgan family had been settled in Iowa, the family had grown quite large. Marcena's mother Elizabeth and his stepfather Martin Skidmore, both 66 years of age, were now running the City Exchange Hotel in Hamburg. Elizabeth and Martin had a total of three girls together, Marcena's half-sisters. Sarah, who had been married to Charles Smith for 12 years, had three children. Nancy, and her husband James Chaney had two boys with another child on the way. Lastly, Mahalia, their youngest, was still single.

Marcena's oldest sister, Ann, had married Elliott O'Neal back in Sangamon County before they left, and Marcena was already familiar with him. Ann and Elliot had two grown children, Catherine and John. Catherine was now a schoolteacher married to a man by the name of Oramel Wing. John was married to a young lady by the name of Lucinda.

Marcena's sister Jane had married George Wolf and they had one daughter, Amanda.

Marcena's youngest sibling and brother Tom Orr Morgan, who was 14 when the family moved from Illinois, was now 37. Tom had been married to Eliza for about 15 years. They had six children ranging from three to 14, and Eliza was due to have another in July. Their three oldest were girls, Sarah, Perlina and Martha. Martha was the same age as Thomas. Then, the next three children were boys by the names of Lincoln (who was the same age as Buck), Bunt and Sene.

When Marcena and Emily arrived in Fremont that summer of 1872, he had a good sum of cash from the sale of his farm. He purchased the Hawley-English farm in McKissick's Grove, possibly on the advice of his brother Tom. It was a 160-acre farm and not far from one of Tom's properties. Tom had been buying up land for years and much of Tom's land was disjointed and all over Madison. Emily was probably not the only one to meet the family members for the first time. Marcena's boys Tom and Buck would also be learning more about this extended family.

Most of these cousins were attending the schoolhouse in McKissick's Grove. At the same schoolhouse, Kate Farmer and her cousins, Edward, Charles and Chesney Baker, were attending, too. Kate and the cousins were much younger than Thomas, Lincoln and Buck. They were closer to the ages of Bunt and Sene and it was during these school years that these children grew to know each other.

Marcena, who had been living up to the expectations of the Austin family for quite some time, would find the atmosphere in Madison quite different. Here the Morgans were the respected ones. It didn't take long for him to make that realization. Marcena would be sponsored by his brother Tom to join the A.F. & A.M. (Ancient Free and Accepted Masons) Fraternity which opened doors to a network of men that would be very beneficial for Marcena and his family. During the following five years, Marcena bought a great deal of land and built a wealth nearly equal to that of his brother Tom. It was a great time of hope for both Marcena and Emily.

Thomas Edwin Morgan

Kate's Aunt Harriet had lived a number of years on her own as a widow. In all that time, she ran the farm operation, raised the kids, and supported her niece Kate. Harriet had experienced the difference between the role of a wife versus an independent woman, a life where she made her own decisions and drove her own success. It might appear that she became comfortable in this lifestyle, but things changed. A man named Theo Sahm approached her for marriage. Harriet may have considered what would happen if she chose to marry again. Accepting his offer meant that everything she worked hard to build would be his. Of course, it may appear it would be "theirs," but that was not the way property was handled in those days. If her husband passed, she would have to fight to regain all that she had. The land and property and money could only remain with her if he wrote it in a will. So, Harriet had to consider these things before she accepted his offer.

Theo was a schoolteacher and an honorable man and maybe that gained her trust and respect. Maybe shifting the burden of responsibility to him would be considered a relief for her. Maybe they made an agreement that he would write a will guaranteeing the estate would remain with her if something happened to him. We do not know. What we do know is that they became man and wife on September 23, 1883.

After Harriet married, Kate was sent to live with Grandpa Joe again. This time she was under the roof of both Joe and Maria. This time it would not be on a farm but rather a grain enterprise with multiple silos spread across his property in Riverton.

Kate was nearly 17 years of age when she attended her Aunt Harriet's wedding. Kate was a much more mature young lady and old enough to hold her own around Grandpa Joe. Joe may not have found this an ideal situation but he may have been far too preoccupied with his new wife Maria to give Kate the kind of grief she had suffered in her younger years.

Kate may not have found the situation ideal for herself, either, not until she discovered she had members of her Farmer family living nearby. Her Aunt Jane Utterback lived in Riverton, too. Jane had married Kate's Uncle John Farmer, the second oldest son of Tom Farmer. Jane was a widow, though. John had died due to complications received in the Civil War. Before his death, they had four children. Kate's cousin George was the oldest and had already left. He left at the age of 16 to go live with his Uncle Billy Farmer in Tulare County, California. Kate's cousin, Mary Farmer, was married to John Samuels and they lived in Riverton with a few children of their own. The youngest cousins, John and James, were closer to Kate's age. It was at this time that Kate became close to the Farmer side of her family and especially close to Mary Farmer Samuels.

During the following two years, Kate continued to grow into a beautiful young woman. At the age of 18, she was 5 feet 6 inches tall. She had jet black hair and dark brown eyes. At that time, Thomas Edwin Morgan had his eyes on her. He was 23 and living with his father Marcena and stepmother Emily on a very comfortable estate. Marcena and Emily had a home with all the fine furnishings which a wealthy family would possess. Thomas was following in Marcena's footsteps when he joined the I.O.O.F. (Independent Order of Odd Fellows). He joined the Modern Woodmen of America and Royal Highlander clubs, too. Having those affiliations was a sort of social resume showing that not only did someone find Thomas special enough to sponsor him, but he had also achieved acceptance from the rest of the members of the organization, too.

During the early part of that year, Thomas' younger brother Buck became engaged to a young woman by the name of Lizzie Thompson. For the first time one of Marcena's children would be marrying. The household would be filled with excitement about their upcoming marriage. When Buck married Lizzie that June, it was clear that it was fully supported by both their parents, Sylvester and Margaret Thompson, as well as Marcena and Emily Morgan. In the county marriage registry, S.D. Thompson and Marcena Morgan signed as witnesses to their children's marriage. The Reverend D.F. Beebe was their officiant.

During this same time, Thomas and Kate became engaged, too. Their marriage would pose a different set of circumstances. Kate did not have parents eager to make her day special. They usually took the burden of the expenses. Instead, Grandpa Joe would be responsible. It's impossible to know exactly what transpired, though. If Kate did not believe Grandpa Joe could step up and provide the emotional and financial support for this event, she may not have felt comfortable enough to ask that of him. If she decided to set aside her concerns and ask Joe to do what was necessary, there was a chance it would not turn out to be the blissful event for which Kate was hoping. Kate was engaged to a Morgan boy and the surrounding community would take notice and hold a certain level of expectations for a Morgan man's choice of bride and how the wedding should turn out. Kate and Thomas both wished to have had an equally lovely wedding like Buck and Lizzie, but they probably knew it was likely impossible.

What transpired may be telling. Kate was allowed to withdraw her inheritance of Mary Farmer's estate before she reached her majority. The rules of inheritance can be overridden if a woman marries before the age of majority. In Kate's case, she received a voucher for the amount of $146.93 from J.W. Chandler, Guardian, for Kate K. Farmer on September 3, 1885, for principle and interest in Kate's interest in the estate of Mary Farmer deceased. Maybe Kate exercised her right to receive the money in anticipation of her nuptials. Maybe she received it in order to cover the cost of the wedding. It is impossible to know for sure why the voucher was given before her majority. It was nearly 4 months prior to her marriage. Was this enough for these two to have a blissful event?

When Kate and Thomas married, the ceremony was held the day before New Year's Eve of 1885 and the marriage registry had two witnesses. It was not Joe Chandler or Marcena Morgan. Instead, it was Mr. and Mrs. Joe Fisher, an older couple who were not related to anyone on either side of the family. There may be some consolation for Thomas and Kate's special day, though. It appears they might have married in a chapel. Their officiate was the Reverend W. E. Howe.

EMILY MORGAN

Kate's mother-in-law Emily might have considered it a blessing that Thomas was married, too. She would finally be free of Purlina's children in her home. Emily was an unusual woman, as Kate would learn over time. Did Thomas share Emily's past with Kate? He could have shared what he could recall, considering he was only 11 when she married his father. She had lived down the road from Thomas since he was 6 years old, though.

Emily Hope Dennison grew up in Old Berlin of Sangamon County, Illinois. She was the wife of John Allen before she married Marcena. She was John's third wife and they were married for five years.

John Allen was a Kentuckian who had moved to Sangamon County, Illinois as a very young man. He built a farm next to the Henderson farm and in no time he took one of their daughters, Elizabeth, as his wife.

Elizabeth bore John two boys, Albert and George. When she was bearing her third child, she passed away. The newborn boy only lasted five days and he passed, too. John had their bodies laid to rest at Antioch Cemetery west of his farm.

John appeared to wait the socially acceptable 12 months, and then took Sarah Skeen, a daughter of another nearby neighbor, to be his wife. She was a young 17-year-old, compared to John's age of 35. It wouldn't be long before she bore him a daughter they named Elizabeth. During the next three years, she did not bear any more children, and in 1860, Sarah contracted scarlet fever and she, too, passed away. John made the trip to Antioch Cemetery once again and laid her next to his first wife and child.

For those living in Sangamon County, they were well aware of the nation's turmoil. They lived a mere 10 miles west of Springfield where Abe Lincoln held a law office and everyone was well aware of what his plans were and the threats the southern states were making if he attempted those changes. It was a tumultuous time and it took no time for the U.S. to be engaged in a civil war. During the next few years, John Allen was on the list of men subject for military duty. Sam Dennison, Harrison Ellis, and Marcena Morgan, all fellow neighbors, were also on that list. It wasn't long before Sam was drafted to serve in the Union Army.

Sam Dennison was Emily's father. Emily and her brother Will were being raised by their mother Nancy, though. Nancy divorced Sam and had married Harrison Ellis. John Allen and Sam Dennison seemed likely friends. Both were from Kentucky. The same was true for Harrison Ellis, who was also a Kentuckian. These families had children close in age with each other. Emily Dennison was close to Albert Allen's age and Will Dennison was close to George Allen. They were all schoolmates in that small rural community.

While the war raged on, John's 15-year-old son Albert became deathly ill and passed away. George was a mere 13 years of age when he lost his older brother and the loss would certainly have had a huge impact on him. Once again John would pay another visit to the Antioch Cemetery where he would place Albert's body beside his mother, Elizabeth. John had four family members in the family plot now.

For John, the loss of an older son, one that would already be considered a young man, would be devastating, especially for a farmer. John had no idea how long the war would run or if he would be called to serve. He was relying on his son Albert to step up if he were called to duty. George would have to be prepared to do this now.

Although John had a young daughter who must have needed a mother figure, John did not look for another wife. Instead, he continued there on the farm grooming his son George in farm management. This was how things were until just a few short days before the Civil War ended. That was when John married again. This time he took Sam Dennison's daughter Emily to be his wife.

Emily might have been socially burned having been the daughter of a divorcee. Divorce was looked down upon at that time and especially out in the rural farming communities. Her mother Nancy would remain under scrutiny by her neighbors, who were uncompromising to any woman who had chosen to leave their husband. It wouldn't be unusual for those consequences to spill over to Emily, too.

When Emily was offered a proposal of marriage, she may not have found John as attractive as the younger men nearer her age. She may not have liked the idea of being his third wife. She might not have had many options, though. John Allen was offering her a stable home. His established and profitable farm would allow her the nice things life could offer. Emily had one uncomfortable truth, though: John's son George, who was then 16, would become her stepson. It was an awkward situation for her, having been a schoolmate of his for so many years. Emily must have put that aside because she accepted John's proposal and on the fourth of April 1865, John and Emily became husband and wife.

Emily was a 21-year-old and John was 44, but this was not the first time John married a woman much younger than himself. Although George was 16, he would have grown accustomed to receiving all of his father's attention. John and George had been working closely on the farm's affairs ever since Albert had passed and George took pride in the responsibilities his father had entrusted to him. Now Emily would be John's wife and George's stepmother and she would have a certain level of power and decision making in that role. George's sister Elizabeth, who was 8 at the time, might have been the only one aside from his father who gladly welcomed Emily into the household.

During those years of marriage, Emily experienced farm life. There would be a certain level of camaraderie with the neighbors. They helped each other harvest, raise barns or build houses. There would be celebrations with food, music, dance and drink. Emily might have received some level of redemption from the community after she became Mrs. John Allen.

John's son George was known to be a very handsome young man. He was becoming highly experienced in stock raising and sales. As he grew to the age of 21, the neighboring farmers would be pushing their daughters on him in hopes he would take one as a wife. George didn't appear to have any interest in marrying, though. He appeared to be satisfied with things as they were.

Emily had remained barren in her marriage with John and when it was just a few short days to their fifth wedding anniversary, her husband John passed away. When the physician examined John Allen, he gave the cause of death as jaundice. Now it could be speculated that John might have been a drinker. Men of that era enjoyed their whiskey and John, after all, was from Kentucky.

The Allen farm would soon be filled with their neighbors and friends who brought food and condolences for their loss. Nancy and Harrison Ellis would certainly have come in support of their daughter Emily. Maybe Sam Dennison, Emily's father, stopped by, too. He remarried just after Emily married John. Marcena and Purlina Morgan were probably there in support, too. John's body was taken to Antioch Cemetery where he was laid to rest next to his previous two wives and his two sons.

It is unknown if John Allen had a will with provisions for Emily. It seems certain Emily had some hard decisions to make if he didn't. If she was not written in a will, then the farm, and home, and belongings she had enjoyed over the past five years would go to George, the heir apparent. Either Emily inherited the farm or George did.

If George inherited the property, then Emily's care would be George's responsibility. She could have returned to her mother Nancy in such a case. The 1870 census revealed her choice. She was still living with George and his little sister Elizabeth four months after John's death. The census taker marked George as head of household, which isn't an admission that he was given the estate. The census taker usually assumes the oldest man living at a home was the head of house. Emily would have had to speak up and clarify she was head of household if the property had been given to her. It seems more likely, though, that George was given the estate free and clear of Emily and he was old enough to create trouble if she fought for any rights to the property.

That summer, Emily's brother Will shared the news that he enlisted in the Army and was heading to Ft. Buford in the Dakota Territory. George and Will were very close in age and it is reasonable to assume they had a close relationship during the five years that Will's sister Emily had been living in George's home. Watching Will head off on a grand adventure would certainly spur George's imagination for his future. If he had indeed inherited the estate, he could sell, and with that, this 21-year-old had enormous possibilities.

Emily's possibilities were not so secure. The comfort and accommodation she enjoyed with John would now be gone. What power she may have had was all removed. She appeared to remain there on the farm and she might have received some comfort from her stepdaughter Elizabeth, but she would have to consider her next steps and decide soon.

Marcena and Purlina were close neighbors to the Allen Farm for many years and it is highly likely they held a close relationship based on events that follow. In a remarkable set of circumstances, two months after John passed, Purlina passed, too. The details of their death can be learned through the mortality schedule that was part of the 1870 census. John Allen was recorded having died of "jaundice." Purlina was recorded on the next line after John and her cause of death written as "unknown."

After Purlina's death, Marcena asked Emily to marry him and she accepted. Their marriage took place 10 months after Purlina had passed. For Emily, it was 12 months and two days after John Allen's death.

It is highly unlikely Emily took possession of her late husband John's farm. If that had actually happened, it would likely have angered George, who would have created a lot of trouble for her. If that had happened, Emily wouldn't have held it for long. Once she married Marcena, the property would have been transferred to him.

Shortly after their marriage, Marcena made a remarkable decision. He decided to sell his farm and move. What would prompt Marcena to leave his equitable farm and a lifestyle to which he had been so accustomed? Was George causing problems for the two? Did they run into problems with the surrounding community? Had the community questioned why Emily, who had never given John a child in their five years, was now suddenly pregnant just a few months after she married Marcena? Or could it be that he had always wanted to move to Iowa but Purlina wasn't permitting it? We will never know the reason behind his decision. We simply know they did move and it was just after Emily had her first child.

Emily might have been quite surprised after she arrived in Iowa. She would soon realize all the problems of her past were left behind. The rumors would not follow. She would not be known as the daughter of a divorcee. The secrets of her life with John Allen were hers to keep. John and Purlina's close deaths would not be questioned. She would be miles from anyone who knew these things. Instead, she was the wife of a Morgan and the Morgan name had ties to wealth and respect there in Fremont County. She brought with her their first-born child, Mollie. They settled in and she became part of a strong family network. She made friends and acquaintances. She enjoyed the life of a respectable woman and became involved in church and social events. She dressed fine and furnished her home with the best things money could buy and over time even she forgot her own past.

A NEW ROLE

On New Year's Day, 1886, Thomas and Kate were celebrating their second day of marriage. If they had married in secret, the news would start hitting the families. Where did they spend their first days as a married couple? We will never know.

That February, Marcena and Emily celebrated their 15th wedding anniversary. Buck and Lizzie were due to have their first baby by May, and Thomas and Kate had just discovered they would be having a child, too. All of this added to the excitement for the family.

The year started off well, and if there were any misgivings about Thomas and Kate's marriage, Marcena and Emily would certainly put those aside when hearing the news. Both sons were bringing the first grandchildren into their lives.

Kate was discovering what it is like to be an expectant mother. She was getting a lot of attention, attention she had never experienced before. As summer just began, Lizzie bore her first baby, a daughter they named Nettie Gertrude Morgan. Kate observed firsthand how a newborn elevated the excitement of the Morgan family household. She also observed the pride Marcena and Emily displayed over their first granddaughter. She watched how the cousins, uncles, aunts and neighbors came to see the delicate new child and showered gifts on the new parents. Kate's heart must have been rushing with anticipation for the day when she would be the mother of a newborn and the portion of admiration and pride they would be showering on her, too.

The year did not end that way, though. At the end of September, on Marcena's 61st birthday, something terrible went wrong.

Marcena Morgan suddenly passed away. It would shock all of the Morgans of Fremont County. Had the family and friends been there with him to celebrate his birthday when he passed? We will never know.

The excitement of Thomas and Kate's upcoming baby would quickly diminish. That excitement would need to be set aside as everyone focused on Marcena's untimely death. They were now consumed with the necessary steps to prepare for a burial. They must choose a cemetery and plot, select a casket, decide on the clothes in which he would be buried, speak with the officiant for the funeral, decide on the flowers, and write an obituary. Did Marcena have special items he wished Buck or Thomas to have? Was Emily concerned about the estate? The untimely death had upended the family.

The family were certainly preoccupied with the burial details and if anyone has participated in preparing for a burial, they know it requires a lot of work. At this same time, Kate would be experiencing all of the uncomfortable aches associated with a woman who was eight months pregnant.

Marcena was placed to rest in the Utterback Cemetery in Madison of Fremont County at the end of that September. The funeral and burial were attended by the large Morgan family, their friends and many others who came to pay their respects to a man who had gained a level of respect from the community.

Hope for a better day and a return to normal routines would not come for Kate and Tom. It could never be the same again. Not for Thomas, who lost his father. Not for Kate, who was excited to receive the same attention for her first born as Lizzie had. Marcena's death would clearly change their lives forever.

Marcena had owned a sizable estate and his younger brother Tom O. Morgan quickly seized the opportunity of handling the division of the estate. On the third of October, the fifth day after Marcena passed, Emily's brother-in-law, Tom O., filed an order in the circuit court of Sidney to be assigned as a "special" administrator for Marcena's estate. When filling out the form, Tom O. marked "intestate" to "testate," striking out the "in" portion of the word. Testate meant the estate had a will and the administration of the inheritance would be conducted under the rules for wills. The bond was set at $60,000, unusually high for 1886. Tom O. took the role as principal, and Emily Morgan and Simpson Finnell, who was the father-in-law of Tom O.'s oldest daughter Sarah, were listed as sureties.

Kate went into labor on the last day of October, just a month after Marcena's death. We do not know what happened during that birth. Did she have any assistance at that time? Had her Aunt Harriet come to be of any help? Did her cousin Mary Samuels assist? Did she have the assistance of a doctor or midwife? We only know that she bore her first child that day, a son, and he lived only two days. The infant was named after his father, Thomas Edwin, and the infant received a proper burial in the Utterback Cemetery, not far from Marcena's grave. It was dark days for this young newlywed couple.

Emily found herself in the same situation that happened when her first husband John Allen passed. She would have to fight to maintain ownership of the home and property to which she was accustomed. Marcena had amassed quite a large sum of acreage, equal to, if not more, than his brother Tom O.'s land. If Marcena did not leave a will, his son Thomas would be the heir apparent with all the rights of property ownership. This time, Emily was fully involved in the estate process. She fought for her rights of ownership. She had a battle on her hands, though. Her brother-in-law Tom O., who carried a great deal of power, was injecting himself into the estate process whether Emily needed it or not.

At this stage of her life, Emily was still caring for four young children, Mollie, 14, Gertrude, 9, Lulu, 7, and her youngest boy, Lyman, who had just turned 3. Could she successfully run a farm and ranch operation, too? Running the farm would not be an easy task. She would have to delegate the operation to someone with experience. All would be contingent on how the estate would be divided, though. If Marcena wrote a will dividing it up to his heirs, then there was little Emily could do but take what portion he planned for her. If he didn't write a will, then the administrator would have to consider the heir apparent, Thomas Edwin Morgan, as a contender to inherit the property. A tough thing to override without reasonable cause.

Tom O. may have discussed with Emily all of those situations. Did they collude together to come up with a plan which was beneficial to them both? Two days before Christmas, Tom O. escorted Emily to the courthouse once again. He assisted in setting up guardianships of Emily's four children. The papers were necessary for minors who might be entitled to an inheritance. In an unusual filing though, both Emily and Tom O. were entered as co-guardians of the children. Tom O. must have wielded some level of power over Emily to be half guardian to any and all monies and property to which these children could be entitled. It was clear that Emily allowed for this, but as a woman in that age she may not have had much choice. She had no other man or family in that county to fight for her sake. Why was Tom O. doing this? He appears to have been motivated to have control over his late brother's estate and wealth. What else would Tom O. do to maintain this control? The bond over the guardianship was set for $50,000 and Emily and Tom O. were listed as principals.

In a strange set of circumstances that occurred the following year, in April of 1887, Tom O. and Emily returned to court to file a new order of administrator of Marcena Morgan's estate. This time Tom O. did not strike out "in" from intestate. Either Tom O. was unable to find Marcena's will, or it was more beneficial to handle the estate process without the rules written for wills. The original order filed that past October had become null and void. This time Emily and Tom O. were both listed as "co-administrators." And the bond was set at $80,000.

George L. Allen

George L. Allen left Sangamon County, Illinois at some point and he eventually made Fremont County, Iowa, his home, but the exact date is not known. Did he sell his father's farm and pocket the large sum of equity for which he was entitled? Did he move to Fremont before or after Marcena's death?

George's life seemed to be in the dark after Marcena and Emily had left Illinois. He was not found in any census records of 1880. He was found on the land ownership map of Madison for the year 1891. The map shows G.L. Allen's 160-acre parcel sitting across the road of one of Marcena's properties; George would sell half of this acreage in April 1892 for $3,200.

Whatever date George had arrived in Fremont County, it took him little time to build a coterie of friends that gave him unwavering support. Bankers, capitalists, lawmen and saloon keepers are just a small sampling of the men George had in his circle. In all this time George had stayed a single man and seemed to enjoy his bachelorhood.

Millard Cooley, a man who referred to himself as a capitalist, was a wealthy man who traveled with George now and then. So did W.T. Davis, a saloon keeper, and his brother Frank, who ran a hardware store. Frank Gillman, the president of the Bank of Hamburg, was a man who was also in the company of George now and then. When George attended the Chicago World's Fair in 1893, Dr. Swiggart and his wife and daughter went along with him.

Peter Wikoff wrote a letter in George's defense after Kate was found dead. Peter was a man about eight years older than George.

Peter also came from Old Berlin of Sangamon County and lived there during the same years George, Emily and Marcena were living in the same town. Peter moved to Fremont County in 1873, operated a grain dealership up until 1890 and then he became the Hamburg justice of peace. He held that title through the end of the 1890s. Peter reveals how close he was with George in the letter he sent to the *San Diego Union and Daily Bee* newspaper just a few weeks after Kate's death. He wrote, "George was an unassuming and honorable gentleman." That, "George had the highest references that could be named for which to prove." He also continued to support the false narrative that George didn't know Kate.

Another man who had a close relationship with George was James Plumb Beach. J.P. Beach took up banking back in 1885 where he stayed and was promoted to the president of the Farmers' and Merchants' Bank of Hamburg. He held on to that title at least until 1893. J.P. continued to hold on to the story that there was a man named "Bernard" that threw off the investigation into the unfortunate woman's identity. It's very telling as to how close J.P. was with George.

George was described as a sport (gambler who frequented bars) and lady killer by someone who was in San Diego at the time of Kate's death. Although George's friend Peter Wikoff defended him over that description, it is likely that it was exactly what George was.

In the newspapers of Fremont County there are numerous mentions of George's stock dealings and it is a testament to the fact that he was indeed heavily involved in the sale and trade of livestock. In any event, George was relatively wealthy. He was held in pretty high regard. He had friends of wealth with ties to banking and he was doing pretty good by the 1890s.

George and Emily also had a past together. In their youth they lived in close proximity to each other and attended school together. Emily was there when George's older brother, Albert, passed away. She married George's father and for five years lived under the same roof with George as his stepmother. It is impossible to know exactly what relationship George and Emily had with each other. They were only five years apart in age. George knew her secrets and Emily knew his and they would have built a certain level of intimacy, not necessarily sexual, during that time. In any event, it is fair to say that George didn't show up in Fremont County by accident.

After Marcena's unusual death on his birthday, Emily was under the microscope by her wealthy brother-in-law Tom O. He injected himself into the role of estate administrator of her property and guardian of her children. Emily was clearly struggling to maintain control over the life and home to which she was accustomed. Could it be that George posed a threat to her, too?

Part III
California

SAN FRANCISCO

There were no records found to learn where Thomas and Kate were living between 1885 and 1889. There were no records to discover Thomas' profession during this time. There were no records to learn if Thomas received any inheritance from his father's estate, either.

What was learned was that in 1889 Thomas decided to take Kate and move away from the Fremont area. Their destination was Burchard, Nebraska. Burchard was in Pawnee County, 70 miles southwest of Hamburg, a location where no other Morgan, Chandler or Farmer members lived. It was an extremely remote place during those years. It is still an extremely remote place. It didn't seem like an appealing location for Thomas, who was more accustomed to finer things.

Burchard was ten miles north of the Kansas border. The village of Burchard was small. Its area was less than one square mile. The only saving grace was a train depot on the Chicago, Burlington & Quincy Railroad. If they intended to do a lot of traveling, the location might have been somewhat appealing, though Hamburg would be far better for that purpose. What we know for certain, as history proves, is that this became the home for Thomas as early as 1889 and it remained his home for many years after Kate's death.

Roughly two years after Kate and Thomas moved to Burchard, Kate was found in California and she probably didn't travel there alone.

When Kate visited her Uncle Billy Farmer, in Hanford, California, she shared a number of stories with him. When Billy wrote a letter to Los Angeles Chief of Police Glass, Billy said that Kate's husband

Thomas was traveling on a "manufacturing business." Could Kate and Thomas have traveled to California because Thomas was pursuing a manufacturing venture? It would seem possible, but Thomas' future wife and daughter never alluded to Thomas having any work in California or involvement with any manufacturing ventures when his obituary was written years later. That doesn't mean he didn't pursue the venture; it could be that they just didn't know, or maybe they didn't want to disclose it.

What was disclosed by the townspeople of Hamburg, Iowa, was that Kate and Thomas had been separated for several months. That was several months just before the time of her death. We know Kate was in Los Angeles for several months and that was after she had spent an undetermined amount of time with her Uncle Billy in Tulare County, California.

What was also learned was that at some point Thomas became convinced Kate was having an affair. We learned of this from an old photo of Kate which Thomas had held onto. On the back of the photo is a handwritten story that claimed Kate had run away with Thomas' stepbrother. It did not spell out the name of the stepbrother but he only had one. Thomas had become convinced she was having an affair with George Allen. When that note was written on the back of Kate's photo, there was no expectation that anyone would ever read it. They had no idea Kate would become famous many years later. In any event, there is a high likelihood that George was in California during this time, too, with or without Tom.

With all of the restrained and simplistic life Kate grew up with in the rural farming region of southwest Iowa, the exhilaration she must have experienced when she arrived in San Francisco might have left her overwhelmed. Chief Clerk Gomer of the Hotel del Coronado shared with the newspapers that Kate was highly familiar with San Francisco's high-end hotels. If this is true, then Kate was not short of money. Either she came with a large sum or someone else was taking good care of her.

How long was she in San Francisco? Long enough to become familiar with those hotels and at least three women who gave Kate their cards. Cards that Kate would hold on to and tuck away in her personal trunk. They were Mrs. Ottinger, Mrs. J.H. McDonough and Mrs. M.R. Abbott.

Mrs. Ottinger was Leila Ottinger, the wife of Adolph Ottinger, and she had a baby, Ella, who was born in 1890. Leila and Adolph Ottinger were both of German descent and oftentimes made trips to Germany when they could.

Adolph ran a railroad ticket scalping business. He had numerous offices not just in San Francisco but in various other states, too. When he passed away many years later his obituary stated he died a wealthy man.

At this time, it would appear Adolph's scalping business was under attack by the Southern Pacific Railroad. They had been pressuring politicians to put an end to ticket scalping. This led to a bribery case where Adolph became a star witness for the state of California. The state was pursuing a conviction of one of California's state legislatures, Mr. Elwood Bruner, for soliciting a bribe. Elwood offered to kill a ticket scalping bill in exchange for $1,500 and it appears that after he killed the bill, he tried to collect from Adolph. Adolph should have received charges on the bribery case but instead he made a deal with the state to testify against Bruner. The trial began in 1891 and ran through 1892, and all of this appears to coincide with the same time Kate was in San Francisco.

Adolph fought the railroad even as late as 1895. In that year, the railroad was in heated arguments with the state of California to have a bill passed to stop scalping. The Southern Pacific Railroad was pushing a bill that would give a $200 fine or one year imprisonment for anyone who bought a ticket and then sold it to another. The punishment was more severe than that for someone who had stolen a ticket or someone who would sell their child on the street. The bill gave no discretion to the judge.

George McKenzie, who was president of the American Ticket Brokers' Association, made arguments against the bill. He laughed at the idea that the bill was out to protect the railroad conductors. He referred to Conductor Massey, who was present in the court, and said "Massey carried me on his train on my bridal tour and now he comes here to protect the people of California. Six years ago (1889), the Southern Pacific came here to lobby for the bill. The railroad, of course, is not here today. It is merely the conductors. Why are they here?" He continued on, "When a conductor does not have sufficient discrimination to lift a scalper ticket, of course he is docked. Brother Massey is frequently docked in this way."

In the courtroom, the governor argued that it just didn't seem right to place such a high price for simply reselling a ticket. He turned to Conductor Massey and asked, "How is it with you, Brother Massey?"

Massey responded in agreement, "Yes, I think it is."

The railroad men were not after the common people, though, they just wanted to stop the men who made it a business to scalp tickets. That was the purpose of the bill they argued about. But the governor refused to sign the bill. Instead, he said, "I know of no power so great as the Southern Pacific."

William Ross of the Southern Pacific, who represented the ticket clerks and the conductors, admitted that the amended law was not a good one. He replied, "In the future we may bring a bill which will catch Ottinger and McKenzie and the rest of the Scalpers." It was a bold statement to be said in front of McKenzie himself.

"And when you do, I will listen to arguments," the governor replied.

Ottinger was often written about in the news. He was constantly pursued by the Southern Pacific Railroad. Details from those news articles are very enlightening. They give a richer glimpse into Adolph Ottinger and the businesses in which he was engaged. Details revealed that Adolph not only owned a ticket broker business, but he also ran a saloon which had a hidden card room located in the back. Adolph was also involved in horse racing. He owned several racehorses for a number of years and raced them in the San Joaquin Valley.

Horse racing was one of the hottest sports at that time. Adolph competed with many other horse owners. Lewis Dalton, the father of the Dalton Gang, was also racing his own stock around Visalia, California a few years earlier. Lewis didn't live in California; he only traveled there for horse racing. He would bring his sons Bill, Cole and Lit along on those trips. It would eventually prompt those three boys to make California their home and at least two of them would stay.

News related to Adolph's horse racing reveals some of his shady behavior. He was sued once for not paying on a claim race. Another time he was sued for not paying out on winnings. He was always fighting to retain money and yet he was never jailed.

How close Kate was with the Ottingers can only be revealed in one's imagination. We only know for certain that Leila's card was kept safe in Kate's trunk.

Mrs. J.H. McDonough of San Rafael was on the next card kept in Kate's trunk. There is quite a twist with this woman's husband. James Henry McDonough was involved in criminal activity as far back as 1878 when he spent time at the Folsom Penitentiary for burglary. He was also known as Virginia Jim, a name after the state from which he came.

James McDonough was also charged in the shooting of Conductor Massey back in 1888 in Borden, northwest of Fresno. At that time, James was using the name Jim Meyers. He revealed he was one in the same during another arrest using the name McDonough, where he admitted he was the one who shot Conductor Massey. When McDonough shot Massey he was living in Red Bluff, California. A witness to the event said, "McDonough boarded the train at Madera and while he was hanging out in the smoking car he took a ticket from a Chinaman's hat and then went to a passenger coach." The act was reported to Conductor Massey, who approached McDonough, and charged him for stealing the ticket. Massey ordered McDonough to return the stolen ticket. McDonough refused to do it, so Massey attempted to take the ticket from him, which resulted in a fight. McDonough pulled a 44-caliber British Bulldog revolver and shot Massey three times. The first shot struck Massey in the breast, but Massey had a ledger with the new train route timetables in his pocket, which protected him from what could have been a fatal shot. Another shot grazed the small of Massey's back. The third struck Massey in the left thigh. Massey was severely bleeding and was taken to a sleeper car by his friends.

When the train reached Tulare, McDonough was placed in jail. During an interview with a reporter, McDonough was told that the shot that hit Massey in the chest did not hit his heart. McDonough breathed a sigh of relief learning that. McDonough told the reporter he was a peddler and that he peddled dry goods. He traveled all over and had a trunk on the way from Chicago, which he had been expecting for some time. McDonough would go to trial five months after the shooting of Conductor Massey and he would be acquitted on a plea of self-defense.

There are two other articles found which could be James McDonough but cannot be confirmed. That would be the one in 1889 where a man named J.H. Meyers (his frequently used alias) was convicted in the murder of John Lowell of El Dorado County. It said that he and two other men were sentenced to be hanged. Then there is another article in 1890, where a man named James McDonough was charged with robbery of a man by the name of Albert Davis in San Francisco.

James McDonough was arrested later in 1902 on counterfeiting charges after a raid of his San Francisco home. In that arrest, he admitted to having been the one who had shot Conductor Massey back in 1888. The police confiscated a number of McDonough's possessions in that raid. There were a few article clippings. One clipping was about McDonough's killing of a man named William Leonard in a shooting in Aspen. It stated McDonough was accosted by Leonard and after a bitterly contested trial where McDonough had pleaded self-defense, he was acquitted. Another clipping was when McDonough ran the Abbey Saloon at Root and Halstead in Chicago. In that article he had complained to the police that his wife was about to leave him and go to California with her brother. They found a marriage certificate between Fannie Dawley and James H. McDonough intermarried at Woodland, California on the third of

September 1884. They also confiscated several of his deeds, one of which was for when J.H. McDonough had purchased property in San Rafael.

J. H. McDonough was convicted and sent to San Quentin on those counterfeit charges. The prison records had two separate records of McDonough, one under the name of James H. McDonough and one of Charles McDonough, but it was the same man, with the same exact picture and same incarceration date.

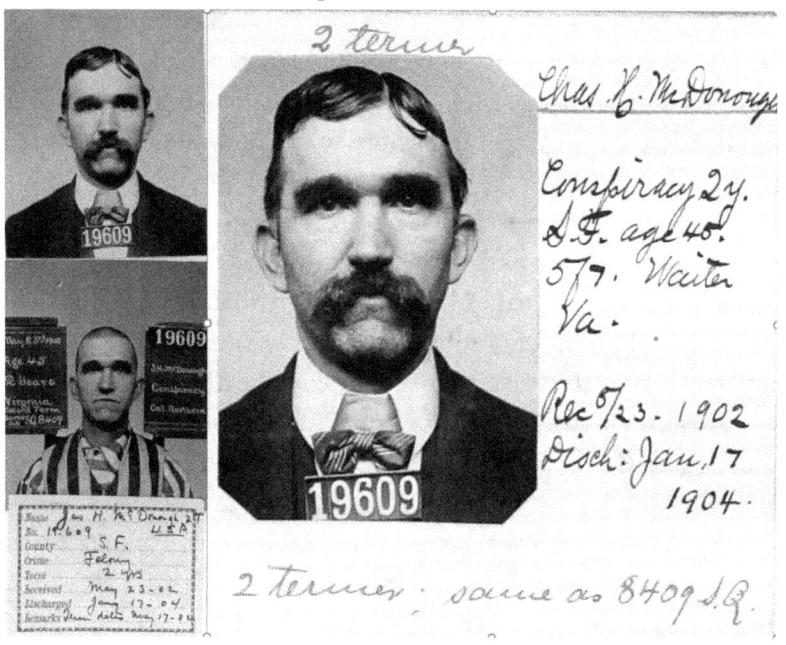

McDonough's prison records described him as having a tattoo on the upper right arm of a rising sun with initials "J McD" tattooed underneath. He had tattooed dots on each finger of his right hand. He was six feet tall and weighed 148 pounds. He went by other names, too. He was known as Jim Meyers, Virginia Jim and James Henry McDonough.

During the years between 1891 and 1892, J.H. McDonough was a 35-year-old who was not incarcerated at that time. There were no news articles of any criminal activity at that time, either. He was either staying clean or he kept his criminal activities undetectable.

It is impossible to know what relationship Kate had with Mr. and Mrs. McDonough. Was she aware of Mr. McDonough's past criminal activity? Did she witness anything unusual about him that might have given her a clue of his character? We will never know. Kate held on to Mrs. McDonough's card safely in her trunk.

The last card was that of Mrs. M.R. Abbott and she had a simple address of Fifth Street and Mission written on it. There is a Mark Leander Abbott found in the 1891 City Directory for San Francisco. He lived at 911 Mission, which is a half block from the corner of Fifth and Mission. Mark initially ran the Grand Hotel on First and K Street in Sacramento back in 1874 where he was the hotel manager. In the 1891 directory, Mark was listed as a hotel runner, a person who would solicit business for hotels by standing outside train stations or other transportation hubs, offering rooms to arriving passengers. A hotel runner was essentially a street-level salesman trying to attract guests to specific hotels, though it is not clear which hotel Abbott was working for during this time, or if he could work for more than one hotel at any given time.

There is an April 11, 1880, news article in the Daily Alta, where Mark was testifying at an inquest on the death of a woman named Enda Hoin. It was a long article on all of the details related to Felix Hoin's murder of his wife Edna. At the time, Mr. Abbott was the owner of a saloon at 1268 Market Street. He ran it with his partner A.M. Byrnes. Felix went into their saloon and having been turned down by his wife to have breakfast with him, he wanted Mr. Abbott to loan him a revolver so he could shoot her. Abbott didn't loan him one, so Felix left the saloon. Afterwards, Abbott left, too, and when Felix returned he was bragging to Byrnes that he had gotten a pistol. He said, "I am going to shoot the 'expletive' and then take my own life." Their testimony led to the conviction of Felix Hoin for murder.

In 1883, Mark and his wife Ella were having heated marital problems, fights that actually made the newspapers. They ultimately divorced but even after the divorce his ex-wife Ella filed charges against Mark because he kept sending her rude letters and giving her unwelcomed visits. He also filed charges against her for stealing a gold watch and other jewelry from his San Francisco room. Both were placed in jail. Mark was unable to secure bail but Ella had and she was released. No more words were found afterwards and it appears Mark remarried sometime later.

On the ninth of December 1886, Mark Abbott and his new wife traveled to San Diego for a visit. They arrived on the steamer Ancon coming from San Francisco. It might not have been a trip for pleasure because Mark and his wife made San Diego their home starting around 1887. He can be found in September of 1888 as the proprietor of the Cliff Hotel in Ocean Beach. He also shows up on the guest list of the Horton Hotel of San Diego during that same year. There are news articles revealing Mark joined the Coronado lodge 328 of I.O.O.F. (International Order of Odd Fellows).

Mark and his wife moved back to San Francisco just before 1891. In September 1891, Mark and his wife were one of several witnesses called on the murder trial of M.B. Curtis, who was accused of the murder of a man named Grant.

The *San Francisco Call* Volume 71, Num. 79, 17 February 1892, wrote a long article. Here is an excerpt of that article:

"WHAT MRS. ABBOTT SAW.

Mrs. M. L. Abbott said that she lived at 249 Fifth Street; that on the night of September 10 there were in her house besides herself and husband, was her sister, a Miss Anderson, a Reverend Dr. Weller, of Santa Monica, and a Mr. Harrington.

Mrs. Abbott heard the pistol shots and sprang from her bed to the window, looking out on Fifth. She saw a man running very fast up Fifth street, towards Howard. This man came from the direction of the fence that had bullet holes in it. When she first saw him this man was under the window of her brother-in-law, Dr. Weller. She next saw two men standing near Creighton's saloon on Folsom Street. She did not see a man running toward Shipley Street, but she was very sure she saw a man running towards Howard Street.

... Mark L. Abbott, husband of the last witness, testified that his occupation was that of a hotel-runner. He corroborated the testimony of his wife."

In March 1892, a month after Mark and his wife had testified, Mark checked into the Palace Hotel in Visalia alone. In June, Mark was up in Red Bluff staying at the Tremont Hotel. Then in mid-August he was back down in Tulare County with a stay in the Grand Hotel. He was then found in the Cosmopolitan in September, near San Luis Obispo. Mark traveled, usually alone, often in the role of hotel runner, as he worked to drum up customers for hotels.

What relationship did Kate have with Mr. and Mrs. Abbott? It is difficult to say. It is also strangely coincidental that during Mrs. Abbott's testimony, a Miss Anderson was there at her home. Could that have been Kate? Abbott traveled a lot and often showed up in Tulare County where Kate's Uncle Billy Farmer and cousin George Farmer lived. There seems to be no articles of hotel check-ins under the names of Kate or Thomas Morgan found in any of the news. We do know for certain that Kate would end up staying near, or possibly even at, her uncle's home in Hanford, Tulare County, California. Of that we can be certain.

TULARE COUNTY

Tulare County, California, is in the San Joaquin Valley, roughly 200 miles south of Sacramento. The Southern Pacific Railroad brought prosperity to that valley. The railroad ran from Sacramento through Fresno to Goshen, continuing south through Tulare, Tipton, Alila (today Earlimart), Bakersfield, Santa Clarita and into Los Angeles.

At the Visalia/Goshen train station, there was a spur line that ran east to west. Hanford was a short distance to the west of Visalia. That line continued past Hanford west-southwest for another 60 miles to reach Cholame, San Miguel and Paso Robles. It was at the Visalia/Goshen station that Kate would change trains to reach her uncle in Hanford.

In the 1890 land map for Visalia, artist drawings depicted an area with large acres of fruit groves and lovely homes dotting the land. The drawings render an idyllic vision of the area. What the artist did not draw were the numerous saloons, gambling establishments and horse tracks found in the area, too. It also did not capture the large number of unsavory types. During the year of 1891, an uptick of train robberies was occurring and the sheriff and other law enforcement were working tirelessly to capture and arrest those men.

The Dalton brothers, Grat, Bob and Emmett, were already wanted for various crimes in Kansas when they left for California sometime around 1890. Their brother Bill had a ranch near San Miguel, California and the brothers hoped to hunker down there to avoid capture. Their ultimate goal was to remake their lives and they brought with them a good sum of cash.

While they received a warm welcome and a nice place to stay with their brother Bill, they weren't always there. They left often, telling their brother they would be looking for work, and meanwhile, they were traveling all over Tulare County by horseback and rail. They didn't find work; instead, they found an abundance of saloons and gambling establishments and it wasn't long before they ran out of cash and returned to crime.

In February of 1891, the brothers attempted a robbery of a Southern Pacific's pay car at the Alila station. Grat was captured and was jailed. When the sheriff went after his brothers, Bob and Emmett, they fled to Oklahoma. The marshals decided to arrest their brother Bill, even though he had a strong alibi, and they placed him in the Visalia jail. Grat was in the Visalia jail, too, already convicted and awaiting sentence. In September, Grat managed to escape the jail. Bill could have joined him but instead remained in his cell and that would turn out fortunate for him, because he would later be acquitted and released.

Grat had fled to the home of a man named Joe Middleton. Emmett would later identify Middleton as a friend of Grat. Joe lived in Hanford but out in the country north of there. Middleton helped Grat by providing him with food and supplies for a hideout to which Grat fled, in a mountain north of Visalia. In February of 1892, Joe Middleton decided to work with Sheriff Kay to show him the location of Grat's camp. Before Sheriff Kay could make an arrest, Grat once again escaped and this time he left California to return to Oklahoma. It would not be long afterwards that he would be killed during the infamous bank robbery of October 1892.

Bill Dalton, who had been acquitted of his charges, might have lived to a ripe old age if he had remained in California. That was not what he did, though. He would later move to Oklahoma and put together his own gang known as the Doolin-Dalton gang. He would ultimately be killed, too, in 1894.

The exact date when Kate arrived at the train station in Tulare County is not known but based on the fact that she stayed there before her time in Los Angeles, it is safe to say she was there between late 1891 and early 1892.

Billy–who was formally referred to as W.T. Farmer–was the oldest brother of Kate's father, George. Billy left his Iowa home for California when he was only 18. In his early years in California, he lived as far north as Napa. When Kate came to see him, Uncle Billy was living out in the country north of Hanford's city center. Would Billy have ever met Joe Middleton? The population at that time was fairly small and it would seem likely he would have at least run into Middleton now and then.

Kate's cousin George Thomas Farmer also lived in the Hanford area. George was the son of John Milton Farmer and Jane Utterback. He was also the brother to Mary Samuels of Riverton, who Kate spent time with during the days Kate had returned to live with her Grandpa Joe and his second wife Maria Chandler.

Cousin George first came to California around 1875 as a mere 16-year-old. In a news story telling the story of George's arrival it said he didn't take the train all the way to Visalia's train station; instead, he jumped off at the Cross Creek switch and walked over to his Uncle Billy's.

When George first arrived, he and his Uncle Billy were living in an area known as Mussel Slough and they lived there during the Mussel Slough bloodshed that occurred at that time. It was over land title disputes between the Southern Pacific Railroad and men who were claiming properties in that area. They had already built homes and barns when the railroad company came to claim the land back. Blood was shed and the disputes took time, but Southern Pacific won and took possession of those settled properties, leaving those original homeowners with nothing. It is known that the men of Tulare County often turned a blind eye to any criminal activity related to the Southern Pacific Railroad.

After George Farmer settled in Tulare, he met and married a woman by the name of Gertrude Ruggles, a native of Woodland, California. Woodland happened to be the same city where J.H. McDonough had married his wife years earlier. There were no records found which could prove the Ruggles family had ever known McDonough, though. When Kate arrived, George and Gertrude had been married for more than 10 years and had five children, all under the age of 10, with the youngest at just one.

1892 was a difficult year for George and Gertrude. Gertrude's brothers, John and Charlie, had held up a Wells Fargo Stage near Shasta, California on the 15th of May. During the robbery, the brothers killed a man named Buck Montgomery. Charlie was injured during the robbery and was captured. John got away, though, and he took with him $3,000 cash and $3,000 in gold.

John Ruggles already had a criminal past. In 1878, he was sentenced to seven years at San Quentin for robbing a man and woman in San Joaquin County. He was released after receiving a pardon in 1880. Afterwards, he settled down and bought a large swath of property across the road from his father in Dinuba of Tulare County. He appeared to have put his criminal past behind him and lived a decent life for many years up until the Wells Fargo robbery.

After John fled the robbery, he stayed hidden for a while and he found his way to Woodland. Deputies were staking out his Uncle Dexter's place north of Woodland but did not find him there. By mid-June, John was noticed, by a hardware clerk, buying cartridges in Woodland. Deputy Sheriff Wykoff and a few other officers followed John and saw him entering a restaurant. Once John sat down at a table, Deputy Sheriff Wykoff and a few other officers went in and sat down with him. John recognized Wykoff immediately. Wykoff ordered his hands up but John did not comply; instead, John reached for his revolver and Wykoff fired, hitting John's neck. John tried again to draw when Wyckoff grabbed him and took his pistol away. John would ultimately sign a confession to the Wells Fargo robbery and the sheriff would recover the bag containing a large sum of money. They did not recover the missing gold, though, and John Ruggles would not give them that location, either.

Lyman Ruggles, the father of John and Charlie, and the father-in-law of George Farmer, was a prominent man who lived in Traver, Tulare County. After John's arrest, Lyman and his son-in-law George Farmer made a trip to speak with his son. John Ruggles was being held at the Redding jail at that time. When Lyman and George made their visit on the 26th of June, Lyman also brought his lawyer, who had drawn up a deed of trust conveying all of John Ruggles' property in Tulare County to his father Lyman. John signed the deed of trust and he also signed papers giving his father power of attorney to transact all of his business in Tulare. It is said that John's property was considerable. He owned a section of fine land, valued at $10,000, two miles from Dinuba. He also had five horses and machinery and other personal effects. John permitted the power of attorney, but he also expressed that after all of his debts were paid, he wished that the remaining go as proceeds to his little daughter Stella. John knew he was not going to come out of this trial alive.

An interesting event followed, possibly unrelated, but the town of Woodland sustained a large fire on the second of July. Many businesses, restaurants and homes were damaged. If John had hidden that gold in that town, it would seem that the fire could have produced the location. Could the fire have been a diversion to have it removed? Impossible to know.

John expected a long trial and a conviction, but things changed. At 2 a.m. on Sunday, the 25th of July, a janitor, who was the only person in the Redding Courthouse at that hour, was startled when a mob of 30 masked men burst in. They forced the safe open and grabbed the keys to the jail. When they opened the Ruggles brothers' cells, John Ruggles pleaded for his brother Charlie's life. It was no use; the mob were determined men and did what they came to do. The brothers were taken, with ropes around their necks and their hands bound behind their backs and walked two blocks to the cross beams at the blacksmith's shop. The beams were used for hoisting and repairing heavy wagons, but that night the mob was using them for a different purpose. The mob's leader said to the Ruggles brothers, "If you want to make a statement, now is your time and be damned quick!"

John Ruggles pleaded with the mob, "Gentleman, spare him." One of the lynchers asked John if he had anything to say concerning the Calaveras stage robbery where a young girl on the stage was killed. The lyncher also asked about the murder of a driver in Siskiyou County, supposed by some to have been killed by John Ruggles. John answered, "I know nothing of these affairs!"

The men attempted to get John Ruggles to reveal where the gold bullion was hidden. John bargained with them that if they spared his brother Charlie, he would tell. They didn't wish to spare Charlie. Instead, they threw the ropes over the cross beams and the two Ruggles brothers were hanged. It was shocking news for the father, Lyman Ruggles, the sister Gertrude, and Gertrude's husband George Farmer.

The lynching occurred approximately four months before Kate would be found dead at the Hotel del Coronado. The newspapers suggested Kate had only been in Los Angeles for three months. Was that true? Could she have been employed by three different employers in such a short period of time? If the news was true, then Kate was likely still at her uncle's when the Ruggles were lynched.

Uncle Billy Farmer had lived in Tulare County for many years and at the time of Kate's visit he was a part-owner of the Excelsior Cheese Manufacturing Company in Hanford. He and four other partners, James Clark, S.C. Fisher, J.H. Dawson, and J.A. Wilson incorporated the company in 1889. Billy made a comfortable profit in this venture. Billy remained single his whole life and was described as a very tall and muscularly built man. Without a family to tie him down, he likely enjoyed his free time in the local saloons and racetracks, too.

When Billy learned later that the identity of the woman from the suicide at the hotel was Kate, he wrote a strong letter to Chief of Police Glass of Los Angeles, refusing to believe this could be Kate. Billy thought that she simply would not have taken her life, that she could always count on him if she even contemplated such an act.

Billy had also written that Kate left Hanford for Los Angeles with a good sum of cash. He did not explain how much or how she came by it. He also wrote Kate a letter of recommendation to help her secure employment. When she arrived in Los Angeles, she wrote to her Uncle Billy to tell him that she had secured a situation for a banker named Mr. Widney on the west side.

Kate held a photo of an older bearded man in her personal trunk. The police believed it could have been her Uncle Farmer. The name on the back of the photo had been carefully removed. The only word that remained was Visalia.

Los Angeles

When Kate arrived in Los Angeles, her future was not certain. She had no job waiting. She had no family or friends to take her in. It had to take a certain level of brevity to do what she was doing in an era when women had so little representation and even less safety without a man to protect them. Her uncle may have warned her not to go alone but she must have been determined because that was what she did. She might have drawn strength from her Aunt Harriet, proof a single woman can be successful on her own. It was a new era and many women were pushing the boundaries for better rights. Kate arrived alone and in no time she secured her first job.

Kate had hoped to get a servant's position that would provide room and board and a level of safety, which she needed above all. It would provide a low salary, but she didn't need too much since she already had a good sum of cash.

There is an article written by Nellie Bly in 1887 named "Trying to be a servant." She went undercover as a woman attempting to gain a servant's job. It is a very interesting read but in short, she reveals the difficulties and degradation to which young women were relegated in order to secure those positions. Most of these girls had little, if any, money and were desperate. They did not have any connections to the wealthy households seeking servants, so they turned to agencies to represent them. These agencies would charge the girls a monthly fee until they found employment. They would also charge the families seeking a servant a fee, too. The prettiest girls would get jobs right away and oftentimes it was the employers who demanded that. The pretty ones were making as much as $20 a month! Employers didn't just want a pretty girl, though; they expected their hire to have experience as a nurse (childcare), seamstress, chambermaid, cook, waitress and parlor maid.

Did Kate ever work as a domestic in San Francisco? If she had, it appears she chose not to disclose that to the Los Angeles employment agencies, maybe to avoid being tied to anything related to San Francisco and whatever nefarious situations from which she might have escaped. Otherwise, maybe she simply hadn't worked as a housekeeper up there and would need her uncle's letter of recommendation in order to get her start in that role. In any case, Kate had secured her first job and it was for the household of Robert Maclay Widney at 416 South Olive, Los Angeles.

If Kate ever participated in farm labor, housekeeping would be easy work in comparison. What Kate may not have been prepared for is the mannerism and etiquette demanded of servants. She would not be alone, though. There would certainly be other servants working beside her who could teach her these things. She would also share quarters with the other servants and her bed would be more likely somewhere up in an attic space or thereabouts.

After Kate settled into her first job, she sent a thoughtful letter to her Uncle Billy. She appeared excited to share with him the news that she secured a job and she gave him her employer's name, occupation and where he lived. This act showed that Kate not only wanted to keep a close relationship with her uncle but she also wanted to ease any concerns he might have had about her safety. She might have also done that as an additional safety net in case anything happened to her.

Mr. Widney had a law degree and in 1892 he was the president of University Bank. Mr. Widney was also a judge in Los Angeles. He was 53 years of age with a wife, Mary, who was 48. The children, Mary, 23, Martha, 18, Joseph, 13, and Arthur, 8, were all still living at the household.

Judge Widney also ran for state senator that year. Pomona and Redlands presented a petition to Mr. Widney to enter the race as United States Senator. They wanted the southern part of the state to have better representation. He would take up their challenge and run, but ultimately he didn't win the seat.

In July of 1892, Judge Widney took part in a delegation to the police commission in hopes of addressing the situation with prostitution in the city.

The *Los Angeles Herald* wrote the story on the delegation and the discussions that took place. It went as follows:

"Dr. Widney said that several nights ago he was on the Santa Barbara train and had been shocked by the open display of prostitution as it is practiced on Alameda Street. He, as well as many others, had witnessed, not one block from Aliso Street, the boldness of painted females whose open windows disclosed their gaudily clad forms, the more visible by reason of big lamps hanging in their dens. The overland Southern Pacific trains carry numerous tourists and pass there every night when these dens of sin are in full blast, and he had made the calculation that no less than thirty trains pass through the street daily. He reverted to the bad impression that such a sight must make upon people visiting this section for the purpose of making real estate investments, or those who are seeking homes. Dr. Widney deplored the publicity of this shocking exhibition of boldness. He thought that the abandoned women who had their abode on alameda street should be forced away from that thoroughfare.

Mr. Mackay - The matter was a very hard one to deal with.

Mr. Widney - The commissioners have the power to drive these women into secluded quarters. If it cannot be done directly, then they should be pushed into other places by indirect means.

Mr. Lewis - The women were first driven away from New High Street. What will we do with them if we now drive them away from the Alameda? Let me remind you of the time when stringent police measures had virtually closed the cribs. The women, thus deprived of the ordinary avenues, became street

walkers and patrolled our principal streets at night, to the great scandal of our citizens.

Dr. Widney - Leaving alone the moral aspect of the situation, the condition of affairs was hurting the business chances of the city. Steps need to be taken to have them ousted as quickly as possible.

Mr. Snyder - I am willing to cooperate with the board for their removal from Alameda but I object strongly to their return to New High Street.

Reverend Mr. Campbell – Another thing. The employees of the railroad wave their pocket handkerchiefs to the women. I have seen it frequently. A lady first called my attention to it. Why cannot the railroad company be directed to build a fence in front of these houses? (Signs of amusement, quickly subdued under the eagle glance of the reverend gentleman.)

Mr. Snyder – I move that the chief be instructed to cause the inmates of the houses of ill fame on Alameda Street to remove their names and door plates from their abodes.

Mr. Shatto - To which I offer an amendment that the women be driven from Alameda Street altogether. They can come into my ward if they want to. I will modify my amendment to read the chief be instructed to disperse them quietly.

The original motion by Mr. Snyder was adopted.

Mr. Shatto - It was strange that the board should so often express the ambitious desire to deal with the question of social evil, but when committees, as the one just departed, came along with their grievances their desires were never properly considered.

Mr. Mackay - Because we do not desire this board shall become the laughingstock of this city. We do not propose to make ourselves ridiculous, sir. I do not care if there were a thousand motions of that kind, I, at least, would not countenance them!

Mr. Lewis - I move that the chief be instructed to use diligence in the premises and order that the women be forced to keep their windows or blinds closed. I will add that the police are not very numerous in that district to attend to the enforcement of this order, a few might be taken from Mr. Shatto's district where, for obvious reasons, they are not so much in demand.

Mr. Shatto - Oh! Yes! What would it avail? The women will remain quiet for a couple of weeks and then they'll give the policemen a dollar or two and that is all it will amount to.

Mr. Lewis' motion was adopted and the board adjourned."

Often women doing work on Alameda actually preferred this over other options of employment. In one story written in February of that year, a brother from Helena, Montana wrote to Los Angeles Chief of Police Glass that his sister was enticed by a Frenchman that he could secure her a position as a cook in Los Angeles. Since then, the brother had learned that she had actually been enticed to a life of shame and the Frenchman was living off her earnings. The brother provided the chief with a picture of his sister. The chief took steps to locate her on Almeda Street and brought her back to the station. The woman gave a different story than the brother gave, though. She said, "My name is Palmyre Guignon and my brother lives in Helena. I was born in Amsterdam of French parents. My brother induced me to come to this country. He said he was rich and had a fine place in Helena. He promised me $8 a month. I came out, but my brother treated me ill and never gave me any money. My brother wanted me to be bad, so I could earn money for him." The woman continued to say that since she had fallen, she was going to keep on the course she was pursuing. As she was of age, the police authorities could not do anything more in the matter.

It may be surprising to know that in 1892, prostitution was not illegal. Single, vulnerable women working in prostitution took great risks. Some had men looking out for their safety, men who used them for their own profitable gain. Some women did business in fine hotels where their clients had wealth and power. Other women worked the trade in "cribs" (small independent rooms rented on a nightly basis) and they carried a much higher risk. They had little control over the clients they entertained and Los Angeles had some seedy areas from which those clients came. One such place was the "Three Mile House."

The Three Mile House was a saloon north of the city near the Southern Pacific tracks that ran between Burbank and San Fernando. The owner, H.F. Parkins, entertained all sorts of unsavory men, but he was no innocent himself. He was charged with fencing stolen property taken from robberies made off of the Southern Pacific freight trains. There were a lot of rowdy men that frequented that bar. Three Mile House's location was not the best location, either. It was so close to the Vickery Slaughterhouse that it had a level, wrenching stench in the air. A man had to desperately need a drink to choose that place as a hangout. They were the kind of clientele who came to Alameda to find a "crib" for the night.

As for Kate, she could have ended up on Alameda. It was extremely difficult for a young, single woman to make it on her own without help from family or some man in her life, and oftentimes, these women took a life in a "crib." It was considered far more profitable than housekeeping. That's not what Kate did. She continued the course of housekeeping, not only for the Widney family, but for two other families, T.H. Hughes, and L.A. Grant.

There seems to be little to be discovered related to T.H. Hughes. There is no T.H. Hughes listed in the 1892 Los Angeles City Directory. That directory included the surrounding towns, too. There are no 1890s census records to look over since the 1890 census records of every state in the U.S. were destroyed by fire many years later. That always added to the difficulties of discovering anything related to this time period. We only know that the news reported that T.H. Hughes was one of Kate's employers.

There was a news article found for Thomas Hughes, who raced horses and worked at the Ninth Street Mill. It is impossible to confirm if he could be the T.H. Hughes the police alluded to employing Kate in 1892.

Her last employer, Lewis Alexander Grant, had quite a history, though. Lewis was a wealthy railroad contractor. He was a partner with his two other brothers, Angus Grant, who was the company's chief, and his other brother John Grant.

All three were originally from Canada. They owned and operated the Grant Brothers Construction Company and made their wealth from the numerous railroad contracts they had won. These brothers were involved in the building of the Santa Fe and Southern Pacific railroads and included the building of the railway terminal in Los Angeles. The brothers also owned a number of properties in Albuquerque, New Mexico, and managed that city's public utilities. The city of Grant, New Mexico, was named after Grant's station whereby the brothers had an encampment during the construction of the Atlantic and Pacific Railroad that ran through New Mexico. That railroad later became the Atchison Topeka and Santa Fe. In 1892, the Grant Brothers Construction Company headquarters were in Los Angeles. Needless to say, Mr. L.A. Grant was not only wealthy but powerful.

L.A. Grant was 40 years old the year Kate worked for him. The year before that, he lived in the heart of Los Angeles at the four-story Victorian Hollenbeck Hotel at Second and Spring Street. When he became engaged to Harriet McPherson, another Canadian, their wedding announcement had him living at the Westminster Hotel. Once they were married, he moved into a home at 917 South Hill St. where they stayed for many years.

In May of 1892, Louis A. Grant's wife Harriet gave birth to her first baby, a girl named Anna. Harriet may have needed additional help at that time. It is understood that Kate was hired by the Grants closer to the Thanksgiving timeframe when their baby was closer to five months old.

What seems unusual is that Kate, who was thoughtful enough to write to Uncle Billy about her first employment for Mr. Widney, didn't choose to write to him with the news of her other two jobs. Uncle Billy received no more letters from her and had assumed she was still employed by Mr. Widney when he received news of her death.

When Thanksgiving Day approached, Kate had something that she needed to take care of and it would require her to be out overnight. She gave the Grants notice that afternoon, assuring them that she would be back the next day, early enough to help with Thanksgiving dinner. When she stepped out, they recalled she was carrying only her gripsack and a shawl.

Kate did not return the next day to help with Thanksgiving dinner and that alarmed the Grant family. Mr. Grant immediately notified the Los Angeles police of his missing servant, Kate.

REFLECTIONS

Kate had been living in Los Angeles long enough to have worked for three different households in the domestic industry. She appeared to have arrived there without an immediate home. No family provided her room and board. Instead, she came as a single woman living independently through her own sheer will. She lived free of the prostitution to which so many other homeless young women turned. She stayed clear from the ruthless, lawless men that were pervasive in the west and on the outskirts of town. She not only avoided so many things in that city that could have corrupted her, but she worked for wealthy families who engaged in the city government, banking, and construction.

Her last employer remembered her as one of the best housekeepers he'd had, never indicating any observation of mischievousness, illness or weakness. Her co-workers at Grant's home recalled her as being quiet and never called on by outside men.

Kate might have experienced a gilded lifestyle in San Francisco, but she turned away from that. She also turned away from her husband, but that might not have been her choice. She did not return to Iowa but instead chose to go to Los Angeles, alone, to seek employment that would give her a level of independence and safety, and a location that provided comfortable winters and sunny summers.

She thoughtfully wrote to her Uncle Billy once she secured her first job in Los Angeles, providing him with her employer's name and his location and showing she wanted to ease any worry he may have had of her. Yet, while out on an errand, one that would only take a day, she came up missing and in less than a week, she would be found dead 120 miles south on the beach steps of an exclusive hotel.

Unfortunately, they didn't know it was Kate Morgan, not for the first few weeks. During that time, the swirling accounts of news and depictions of the mysterious woman took on a life of its own, a protagonist in a story told through the lens and perceptions of people who didn't know Kate as a person and had no vested interest in her.

It was a matter of consequence. She came down to a town that didn't know who she was, using a name that was not hers. Her identity was left up to the coroner, undertaker, news writers, and the general public to determine who she was. Without her family or friends stepping forward to clear the clutter, the mounting false depictions tagged on to the mysterious woman developed an identity of its own. A new optic filtered through prejudices, opinions, emotions, and deceit were developed in the consciousness of the public mind. After a long and extensive search revealed it was Kate Morgan, those depictions stuck to Kate's legacy, even to this day.

It is said that a single spoken story is interpreted in a multitude of ways. Each person listens and interprets, using their own experiences and understanding. What starts as a single truth transforms into endless variations, memorialized by each individual in their own way.

What is the truth of Kate's last days? That will remain in the grave with her.

To understand Kate's last days, we have the stories and evidence left behind by individuals who gave what they recalled. The information and evidence is overshadowed by embellishments and interpretations the writers at that time understood to be correct. Somewhere in all that minutia lies fragments of truth.

The following will be another interpretive story to depict her last days. It will include another layer of bias from yet another lens. A lens that will attempt to pull together knowledge of her past history and the new evidence found from recent research.

Let's unpack.

Part IV

Arrivals and Departures

Elizabeth McGovern

THOSE LAST DAYS

For the past week, Kate had not been herself. She was anxious, jumpy and somewhat distracted. Her fellow workers at the Grant's home were curious. This was not like Kate, but they knew she was a private woman. Kate didn't like to talk about her personal life. They only knew she was married to a gambler and she had no idea where he was. As much as they wanted to intervene, they respected Kate's space and didn't pry.

It was the day before Thanksgiving. Once Kate had finished her chores she quickly went up to her space. She opened her trunk and grabbed her satchel. She picked up some fancifully embroidered handkerchiefs and placed one in her dress pocket and a few in the bag. She picked up her coin purse, opened it to see how much she had, then placed it in her pocket. She grabbed a black shawl and wrapped it around her shoulders and neck. She pushed other items around and looked down at a tin box. It contained her uncle's letter of recommendation, some family photos and her marriage certificate. Her hand edged toward it but she drew it back. She decided she had what she needed and closed the trunk. Holding tight to her satchel, she headed downstairs.

Kate found Mr. and Mrs. Grant and gave them a smile. She explained she had an errand she needed to attend to and it would not take her long but she would be gone overnight. She promised she would be back the next day in time to help prepare Thanksgiving dinner. Without any worries, the Grant's gave her permission and she took off along the walkway in front of their home.

That afternoon, Kate acquired a beautiful black dress. The dress sat on top of a black corset she was wearing underneath and it gave her a flattering hourglass figure. There were no protruding bustles in the back of the skirt. That was too old fashioned now. This dress was part of the "New Woman" fashion of the day. The dress hung smoothly over her hips and was just long enough to lightly graze the ground. It had gigot sleeves which had pronounced puffing above the elbows and hugged her lower arms down to the wrists. She chose a beautiful black narrow brimmed hat that was neither a riding hat or a fedora but had similarities to both. It had plumes of black feathers on one side along with soft black netting that wrapped around the crown and ever so slightly trailed. The hat was becoming very popular with progressive women. Women who wore such hats were the boundary breakers and seekers of independence. Underneath all of this she wore a pair of Louis-heeled, pointed-toe boots of black leather that laced up just past her ankles.

Kate wore those fine clothes that morning as she waited at the Los Angeles train depot. She felt beautiful as she watched others waiting on the train. Men gave her respectful tips of their hats as they passed by her. She was no longer seen as a domestic but a woman of high society and independence as she anxiously awaited the train.

The Southern Pacific train began every morning from San Bernardino at 7:30 a.m., then Colton at 7:38 a.m., Riverside at 7:55 a.m., arriving in Los Angeles at 8:15 a.m.. It would then continue on to Orange arriving at 9:23 a.m., Santa Ana at 9:31 a.m. and Oceanside at 11:17 a.m.. When it arrived in San Diego it would be 12:50 in the afternoon and its final stop was National City at 1 p.m. before it began its return trip back to San Bernardino.

When the train stopped in Los Angeles, it was carrying trunks, trunks that had tags showing they were coming from Omaha by way of Denver. One particular trunk was filled with Kate's belongings, a trunk that had a peculiar French lock. Kate was so familiar with it, she could name every single item it had and she held its key in a small coin purse in her pocket.

When the train stopped, something compelled Kate to board. She was not alone, either. Another man was there and he was as well dressed as she was. Boarding that train was going to come with consequences, consequences of which Kate seemed unaware, consequences she would bear the moment she placed her black leather lace up boot on that first steel step. Boarding would add a level of complexity to her day as she took a seat with the man and the train slowly pulled away from the terminal. The next stop, Orange California, was just a little over an hour away.

While they rode, they engaged in small talk. Their conversation went smoothly but the topic changed and gradually the discussion escalated into an intense argument, so much so that it attracted the eyes and ears of the other passengers. Orange Station stop was just five minutes away and Kate began to plead with the man that she was sorry. He was unusually angered by the discussion, though, and when the train made its stop, he grabbed his things and left the car.

Kate could have chosen to get off, too. She could have gotten off to mend whatever disagreement she had with the man. She could have gotten off and returned to Los Angeles, keeping the secret of this failed attempt and saving her job. That is not what she did though. She stayed steadfast in her seat.

The next stop was Santa Ana, only 10 minutes farther down the tracks. It gave time to process that sudden exit of the man and a chance to reconsider whether the idea she had planned was worth sticking to. She had one last chance to return to the safety of her job and independent life. That was not what she did, though. She stayed in her seat and continued on.

Something was going through her mind and maybe the trunks were partially to blame, but something else seemed to be part of her reason to stay, some grand plan that she became so convinced was necessary that she was willing to abandon her job and independent life to achieve. She was not doing this alone, though. This plan involved a man. A man she trusted. They had a disagreement and they certainly argued, but she trusted he would not be gone for long and he would return for her, so she stayed in that seat and the train slowly rolled forward.

For two long hours, Kate sat on the train after leaving Santa Ana. It was a good time for her to reflect on her situation. Was she certain the man would not be gone for long? That he would take the next train down? That train made two trips to San Diego daily, the morning run which Kate was on and an evening run.

The tracks ran along the California coastline. The Pacific Ocean would be shimmering from the midday sun. It was nearly 11:30 a.m. when the train stopped at Oceanside. San Diego was the next stop and only an hour away.

When the train pulled into the D Street Station in San Diego, the baggage clerks unloaded everyone's trunks. The passengers were picking them up and loading their things on nearby wagons. When Kate asked for help to pick up her trunks, the baggage clerk asked her for her claim tickets. Kate may not have considered a need for proof to take her trunks. He didn't seem to ask the same from a man nearby. Kate suddenly became concerned; the man she traveled with had those tickets. Kate was frustrated and she offered all sorts of arguments with the clerk but he would not budge. Instead, he assured her the trunks would be safe at the station until she returned with the tickets.

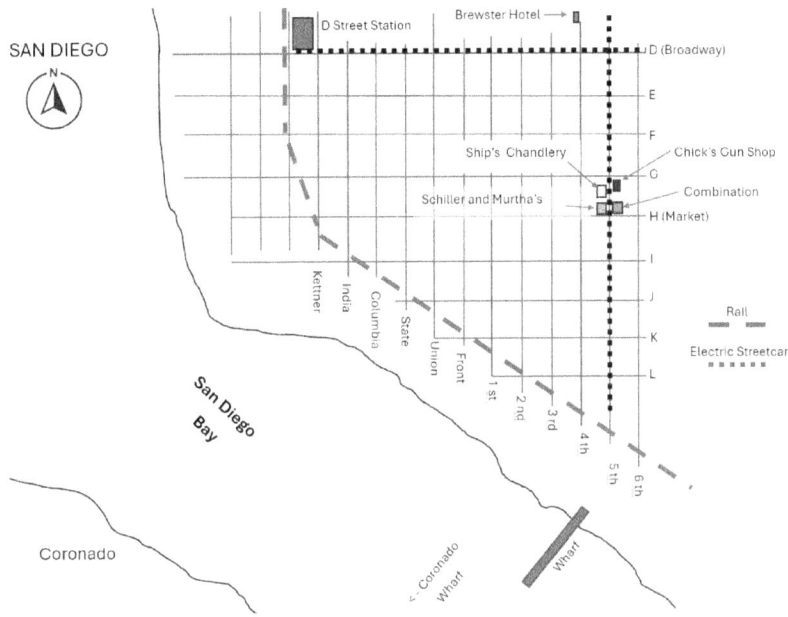

SAN DIEGO

D Street Station

Brewster Hotel →

D (Broadway)

E

F

Ship's Chandlery

Chick's Gun Shop

G

Schiller and Murtha's

Combination

H (Market)

I

J

K

L

Kettner

India

Columbia

State

Union

Front

1 st

2 nd

3rd

4 th

5 th

6 th

San Diego Bay

Coronado

Coronado Wharf

Wharf

Rail

Electric Streetcar

143

Thanksgiving Day

"CORONADO NOTES:
Thanksgiving Day was observed at the Hotel del Coronado in a quiet manner. The guests gathered in groups on the verandahs and visited with one another. Some went sailing, others went horseback riding, while the younger generation rollicked in the surf and basked in the sun on the beach."
***-San Diego Union and Daily Bee*, 25 November 1892**

It would seem pointless for Kate to turn back now. Her job at the Grant home certainly seemed lost. She could have, though. She could have returned and begged forgiveness from the Grants. She didn't do that, though. She couldn't leave the trunks behind, especially the one fitted with a unique French lock.

It was nearly 1 p.m. when Kate was given instructions on how to get to the San Diego wharf. She boarded the D Street trolley and rode it east towards Fifth Street. She had a chat with a fellow passenger who suggested where she could get ferry tickets for a mere 25 cents, so Kate stepped off the trolley at 4th Street to find the Hotel Brewster.

The Hotel Brewster had been advertising the sale of round-trip tickets to Coronado at a drastically reduced price of 25 cents. The typical price was 60 cents.

Kate entered the Brewster early that afternoon. She sauntered up to the check-in desk with the confidence only displayed by an independent, financially-entitled young lady.

The clerk looked upon her and gave her a warm smile. "Hello ma'am, how can I help you?"

"Good afternoon. Would you please tell me if Mr. and Mrs. Anderson have checked in?" She felt exhilarated with this move.

"Let me have a look," the clerk said as he pulled the book out to search through the last few days of hotel guests' signatures. "I'm sorry, there is no Anderson checked in here."

Kate gave him a warm smile back. "Oh, they must have gone to the Hotel del Coronado. I'll go find them there," she said as if she and her friends were from that kind of wealth.

"Yes, ma'am. We sell round trip tickets to Coronado at our pharmacy just down that hall," he replied, as he pointed down a nearby corridor.

"Thank you. That is very kind of you!" she said and headed off to the hotel pharmacy with a flair of importance.

Kate had been testing the societal norms for women pushing the boundaries of independence. She was also clever with her little stunt. If "the man" who had left her arrived late on the next train and decided to check into the Brewster, the clerk there would share with him that a woman asked for him and she went to the Hotel del Coronado. It was her way of leaving a virtual calling card.

The round-trip tickets Kate bought could be used in one of two ways. Either she could go by way of the Coronado Ferry or the Coronado Belt Line.

The Coronado Belt Line took an hour and 30 minutes from the foot of Fifth Street to the Hotel del Coronado. It followed along the San Diego Bay edge, first south until nearly one mile of the Mexican border, then swinging west for a mile or so before it turned back north on a very narrow stretch of land known as the silver strand. The strand had areas so narrow that often it was only a quarter mile wide. The Pacific Ocean could be seen on the left and the San Diego Bay on the right. The Coronado Belt Line ran two times a day: in the morning at 8:25 a.m., arriving at the hotel at 9:50 a.m., and in the afternoon at 5:10 p.m., arriving at the hotel by 6:30 p.m. The Coronado Belt Line ended just a mile from the hotel steps. The hotel provided horse-drawn cars and buses that would bring the hotel guests to the main entrance.

If Kate was given her trunks, then the Belt Line would be her best choice and she would have to wait until 5 p.m. But she was only carrying her satchel and it was still early afternoon, so the Coronado Ferry would be her best choice. The Coronado Ferry ran every 30 minutes from the foot of Fifth to the Coronado dock. She would then transfer to the Orange Street electric trolley that would take her about a block from the Hotel del Coronado.

The San Diego Bay was busy that afternoon. There were various sailboats scurrying around. A large freighter was anchored in the distance and a three-masted schooner loaded up with lumber was sailing towards a San Diego dock. The Coronado Ferry would be a fairly pleasant 10-minute ride. The bay would give off a salty smell and the gulls above would follow along high above, screeching out in what can only be described as a taunting laughter.

As Kate looked out toward San Diego, she could see rolling sandy hills, colorful homes of white and pale-yellow stucco, homes of ornate Victorian wood framing painted in blues, oranges, or green clapboards dotting the land. She would soon be nearing the Coronado dock and the Orange Street electric trolley. The trolley ran in sync with the Coronado Ferry schedule. The trolley rode west along Orange Street for a mile and a half to reach the Pacific side of Coronado where it stopped within a block of the massive hotel.

Kate's eyes were transfixed as she approached the Hotel del Coronado. The trolley conductor called out, "Next stop, The Del." The locals affectionately called the Hotel del Coronado by that name. The huge white fortress dominated over the stark blue backdrop of the Pacific Ocean. The sun lit up its red roofs with its cone-shaped corners topped by fluttering flags. It was beautiful and it took her breath away. She felt the fluttering of her heart and it made her a little nervous.

Kate usually didn't do hotel check-ins by herself. She was well aware hotels did not like to do business directly with women. This concerned her. Hotels had preconceived notions about unescorted women. There were good reasons. Most women didn't have access to bank accounts. Women usually didn't have credit, either. It was not impossible for unescorted women to get a room by themselves. Prostitutes did it all the time but they wouldn't be accepted at high end hotels such as The Del, or the Brewster. Kate was nervous with good reason. She must be convincing to successfully get a room at The Del on her own. She hoped the clothes she wore could help prove she was a woman of wealth.

After Kate arrived, she climbed the 12 or so wood steps to reach the front veranda. The door attendant had stood there with a wary look as he watched her approaching.

"Hello, may I help you?" the attendant asked.

"Yes, I'm here to check in with my brother," Kate said.

"Is your brother here already?" the attendant asked.

"He will be here shortly," she answered.

"You will need to enter those doors at the other end of the veranda. The clerk will come see you there," he explained to Kate as he pointed towards the other end.

She expected that. She entered those doors into the large women's reception area. The room was an immense space about 30 feet by 40 feet. It was just enough distance from the main desk for the hotel clerk to engage in a more private and oftentimes awkward conversation with an unescorted woman.

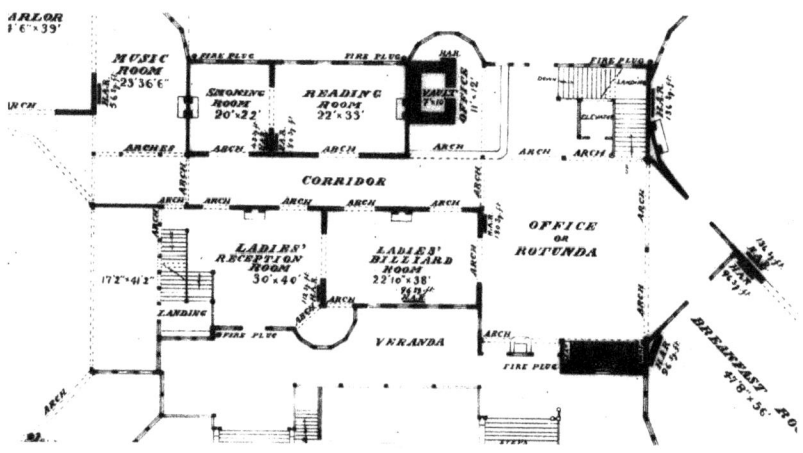

Kate waited there as she listened to the sounds of music softly bouncing off of the walls. She took a better look at the space she was in. It was very ornate and wide open. She could see through the large, elaborately-carved archways, straight past the adjoining billiard area and into the rotunda where she watched the other guests check in. The rooms had 14-foot-high ceilings with beautiful, thick wood gridwork, and there was a set of stairs beside her that led to the second floor. The reception room was filled with well-appointed furniture, mirrors and tables and she took a seat.

It was mid-afternoon, and the sun wouldn't be setting for a few more hours, but the hotel chandeliers and sconces were lit anyway, and it gave the room an inviting glow. Kate could now see the room was lit by electric lights. She looked about and realized the whole hotel was lit with electric lighting. She became nervous again. *This hotel must be very costly*, she thought. The hotel wasn't her choice, though. The man she would refer to as Dr. Anderson had targeted this place for their stay. *Anderson must have known this was going to be an expensive place to stay*, Kate thought.

The Del had just over 400 hundred rooms and if it were only half full, there could easily be 300 hundred guests checked in. It had already gained notoriety across the country as a premier destination. The Del also provided their principal staff members with special accommodations within the hotel.

Among those staff members were: chief hotel clerk, A.S. Gomer; hotel clerk, I.W. Tucker; hotel clerk, George H. Arnold; the bellboy captain, P. Artigue; hotel cashier, A.G. Bettens; assistant hotel cashier, K. Pinkham; head waiter, Mr. J. Havery; hotel bookkeeper, A.M. Hart; head bartender and proprietor of the hotel pharmacy, T.J. Fisher; housekeeper, Della Fisher; head of laundry, William Burns; chief engineer, F. H. McIntosh; superintendent of gardens, F.W. Koeppen; Western Union telegraph operator, W.H. Jackson; and sometimes Harry West, the bellboy who often stayed overnight.

The hotel employed roughly 250 people at the time of its debut in 1888. Some staff members were given a room and board at the hotel but not all of them. Some lived in San Diego. Coronado land and homes were at a premium and the staff members usually could not afford to live there.

Kate waited in the reception area but she was not alone. The hotel was filled with guests, affluent guests, guests who could afford to receive this level of catering that the exclusive Del had to offer. Some came for its remote location and discrete stay. Some came for the personalized and tailored experience they expected. The halls echoed their laughter and long conversations. Everything they could possibly need could be found within the walls and grounds of The Del and they would feel a level of comfort and security there. The enchantment that the guests experienced was intoxicating and addictive and many would make her their regular destination year after year.

Kate was bored, though. She waited patiently for what seemed to be a very long time. She tried to listen in on a conversation a few folks were having just past the stairs and slightly down the hall as they kept laughing. Across the hall she saw three men sitting in a dark lounge. They were having some sort of serious discussion but they kept their words low. They puffed at pipes and the sweet smell of tobacco was intermingling with the sweet smell of Thanksgiving dinner from a dining hall that Kate knew was not too far away. Kate felt a pang of hunger. She turned her attention past the adjoining billiard area that held two large pool tables nobody was playing. She could see into the rotunda. There were no guests checking in and she wondered what she was waiting for and she was losing her patience.

At that moment, the hotel clerk made eye contact with her and he started to head over.

"Hello, miss, are you waiting for someone?"

"I've been here waiting to check in," she said with a tone she didn't mean to use but it was too late. She took a breath to calm down.

"Oh, I'm sorry, I didn't know you were checking in. Who are you checking in with?" he asked.

"My brother, Doctor Anderson. Unfortunately, he was called away at Orange. He will be here either tonight or tomorrow," Kate said as she braced for the worst.

"Please follow me, I'll look at our records for his reservation," he said as he began to walk back to the main check-in desk. The hotel was bustling at that hour. Guests were already making their way to the dining room (Crown Room today) that adjoined the rotunda. Kate caught a glimpse of white linen-clad tables through the dining room's double doors.

"I do not see any reservation here for Doctor Anderson. Are you sure he was expected to stay here tonight?" He asked as he looked back at Kate.

"He told me this was the hotel we were supposed to stay at." Kate pulled out an invitation to the hotel to prove it. In a pleading voice she continued, "He told me to come and get checked in and he will be coming along as soon as he can." She hoped he would respect a doctor being called away.

"I see. Where are your bags?" he asked.

"Well, he didn't expect to be called away and when he left the train he forgot to give me the baggage tickets. The bags are still at the train station. They wouldn't let me take them without the claim tickets," she explained.

The young clerk couldn't help but feel concern now. The story was unusual and it raised red flags. He wasn't sure what to do. He looked at Kate. She was well dressed and she spoke well. He was still nervous. It usually wasn't a decision he could make. The chief clerk usually managed situations like this but he was away. He began to run various scenarios in his mind. If he turned her away so late in the day it could be very difficult for her. If her story was true, her brother would arrive and he would create a lot of trouble for the hotel if they had turned her away. It was Thanksgiving Day, and the hotel was filled with music and good spirits and the young clerk decided to take a chance and he let her check in.

"Don't worry mam, I'll check you in," he said with a smile.

Kate suddenly felt relieved and excited. She took a deep slow breath, hoping it wasn't obvious.

"What is your name and where are you coming from?" he asked.

"My name is Lottie Anderson Bernard, Detroit,"

CHECKED IN

"The interior of the Hotel Del Coronado will be seen at its prettiest in honor of the day. The Parlors, reception, billiard, reading rooms and dining room are very tastefully decorated with palms, tropical plants, smilaxes, and a variety of choice flowers. The fireplaces are all banked with a mass of vines, golden rod and marguerites, which will be in a marked contrast with those in the east. After the annual Thanksgiving dinner, there will be an informal dance in the ballroom."
-*San Diego Union and Daily Bee*, Thursday 25 November

He wrote her name in the registry for her and called over the bellboy, Harry.

Kate looked over her shoulder to see a young boy who didn't look a day over 15. He wore a grey uniform that seemed a little big for him. The vest had a single row of silver buttons and on his head he wore a round grey hat that reminded her of a wooden drummer boy with which her cousin used to play with. Harry avoided Kate's glance as he tried to hide his blushing face.

The clerk handed Harry a key and said, "Put her in room 302."

Kate was not the only one placed on the third floor that day. More than half of those who checked in that day were placed there. One man from New York City, a couple from Denver, another couple from Coronado, a man from New Mexico and a man from Boston. The rest of the check-ins were assigned rooms on the first floor, a floor for the highly privileged who could afford the extra expense. Kate's room would run about $3 a day. To put that in perspective, rent for a six-room house in San Diego ran about $12 a month in 1892.

Harry collected Kate's satchel and she began to share that she suffered from neuralgia. Neuralgia was a term often used for any ailment from arthritis, general aches, all the way up to a debilitating problem with the nerves. Kate's Uncle Billy had also commented in the letter that he wrote that Kate suffered from rheumatism, another loosely coined term for body aches in those days. Kate was not remembered like this by the Grants, who said she was a hard-working staff member that was considered one of their best.

Harry probably already planned to use the elevator but upon hearing her complaint he led her inside the small, caged space. It was an ornate electric Otis Brothers birdcage elevator built exclusively for the hotel.

In 1892, that elevator was still in the first years of production by Otis Brothers and The Del has kept it operating to this day. At least two other locations have operational Otis Brother elevators, the Biltmore in Asheville NC, and St. Mark's Church in Jim Thorpe, PA.

The elevator glided up two floors and when they stepped out onto the third floor, they made an immediate right, skirting around the side of the elevator towards the outside veranda. The veranda overlooked an interior courtyard. Harry led Kate to the right along that walkway as it curved to the left. Kate peaked over the rail edge to see the exotic plants that filled the yard. She looked at the stack of floors that surrounded all four sides of the courtyard space. Each floor had a veranda that overlooked the courtyard. Soft lights glowed from the guest room windows and it all distracted Kate until she nearly walked into an oncoming guest. Harry led Kate into a passage on the right, stepping away from the courtyard veranda into an interior leading hall. A large stairwell was on the left, which they skirted around to another hall, and Harry stopped at Room 302, the first room on the right. He sat Kate's satchel down and unlocked the door.

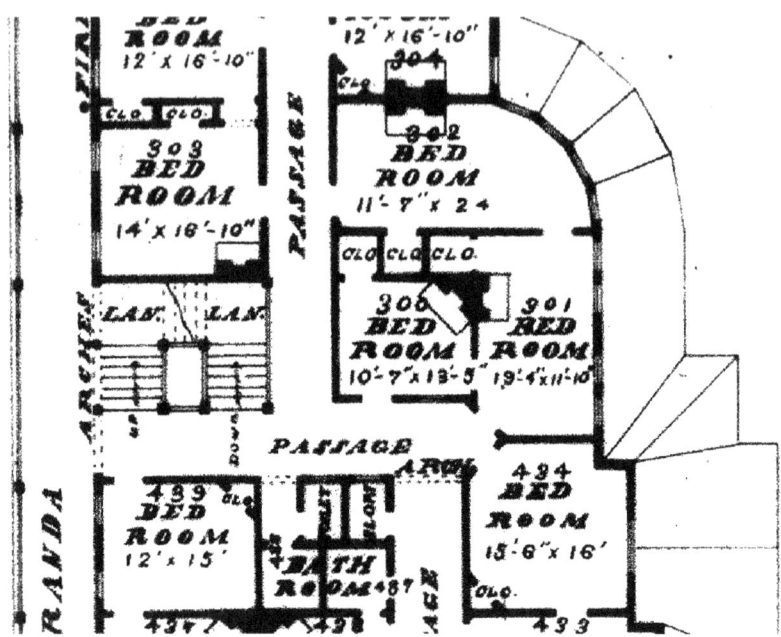

Kate now realized how close her room was to the stairwell. The stairs were midway on that wing of the hotel and it led down to the main floor where a turn to the right led to the interior courtyard and a turn to the left led to the east facing entrance. It was not as grand an entrance as the main entrance but it had a good-sized porch. The porch was on a circular dirt road where guests could catch a horse drawn car or the hotel could receive supplies. Connected to the porch was a wraparound veranda that went along the back part of the hotel's perimeter.

When Harry opened the room door, Kate noticed its unique shape. Standing in the doorway she could see that it was not a typical rectangular room. Opposite the doorway was a chamfered corner that had four large windows with the two middle ones pointing due north. It was a pretty architectural feature and it would bring in a lot of light on a summer day, but it was November and it now lay in the hotel's shadow. On the left wall was a fireplace followed by a path that flowed around the foot of the bed to those windows. Against the wall by the room door was a small desk and chair. The bed sat against the right wall and just past the bed was a door that led to an adjoining room. This room was much larger than many of the rooms on that floor, though Kate did not know that. It was 24 feet long by a little over 11 feet wide. It was a comfortable size but Kate found the electric lighting the most remarkable feature. The sun was setting and the room had a warm glow from the lamps. There would be no smells of burning lantern oil and Kate found that quite a treat!

Harry opened the closet door that was just past the opened door and placed her satchel there. "Over here you have a phone. It will ring to the front desk. Over here is a bell ringer, just turn the knob. If you ring it I will come as fast as I can," he explained nervously. "Breakfast is available starting at seven in the morning, and lunch is between eleven and one. Dinner starts at six and runs until nine. Your meals are included in your room charge. Tonight is going to be a Thanksgiving meal and you have plenty of time to make that." Then Harry opened her room door and stepped into the outside hall. He pointed to an arched opening opposite of the stairs and said, "Through that arch in that little hall is the toilet. It is through the door on the left. The other door is a bath. If you need a bath just ring me and I will prepare it for you." Then Harry pointed down a hall left of the toilet and explained, "There is another toilet there, too."

Down in the rotunda, Chief Clerk Gomer had just arrived at the desk and was looking over the day's signatures in the registry. When he saw the name of Lottie A. Bernard, Detroit, he looked on the page to find who she checked in with.

Holding the registry, he turned to the young clerk and said, "Tucker, you have here a Lottie A. Bernard that checked in today. Who is she with?"

The young clerk hoped Gomer wouldn't notice that. He became nervous as he began to explain. "Yes, sir, she is here with her brother but he hasn't checked in yet." Tucker knew he was going to be questioned on this for sure now.

"What? How can she be checking in with someone who hasn't checked in yet?" Gomer said, demanding a full explanation.

"Yes, sir, I'm sorry, I mean she came here, and she explained she was going to be arriving with her brother, but he is a doctor and he got called away. She said in a very convincing way that he will arrive tonight and if not tonight then tomorrow. I didn't want to turn her away and then have the man show up angry that we turned his sister away," he explained. Tucker knew his actions might come with consequences and hoped Mr. Gomer would understand and let this pass.

Mr. Gomer was the hotel's chief clerk and he directly reported to the hotel's general manager Mr. Babcock. Gomer was responsible for managing the other clerks, the books for room charges and ensuring the expectations of the guests who were promised an experience from a hotel of that caliber were met. Gomer was also new, having just been there a little over a month and he was still proving himself to Mr. Babcock.

Elisha Babcock was the general manager of the Hotel del Coronado. He was also one of the original builders of the hotel. He and his partner Hampton Story built the hotel from the ground up. Babcock and Story went into debt and took a major loss after the land boom collapsed. They sold the hotel to one of their creditors, John Spreckels, who made his wealth in the sugar industry, and Babcock was asked to remain as the hotel's general manager. Babcock accepted the job even though he didn't need the extra money. He owned and ran many other businesses including the Coronado Beach Company. Nearly all the contractors used at The Del were hired through a business Babcock owned.

Mr. Gomer wasn't the chief clerk for just any hotel. This was one of the nation's finest. The guests they catered to were wealthy, high-class individuals, prominent men, captains of industry, and oftentimes business partners with Babcock and Spreckels.

Mr. Gomer was nervous and suspicious with the story of Lottie, a woman who was allowed a room at this hotel with just a story that she had a brother who would be coming along. This left Mr. Gomer anxious as he demanded Tucker point her out as soon as he could, because, as much as he disliked keeping an eye on a guest, this situation required it.

After Harry left Kate's room, Kate was hungry and the thought of having Thanksgiving dinner at The Del distracted her from all the feelings of anxiety she was experiencing. She readied herself and made her way back down to the rotunda where the dining entrance was.

As Kate walked towards the dining entrance, Tucker quickly turned to Gomer and pointed her out. Gomer looked her up and down. He noticed how young she was. He noticed she was well dressed and beautiful. She appeared to carry herself well and all this gave him some level of relief as she seemed to fit in with the look of their guests. He looked at Tucker, "Her brother had better arrive here soon," he said in a threatening way.

The dining room entrance was just off the rotunda and as Kate stood there, she was in awe of the immensity of the room. Wood paneling with a thick wood gridwork continued up into a very high curved ceiling. It was rich and polished with huge dangling chandeliers, not the fancy "crown" chandeliers found today, but beautiful chandeliers, nonetheless. Rows of tables were dressed in white linen and plated with fine bone china, shiny flatware and carved crystal glasses. Guests were dressed in their finest clothes, sparkling jewels, gold watches, coiffed hair and well-trimmed beards. The smells were much stronger and all this would increase anyone's anticipation for what was in store. Kate was amazed that such an experience was included in her room charge.

Then it all came to an abrupt stop. Once she revealed to the door man that she would be the only one in her party he waved over another staff member to guide her away. She felt like an unentitled waif who had lost her way. The staff member explained to her as he led her past the elevator that women must have an escort to dine in the dining room. Just past the elevator he took her to the right as they followed along the courtyard walk and he showed her into a dining area on the right.

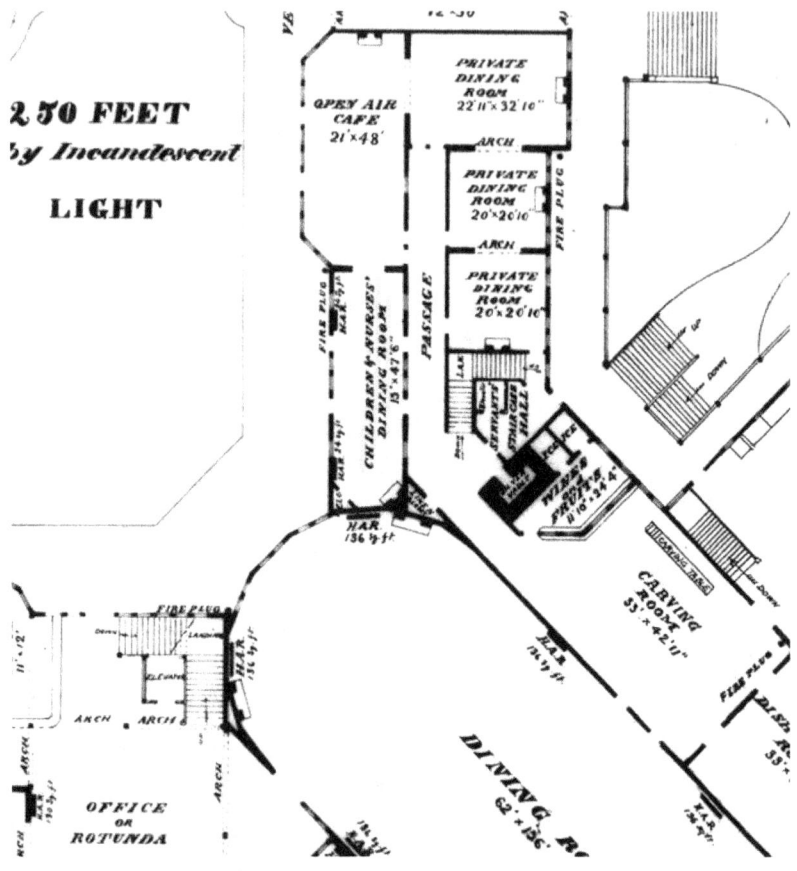

It was a long narrow room of about 15 by 40 feet that was next door to the open-air café. When she entered she saw other women there but quickly recognized they were nursemaids and they were attending to children. Kate was given a place to sit, not with fine draped linen but at a table which could withstand the daily grind of children banging their bowls and flatware. The abrupt manner in which she was treated was no different than what she had experienced in her domestic work. She sat there alone, startled by the treatment, and was served her Thanksgiving meal.

Having her Thanksgiving meal alone alongside other domestic servants created a heavy heart for Kate. Was this going to be the level of service she would expect going forward? Is this how it was for single unattached women? She certainly had a heavy heart but she also felt anger. Anger for Mr. Anderson, who not only left her to do her check-in by herself, but now this. She could have been dining in that beautiful dining room with him but he left her, and as much as she expected it to be somewhat difficult for her until he arrived, she still blamed him for how she was feeling right then.

It had been an extremely long day and she truly had little to eat. When she thought of it all, she was just thankful. A Thanksgiving dinner, no matter how she received it, left her satisfied and with a new level of energy, and she returned to her room.

She unlaced her boots and took them off. She emptied her dress pockets, placing her coin purse and handkerchiefs on the night table. She hung her dress in the closet along with the black corset. She kept the chemise on. It was light and airy. After removing the weight and burdens of her day clothes, she could truly relax in the simplicity of her underclothes. She slipped under the covers and laid her head to rest.

Sleep would not come easily for her that night. So much had happened. She was in a dark area of her life now and had no idea what lay ahead. She had certainly crossed a line and it might be impossible to recover from the decisions she made that day. What were her chances of retrieving the trunks without the claim tickets? Would Anderson come through for her? That was still swirling in her head. Maybe the hotel could be of help? She closed her eyes while trying to convince herself that it could wait until the morning. Although the weight of the dress was off of her, she still bore a great burden that wasn't so easily lifted.

When Mr. Gomer finished his work that night, he headed to a room near the kitchen. Mr. Gomer was looking forward to the fine Thanksgiving dinner that was served earlier. He was not the only staff member there. T.J. Fisher and his wife Della were also there. Harry, who was not supposed to be staying at the hotel, was probably there, too. Several employees who lived in the hotel would be there after their shifts ended. It was a secluded area where they could relax, have food, socialize and unwind.

T.J. Fisher had been a staff member ever since The Del had opened. He had been promoted to head bartender by John Seghers, the original general manager, but after Babcock took that role, T.J. tendered a resignation. His friends presented him with a gold-headed cane as a gift, including a note wishing him well. He didn't leave, though. Maybe Babcock gave him an offer that convinced him to stay. T.J. was a man of some wealth. He was a cocky and entitled man who pushed against the established rules. T.J. was arrested in April of 1889 for serving liquor at the hotel on an election day. It was against the law in San Diego to serve liquor on an election day but those in Coronado did not consider themselves part of the city of San Diego. That arrest was contested for well over a year and those in power in Coronado eventually proved Coronado did not have to comply with the laws set in San Diego. Afterwards, T.J. became involved in politics and was elected as a Coronado trustee in early 1892. T.J. continued to manage the hotel's saloon and billiards room up until the first of November 1892. That was when he won a closed bid for a five-year lease on The Del's pharmacy. He and his wife Della remained residents of the hotel for many years, up to and past 1900.

Della was appointed to the position of hotel housekeeper sometime around 1890. The housekeeper was the head of the hotel's housekeeping staff. She managed the maids, chambermaids and anyone responsible for cleaning and maintaining a guest room. The role was appointed by the hotel general manager. She received the role when John Seghers was the general manager. Della was of Canadian origin and she was in her thirties in 1892. She was a diligent manager who was held in esteem by the other staff members. Della was also a devout Catholic. She had a lot of energy and was very active with her local Catholic church.

Mr. Gomer was new to these staff members. They probably found him talkative and full of self-importance. Mr. Gomer would be in the process of building a rapport with the hotel staff. He might have done favors for them, and they would do the same for him. He was a storyteller and that night he already had a story stirring in his head, one about a woman named Lottie A. Bernard, a woman clerk Tucker happened to have taken it upon himself to check in that day.

Upstairs, on the third floor, Kate would be nearing sleep. She was extra sensitive to sounds as she anxiously listened to hear whether someone was being placed in the adjoining room. The room "Anderson" would be given when he arrived. It was late and it should have been quiet, but the faint sounds of talking and laughter were coming up through the walls and shafts of the hotel. Sounds of quiet creeks from the stairwell and the whisking sounds of hotel guests heading to their rooms or the bathrooms arose outside her door. She listened for as long as she could until even those sounds could not keep her awake and she faded off to sleep.

FRIDAY, NOVEMBER 25

"CORONADO NOTES:

The schoolchildren of National City spent their Friday half-holiday on the sands at Hotel del Coronado. The temperature of the water at the Coronado bath house yesterday was as follows: Warm plunge, 84 degrees; cold plunge, 66 degrees; bay, 57 degrees; ocean 58 degrees. Miss Kate Pinkham, who has been enjoying a long vacation in 'the woods of Maine,' her former home, returned to Coronado Thanksgiving Day, much improved in health. She will resume her duties as assistant cashier at Hotel del Coronado on December 1."

- San Diego Union and Daily Bee, Saturday 26 November 1892

The east side of the hotel was one of the busiest areas, especially in the morning. This was the main entrance for the delivery of hotel supplies. It was where the ice trucks came to place ice in the refrigeration room by the kitchen where wines and fruits were kept cold. Horse drawn trucks arrived to supply the chefs with fresh fish, meats and vegetables. Wagons carrying clean linen from the hotel's laundry pulled in. The chatter of the workers could be heard, sometimes in Chinese, or Spanish, or a strong brogue English that only an Irishman could discern. Chatter could not be avoided and Kate woke up after her first night's sleep. The early morning sun streamed through the east-facing window as she sat up, squinting from its bright beams.

That morning Kate would meet the housekeeper Della. It was unusual for Della to personally meet a guest. She probably arrived alongside the chambermaid who would be the one who would make the bed and take care of anything else Kate might need.

It is likely that The Del had at least 10 chambermaids to clean rooms at that time. The Del was struggling to be fully booked in the early 1890s and more than likely the cleaning staff was handling around 250 rooms on any given day.

"Good morning," Della said in a cheery voice.

"Good morning," Kate said, and she crawled out of her covers to allow the chambermaid to make the bed.

"Where are your trunks?" Della asked.

"They are at the train depot. They wouldn't let me take them without claiming tickets which my brother has, but it's ok, he will be here today," Kate replied.

"Oh, I see. You should bring it up with the chief clerk," Della said. "Maybe he can help you get them."

"Oh, can he do that?" Kate asked.

"I would think so," Della replied while the chambermaid was finishing the bed.

"There, your bed is made. Is there anything else we can get for you?" Della asked as the chambermaid left the room.

"No, thank you," Kate replied.

Della closed the door behind her and Kate was alone in her room once again. Kate put on her dress and boots. She fixed her hair and then headed downstairs.

Della would check on Lottie every day during her stay. It was probably a request from the chief clerk, Gomer, to keep an eye on her until her brother arrived.

The weather that Friday morning was a little hazy. A light gray marine layer sat over Coronado and the high would be 55 degrees. For someone from Fremont, Iowa, it would be considered spring or fall weather. For Southern California, it would be considered a little chilly. If Kate wanted a little breakfast to start her day, she could return to the children's dining area or possibly even the outdoor cafe.

In the *San Diego Union and Daily Bee* newspaper there is an article taking up half of page 6. It was titled "WOMEN AND HOME. A story about women and their choices.":

"The woman who complains that she has no place in the world has only to open her eyes and in most instances she will readily see what is waiting for her. The fact that she does not like that particular field is no argument against its usefulness for her...If women dislike needlework, even if it is not pleasurable, it is useful and they should be content to follow what they are best fit to do..."

The newspaper would be available there at the hotel every morning. Kate didn't have time to read that morning, and maybe that was a good thing. She was anxious to get her trunks. She seemed certain the man would arrive but she might have figured that if the hotel could be of help, she was willing to give that a try.

Mr. Gomer was not expecting to meet Lottie face to face and his face showed it as she approached him.

"Hello, I arrived in San Diego yesterday on the train but when I went to get my trunks the baggage clerk wouldn't allow me without the claim tickets. Is there any way you can help me get them?" Kate asked directly. She didn't even think of saying hello, introducing herself, or offering other nice things to say first. She was on a mission to get her trunks and that was all she was thinking about.

"Well hello.. miss..?" he asked. He knew exactly who she was, but he wanted her to say it. He also wanted to extract as much as he could about her brother.

"Oh, I'm sorry. I am Lottie Bernard."

"Hello, I'm Chief Clerk Gomer," he said with an emphasis on "chief."

"Hello. I checked in last night, but I do not have my things. My brother has the claim tickets for my trunks and hopefully he will be checking in here today but, if you could call and ask the baggage clerk at the San Diego train depot to have them sent here, wouldn't they do that for you?" Kate reasoned.

"You don't think your brother is going to arrive today?" Gomer asked, a bit confused. He was told by clerk Tucker that Anderson would arrive either last night or today and now Lottie was saying he would "hopefully" be there. That was totally unacceptable and he was trying hard not to show his anger.

"Yes, he should arrive today, but he is a doctor and when he was called away in Orange I didn't know exactly how long he would need for that call. Once he is done, he should head here immediately," Kate explained. She could clearly see that Chief Clerk Gomer was becoming concerned and she realized she needed to be more mindful of what she said to him.

"Your brother is a doctor? What is his name?" he asked.

"Doctor M.C. Anderson. He is a doctor from Minneapolis. I don't mean to bother you but I am just looking for a way to get my things sent here this morning rather than wait until he arrives. I was hoping you could help me get them. Could you help? I do not have anything until I get my things," Kate reasoned with a sense of serious concern now.

"Well, I am sorry, there is nothing I can do. They will not let trunks go to just anyone simply because they asked." Gomer said, though he knew if he asked the baggage clerk they might send them simply because it was The Del making the request. Gomer did not want to accommodate her. Not yet. Not until he was assured her brother would arrive and then he would extend to her the respect he usually gave to a Del guest.

When Kate walked away, she was annoyed that the hotel didn't pull some strings to get the trunks transferred over. She decided to go back over to San Diego and try once more. She also wanted to look and see if Anderson might have arrived in town last night and possibly stayed at a San Diego hotel. With the other half of her round-trip ticket, she headed out to catch the Orange Street trolley and head back to the city.

Once she was back in San Diego, she went to the D Street station where she was once again disappointed. She grabbed the trolley back to Fifth Street. Kate had thought all night about the man she had been referring to as "Anderson." Did he get in too late to get across the bay last night? Did he check into the Brewster? If he had, he would have been told that a woman asked for him and that she went to the Hotel del Coronado. Kate was concerned, though. It was still early; he could be arriving on this day around noon if he didn't leave on last night's train. She wanted to stay in town at least until noon to see if he would arrive on that train. Meanwhile, she considered looking around, but not by foot. She wanted a horse.

In San Diego there were at least 18 livery and stable companies: Alta on Third and Grape, Fashion on First and H, Fifth Avenue Boarding Stable on Fifth and B, and the list goes on. Many were within close proximity of Fifth Street.

Kate went to Star Stables, located on the corner of Seventh and J, and she rented a horse. Kate had handled horses before; she was quite an experienced rider having lived in rural Iowa and having had Grandpa Joe's and Aunt Harriet's horses available. The horse that Star Stables rented her was unusually unruly and misbehaved and she simply could not get it under her control. Charles Stevens, a stable hand, noticed her trouble and rode to her. He quickly got her horse under control. He then introduced himself and offered to ride along with her.

Kate was grateful for his help, but she was hoping to ride alone. She didn't want to appear rude though, so she allowed it. They rode together for several hours along Fifth Street while Kate kept a keen eye out for Anderson. Kate stayed mainly on Fifth Street since it was there she would expect Anderson to head. It was the road that led to the wharf. She decided to stop at Marston's and she bought a pair of gloves. She was flattered by Charles' attention and she smiled often.

Kate kept an eye out for Anderson but there seemed to be no sign of him, not even from the noon train. She needed to return to the hotel. She hoped she simply missed him and hoped he was already there. Charles would not leave her side though. He persistently stayed with her. When she told him she needed to return to the hotel, he rode with her to the wharf. Then he bought two round trip tickets so he could accompany her to the hotel.

They boarded the ferry and rode across and although Kate was nervous about his persistence, she did enjoy his company and it was a beautiful sunny day. They boarded the Orange Street trolley and took it to the end. They both stepped off and Charles walked her to the hotel's side entrance. He knew his time with her was coming to an end. Smiling, Charles handed her his card and said, "The next time you need a horse, come see me. I will make sure the next one will be a gentler one."

Kate extended her hand and took his card. She gave him a soft smile. "Thank you Charles, I will be sure to call on you the next time."

She stood there watching him as he headed back towards the Orange Street trolley. Kate enjoyed the attention the stable boy gave her and she relished the delicious sea breeze as she entered the hotel's side entrance.

Up in her room, Kate sat down at her desk. She felt enchanted by the afternoon ride and how impressed Charles was that she was a guest at The Del. She pulled out an envelope and wrote Denman Thompson and addressed it with *The Old Homestead*. She smirked. Kate loved the theater and that was her favorite play. Kate was feeling good. She was flattered, but she was also distracted by the fact that she did not find any trace of Anderson in town.

Kate went back to the front desk to see if Mr. Anderson had checked in. No was the answer. She asked if she received any messages or mail. That answer was also a no.

Kate started to think to herself, *Where is that man? Couldn't he at least send me word of what is going on? Couldn't he at least mail the claim tickets to me?* She was anxious and concerned and a little upset.

As she headed up to her room to get ready for dinner that evening, a lot was going on in her head: *What if he never shows up? What if something happened to him?* She wanted to push those thoughts out of her head. She was certain he would show. The idea that something might have happened to him troubled her, though. She could not set that thought aside.

Could I ever return to Los Angeles and find new work? My name is probably ruined in the domestic circles now. She was certain of that. *Maybe I can stay here in San Diego and find domestic work. Would that even be possible? Many know me as a guest of The Del, though. No, that couldn't be possible either. Should I go back to Nebraska and work things out with Tom?* She shuddered to think of that. *What about Uncle Billy? Maybe I should return to him. Could that be possible?* She would keep that in mind if all else failed. There was a lot going on in Kate's head and she began to feel very alone.

After dinner, Kate looked forward to a good night's rest. She had unusual aches after her day's ride, though. She would have to scale two flights of stairs first. There was only one elevator and too many guests were already waiting for it.

Saturday, November 26

"CORONADO NOTES: James A. Jones is another contended sojourner hailing from the Hub at the Hotel del Coronado. Mr. Jones is a member of the large importing firm Arnold, Cheney & Co. of New York, and was for years the resident partner at Aden, in Arabia, in the heart of the coffee plantation region."
-San Diego Union and Daily Bee, p. 8, Nov. 27, 1892

Kate woke up that Saturday with the same typical noise of deliveries of ice and various things brought for the kitchen. Kate also woke up with pain. She wondered if the horseback ride exacerbated an old back injury she had after giving birth many years earlier. The pain worsened depending on how she turned her body. So, she decided to make her way downstairs and find the pharmacy.

As she headed downstairs, she saw Harry. He was signaling to her at a nearby hall off the second floor.

"What is going on?" Kate asked as she met up with him.

"Well, I thought I'd tell you that your brother has still not shown," Harry explained with some concern in his voice.

"I don't know what happened to him and I have been worried, too," Kate said with some concern. "Have I received any mail or telegraphs today?"

"I don't think so, but I wouldn't know for sure. They give those directly to the front desk," he said to her in a low voice.

Kate was wondering why he is being so secretive. "What is really going on? Why are you telling me this here? I was just heading to the front desk to ask myself," Kate asked prodding him for information.

"I know, but Mr. Gomer is mad. He is mad that your brother hasn't shown and he is mad he hasn't sent any telegrams to him, either. I heard he doesn't believe you have a brother, Harry explained as his eyes continued to scan around to be sure he wasn't overheard.

"Oh?" Kate said in surprise. She was speechless. She didn't think she would have to worry that the hotel would question any of this, or at least not yet. She had a lot to think about. The man Anderson appeared to not care one way or the other what position he had put her in, she thought. He had not seen fit to at least send her a message to explain himself. He had not seen fit to at least mail the claim tickets so she could get her things, either. Her hope was turning to anger. She wanted to hold on to hope, though. Maybe he'd arrive on this day. Maybe she should give him one more day; she envisioned what she was going to say to him once he arrived. *He will pay for putting me through this.*

Downstairs at the front desk, Mr. Gomer was angry. He had been growing angrier ever since Tucker allowed Lottie to check in. *There is no way a man who was planning to spend a week at this hotel would leave his sister here alone without any word of when he would arrive. No honorable man would put a family member in such an awkward situation.* Gomer knew a man who was planning to be a guest would at least send some directions or expectations to assure the hotel of his intentions.

Mr. Gomer had already been suspicious of Lottie's story, that it was a ruse. He was now feeling convinced of it. *Who is this woman? Who does she think I am?* Gomer was taking it personally. That young woman by the name of Lottie was playing him and he would not be played!. He started thinking of ideas. *I need to do something about her. Who can she turn to? I don't think she knows anyone, not in this hotel, city, county or really anywhere!*

Kate entered the elevator on the third floor and rode it down, past the main floor where Gomer would be at the check-in desk, to the floor just below the main floor. She entered the wide hall that was lined with numerous shops: a barber shop, a flower shop, a clothier, the Western Union Office and finally, the pharmacy. She was close to the end of the hall where a strong light came in. The light came from the hotel bar where she heard men talking, laughing and banging shot glasses on their tables as a sign they need more. She heard the smack of cue balls from nearby billiard tables. T.J. Fisher saw her peeking into the area before she turned to step into the pharmacy.

Kate walked around, looking at all of the items on the pharmacy shelves. T.J. was curious about the young and beautiful woman and decided to introduce himself to her.

"Good morning, young lady," T.J. said, looking into her dark brown eyes. "I'm T.J. Fisher. Can I help you?"

Kate looked back into his light grey eyes. Kate was used to men being drawn to her and wasn't surprised by his approach. "I suffer from neuralgia and it is really bad today. Is there anything here I can buy to ease the pain?"

T.J. felt helpless. He didn't manage prescriptions or drugs. Mr. Fosdick was the pharmacy manager who could help her with that. T.J. introduced her to Mr. Fosdick and she explained her maladies to him. Mr. Fosdick felt a strong pain reliever would be best for her but he couldn't sell her pure opium or cocaine without a doctor's prescription. He suggested she see the hotel physician who could provide her with that.

Kate brushed that idea off and explained, "My brother is a physician and he is coming along soon."

It was unfortunate for those living in 1892. Aspirin had not been discovered yet. It is unlikely that Kate was an addict. Some might consider that, but an addict would not have turned down the hotel physician or any opportunity if it meant they could gain drugs. Kate must have been in some sort of pain, though, enough to drive her to the pharmacy looking for relief. When Kate left the pharmacy, she had a small bottle, likely a tincture of laudanum, which had a very small percentage of opium in the ingredients. The druggist wrote a small note which he wrapped around the bottle. The note said, "If this does not relieve you, you better send for a doctor."

After Kate returned to her room, she rang for Harry. She asked him if he could bring her an empty pint bottle and a sponge. Harry returned with those items.

When T.J. returned to the bar area, a man who had observed T.J. talking to Kate asked, "Do you know that woman?"

"Not really, I just went and asked her if she needed help, why?" T.J. asked.

Mr. Jones explained, "I don't know who she is either, but I remembered seeing her on the train I rode down on." T.J. was curious and the two continued to talk over a few drinks.

SUNDAY, NOVEMBER 27

"SUMMARY OF THE NEWS:
Few days in the year are more pleasant in this land of pleasant days than that of yesterday. The bay was dotted with sails and Coronado Beach with visitors. Bright skies and an exhilarating atmosphere are the signs by which November is recognized in California. Who would change them for the frosts of the north, the wintry blasts of less favored spots?"
-San Diego Union and Daily Bee, **Monday, November 28**

Kate woke up Sunday morning and she was not well. The pain she had the day before was stronger that morning.

She rang for the bellboy Harry and when he dropped in she asked if her brother had arrived yet. Harry told her no and there were no letters or telegraphs, either. He said he was sorry but he had a number of guests waiting on him that morning and he continued on down the hall.

Kate groaned as she turned in the bed. The news of Mr. Anderson was not surprising her anymore, instead she was hurt by it. *He knew how much I was looking forward to having my things! He knows I can't have them without those claim tickets! He is purposely keeping them from me!*

It was the fourth day and Kate was realizing the man was off enjoying himself somewhere else without any consideration for her. She felt invisible, alone and discarded. The thought put a hard squeeze on her heart.

Kate had learned how to deal with a lot of emotional experiences. She had been hurt before. She had learned how to ignore the children at school who reminded her constantly that she didn't have parents. She had learned to ignore Grandpa Joe's attitude about her father and the Farmer family members. She learned to set aside the strong feelings she would have when Grandpa Joe disrespected her grandmother, who Kate loved very much. She learned to avoid Grandpa Joe after Grandma Matilda died. She learned to get by and make do and she thought she was good at it. But there was a weakness within her. She knew it, she avoided it, she tried to guard herself from it. She did not do well when she felt discarded.

Memories flooded back to her like a grand reunion: memories with a common thread, memories that found a sense of familiarity with each other. They all came at once.

There she was, watching her Grandmother Matilda's smile as Kate's love swelled, and then she saw her grandmother's casket lowered into her grave and the tears welled in her eyes. She recalled hearing the news of her father-in-law Marcena while she was eight months pregnant and how invisible she felt to the family who were too busy with the burial. Kate wiped the wet off her cheeks as she recalled the moment she was alone, holding her newborn who had just taken his last breath. Kate took a deep breath and a whimpering sigh snuck out. She saw her husband Tom, who made her feel personally responsible for the loss, and guilt and anger welled in her. All these thoughts squeezed at her heart in such a strong way.

I must stop this flood of memories, she thought. She recalled her excitement the first time she arrived in California. The state was beautiful, with lush hills and beautiful flowers. Then she realized the future she had dreamed might not be possible. She could never get work again in Los Angeles. She had ruined her chances in domestic services. She couldn't work in San Diego, either. They would question what she was doing at The Del. Would she ever get hold of her trunks? She might never be able to get her belongings back from the Grants, either. *How could I have let that man deceive me like this!* The sadness was turning to anger and the anger pulled her back from despair. Back to reality. A passion formed in her heart, a passion to figure this out and win, a passion to prove to all those who never believed in her that she was a strong capable woman. She would come up with a solution.

She took out her handkerchief and looked at the embroidered name on it. She gave a self-mocking chuckle and then dabbed her eyes. She took a deep breath and peered out the windows.

Could she return to Hamburg? She was always fond of her cousin, Mary Samuels, but Mary lived too close to her Grandpa Joe. Could she return to her Uncle Billy? She thought deeply on this. She liked Uncle Billy and he always told her he was there for her. Kate felt hopeful. *Maybe I shouldn't have left Hanford in the first place. Maybe I will return.*

Kate was emotionally exhausted and decided to spend Sunday in her room and come up with a plan. She was also still sore and she hoped some rest would help her recover from her back pain, too. Della stopped by as she did every day. Della recognized how down and depressed Lottie appeared.

"Is everything ok?" Della asked with deep concern.

Kate couldn't share with Della the situation with which she was really dealing. "It is my heart. I am troubled with heart disease," Kate said. Kate could see Della truly cared and it meant a lot to her that she had a fellow woman who cared enough to check on her every day like this. Kate did not feel entirely alone between Della and Harry's regular visits.

Della was concerned about Kate. She originally checked on Kate as a favor for Chief Clerk Gomer, but it didn't take her long before she grew fond of Kate and only shared with Gomer the bare minimum to prove she was keeping an eye on her.

Kate ordered food and had it sent to her room and then crawled into bed where she gained a level of comfort in the warm wraps of her covers.

When the 6 p.m. train arrived in San Diego that evening, a man stepped off, a man with whom Kate was familiar. He arrived at the D Street station alone. A reporter took down a note of his arrival but this time the reporter would not report at which hotel the man was planning to stay.

Monday, November 28

"PERSONAL MENTION,

   M. L. Abbott, a former San Diegan, arrived by rail last evening and is registered at a downtown hotel."

-San Diego Union and Daily Bee, **p. 8, 28 November 1892**

On Monday, Kate woke up weak, sore and quite deflated. She peered through the four large windows. The bright morning rays that usually beamed in every morning were now muted by a gray layer of clouds. It wasn't the marine layer, either. No, it was a sign the day would bring rain.

She lay there in bed for a long time, and then Della showed up. "How are you this morning?"

"I'm feeling poorly. I think I will take a bath," Kate said with some level of hope.

Della shook her head and said, "No, that is not a good idea. That will only make you weaker." Della's concern was not about Kate's health. She was more concerned with the bath cost and how that might anger the Chief Clerk Gomer.

Kate strongly disagreed, "A bath would help relieve the pain."

Della breathed a sigh, "I really do not agree but if you insist I will call for the bellboy so he can prepare it for you."

"Thank you," Kate said and the thought of a nice bath lifted her spirit.

After Della left, Harry dropped by. "I was told you asked for a bath?"

"Yes," Kate replied

"OK, by the way, you still haven't received any letters or telegraphs and your brother is still not here."

Kate gave a heavy sigh, "Oh, no one comes to me anymore!"

"I'm sorry," Harry empathized. He, too, had become very fond of Kate and as much as he tried to see her as another hotel guest, he was just as troubled as she was about her situation.

"I think I'll stay in the bath for a while, maybe as much as two hours. Is it too early to ask for a glass of wine, too?" Kate asked hopefully. She was looking forward to relaxing in a nice hot bath with a glass of wine.

"I'll take care of it at once," Harry said in a thoughtful way. He left feeling poorly for his room guest.

When Harry returned, he handed her the wine and brought her a robe and two towels. He left saying he would be right back. She drank some wine then slipped on the robe. When he returned, he was carrying a pitcher of ice. She followed him down the hall to a small room that had a deep clawfoot tub, a hook on the wall and a small table. Steam rose ever so slightly off the water's surface. Harry sat the pitcher of ice water on the small table and asked, "Is there anything else you need?"

"I don't think so," Kate replied. Kate pulled a gold dollar piece and handed it to him.

"Oh, I couldn't take this," he said with astonishment.

"Take it, I have plenty of money!" Kate said.

After Harry left, closing the door behind him, Kate sat her glass of wine down and felt the water. It was too hot. She poured some ice water into the tub to cool it off a little. She then slipped in. It felt good and she sat there feeling the warmth surrounding her. It was very comfortable and her aches seemed to melt away.

Mr. Gomer was at the desk when Harry returned to the first floor. Gomer called him over and asked him what he was doing. Harry explained he prepared a bath for Lottie. Gomer felt the anger building but contained himself. There were other guests nearby. Nobody could tell, but his mind was swirling with angry thoughts.

She knows she is not going to pay for this stay and now she's taking baths! I really need to stop this. Something needs to be done!

"Oh, hello Mrs. Hoffmann, did you say you need more pillows? Let me get the bellboy for you," Gomer said to a frumpy old woman who was wearing way too many pearl necklaces. On the exterior Gomer went about his business, but inside he was trying to solve a problem. *I'll figure out something with Lottie, but first I must take care of this couple who are about to check out.* "Hello, Mr. and Mrs. Martin, I hope you had a good stay," Gomer said with a smile.

After an hour passed, Kate was ringing for Harry from her room. When Harry arrived, Kate stood there in the robe with drenched hair. She was also unstrung and nervous.

"Could you please help me? I need to dry my hair but I am just too weak," she asked with a quiver in her voice.

Harry was shocked, and asked, "What happened?"

Kate paused to think of a reasonable explanation. "I was just standing beside the tub and I was so weak I just fell in."

Harry was worried. She always complained about her neuralgia but he had no idea how bad it was getting. He worked the hair gently and tried to dry it, but he could see it was not going to get completely dry, not by towel, not hair wet to the very roots like that.

"It's ok, Harry. That will be enough. Could you do me one more favor? Could you bring me a whiskey cocktail?"

"Yes, ma'am, I'll get that for you at once!" With that Harry left.

Harry headed downstairs and once again was spotted by Mr. Gomer. Gomer asked, "Harry, the couple in room 311 have been ringing for you, where have you been?"

"Oh, I'm sorry, I'll take care of them right away!" Then Harry started to take the stairs down.

"Wait a minute. Where are you going?" Gomer asked, confused.

Harry explained, "Oh, Lottie asked for a whiskey cocktail and I'm heading to the bar to put the order in."

Gomer was shocked and angered by her request. "A whiskey cocktail?"

Harry explained, "She fell in the tub this morning and it drenched her head and hair so bad I had to help her rub her hair." Harry knew he was in trouble for spending so much time with Lottie.

Mr. Gomer's anger had been building, but when he heard that she ordered a whiskey cocktail that was enough. No excuse mattered.

"Do you want me to stop the order for the cocktail? She really looked bad and in pain." Harry said with a sign of worry he couldn't mask.

Mr. Gomer responded, "No, I'm going up there to talk to her myself."

With that Gomer entered the elevator and Harry continued heading downstairs to the bar.

Kate was trying to pin up her hair which had become a damp mess when she heard a knock at the door. She was surprised Harry had the drink already. Kate quickly shot under the bed covers and called out, "Come in." It wasn't Harry, though. Instead, Mr. Gomer entered and stood over her bed and she became quite uncomfortable.

"Did you just order a drink?" he asked angrily. "Is there anything else you want us to do for you? How about a fire? Certainly, you would like a fire to keep warm on such a cold, awful day like today!" Gomer said in a very sarcastic way.

Suddenly a noise was heard from down the hall. Gomer peered over his shoulder at Kate's room door, which was still open by a few inches, and he softly shut it. A concerned look came upon his face, as he hoped nobody overheard him.

Kate was very uncomfortable now, alone with this mad man. *What does he want,* she wondered.

"Where is your brother? Where is he?" Gomer demanded.

Kate pleaded, "I don't know where he is, believe me! He could be anywhere, Los Angeles, Frisco, I just don't know!"

"Ok, calm down. Tell me what hotels he typically stays in? I have connections, I can help find him for you." Gomer said trying another approach in hopes of gaining more information.

"You don't need to do that, he will come, he always does," Kate said, but she wasn't certain of that now. She was concerned, too, but she had to keep that to herself. What she couldn't keep to herself was the pressure Gomer was applying in his questions. She needed to give him something to assure him so he could go.

"Well until he shows, I want a name. I need someone else who will be responsible for you and this hotel stay," Gomer said. "Who else, other than your brother, do you have?"

Kate needed to give him a name. One man was all he wanted. One man she knew could teach a big bully like him and he would regret ever asking for the name. "G.L. Allen," she called out but the moment the name was spoken she immediately regretted it. George would not forgive her for that. He didn't even like using his own real name if he didn't have to. She became worried.

Gomer looked at her, "Ok, ok, how can I reach him?"

She took a pause, afraid to say more. She didn't want him to reach him.

Gomer started peering at her papers, pushing them back and forth to get a better look. Then he turned towards her satchel.

She became very nervous and stopped him, "OK, stop. He lives in Hamburg, Iowa. That's where you will find him"

He looked at her, and something inside him didn't believe her. "OK, I'm going to send a telegraph to Hamburg for G.L. Allen and I better get a response!" He stared at Kate to see if she had a response to that, but she didn't. She just stared back at him.

With that, he left her room.

Kate turned her head into her pillow and wanted to scream. *What have I done? He will never forgive me for giving his name to a hotel clerk!* Kate heard a knock on the door again and her heart skipped a beat. Softly she called out, "Who is it?"

"Harry, ma'am. I have your cocktail."

Kate took a deep breath of relief and called him in.

Harry stepped in, while carefully holding a whiskey cocktail in his hand.

Kate had never been so happy to see him. She moaned from pain as she sat herself up in bed.

"Harry, would you do me one more favor?"

"What is it?" Harry asked, confused and a little concerned.

"Enjoy the whiskey in your hand, you deserve it!" she said.

Harry turned a deep shade of red as his mouth suddenly grew into a huge smile. He turned his attention to the deep gold elixir. He wasted no time in turning the glass upside down as he emptied it straight down his throat! He coughed and then took a huge breath and then coughed again followed by another heave of air.

"I didn't think you would drink it all at once! I hope you are alright!" she said and then couldn't contain the giggle that followed. "I just wanted to thank you for being there whenever I called," Kate said with all sincerity.

"You are more than welcome, ma'am. Do you want me to make you a fire? It is a little chilly here today," Harry asked.

"Not now or at least not yet. I need to take care of some things first," Kate answered.

"Let me leave you some matches," he said as he dug around his pocket. He found a small pile and placed them on the mantle. "Ring me when you are ready for a fire and I'll bring you some firewood." He then gave her a wide smile, took the glass, and left.

Kate got out of bed. Her hair was a total mess. It had been drying in the most unflattering way. It made her feel the chill in the room even more and exacerbated her body aches. She did all she could to comb and straighten her hair out so she could pin it up again. She looked at the bottle of medicine she had received on Saturday. It was empty now. She grabbed the black dress from the closet. It was starting to show signs of wear from being worn day after day and she started the process of dressing up. The sounds of soft taps were heard on her windows. It was a reminder of the weather rolling in.

Kate went to the bottom floor and made her way to the pharmacy once again. It was almost one in the afternoon now; she needed to go into San Diego and hoped she could get one more vile of pain relief.

"Are you ok?" T.J. asked. He could see something didn't look right. She looked a little rough and not so good.

"It's the neuralgia again. It is really bad today. I need to go to San Diego and some pain relief would be very helpful," Kate answered, but she could read in his face that she must not have done a very good job of putting up her hair.

T.J. looked puzzled, "Why do you want to go into the city? It's such a dreary day."

Kate looked at him, "I must, I need to get my trunks. I think they will let me have them if I can prove I can identify the contents. I just have to go and do this personally."

T.J. pulled out a small tin from his pocket and handed her something. "That may help for now."

"Thank you." she said, as she placed it in her mouth. She said her goodbye and headed back upstairs to head out for the trolley.

Kate wanted to take the train instead of the trolley and ferry but the Coronado Belt line wouldn't be available till 5:10 that afternoon. The schedule was never on her schedule. It was rainy and the trolley and ferry may not have been ideal, but she needed to get into the city before dark.

When the trolley arrived, Kate boarded. As the conductor drove, she asked him if he knew of any hardware stores in San Diego.

"Todd and Hawley is where I go when I need anything of that sort," he told her.

When they reached the ferry landing, Kate asked the conductor if he would be so kind as to help her down. She was concerned that the steps would be wet and slippery and he helped her down.

The ride on the ferry was not as pleasant as her previous trips. It was gray and rainy. There were wind gusts. As the ferry rode along the water, the wind sprayed sea water over the bow. Kate rode inside, though, and the smell of burned engine oil was enough to make anyone nauseous. She reached the dock in no time and headed towards the Fifth Street trolley. It was almost 2 in the afternoon now but the dark clouds and rain made it feel much later.

Todd and Hawley were near the intersection of D and Sixth Street. It would be on the same trolley line that led to the D Street Station.

Kate had time to go to Todd and Hawley. Kate had time to check on her trunks. Kate had time for a bite to eat or to visit some shops. There were a number of things Kate could do before she returned to Fifth Street. In all that time, did she discover Mark Abbott was in town? If Kate became aware Abbott was in town, did she greet him or did she avoid him? Would an encounter with Abbott be of concern for Kate? During this short period of time, Kate was now in possession of a seal skin coat, one that wore on her longer than the fashion of the day.

When it was just past 3 p.m., Kate was walking along Fifth Street. The wagons and horses kicked up dust and mud and the wind was strengthening as the rain fell softly, then heavier, and then back to soft again. It wasn't the best of days to be out in town but that was what Kate was doing. Kate was shopping and she was now looking to buy a gun.

Kate headed to Chick's Gun Shop. The shop was on the east side of Fifth. closer to G Street. Martine Chick had owned the shop for years and sold all types of guns, ammo and accessories. Kate entered and strolled slowly to the gun counter. Martine was used to doing business with men and occasionally women, too. He may have been a little surprised with Kate, though. She was very young.

She asked Martine if he had a gun that was inexpensive.

"Yes, I have a pocket revolver here that would be perfect for you." He placed on the counter a 44-caliber American Bull Dog revolver and then said, "This one here can be yours for $3."

32, 38 and 44 Calibre, Centre Fire, 5 Shot.

NO.	DESCRIPTION.	EACH.
1532	32 Calibre, Centre Fire, S. & W., 2½ In. Octagon Barrel, Rubber Stock, Nickel Plated,	$3 50
1538	38 " " " " " " " " "	3 50
1544	44 " " " Webley or Bull Dog. " " " " "	8 50

Kate was nervous. She did not like handling guns. "How is it loaded?" she asked timidly.

Martine picked up the gun as if it belonged in his palm, as if he had held it all his life. He turned it with the handle pointing to Kate and showed her a metal flap on the gun's right side of the back of the barrel. He swung it down and there she saw a chamber. Then, he swung the flap shut.

"Let me show you," he said and he reached for a box of cartridges. Taking one, he swung the chamber flap open and slid a round in. "See? It's easy." He removed the round, then swung the flap open again and rotated the cylinder, showing her how she could see each chamber. "That's how you fill each one."

"Here. See how it feels," he said, as he handed it over to Kate.

Kate felt its weight. It was a pocket-sized gun and she liked that, but it was heavy in her hand. She slid her finger in and pressed on the trigger. It didn't budge. She squeezed harder, still nothing. "Isn't it hard to pull?" she asked, frustrated.

Martine took the gun back and he put his finger in. With a squeeze, it clicked. He squeezed it a few more times just to be sure it wasn't a mechanical problem. Click, click, click. "No, it fires just fine," he said.

Kate was nervous; she turned her head slightly and saw something move. There was someone else there and that added to her nervousness. Martine gave her the gun again. She took it and pulled hard and it clicked.

Martine said, "See, it works!"

"Ok." and, with some hesitation, she said, "I'll take it. I'd like some cartridges, too, please."

Martine said, "How many? They are not cheap. Two bits (25 cents) will get you ten."

"Two bits will be fine." Kate answered, turning her head slightly to see if that stranger was still somewhere in the store. "Could you load it?"

"I'm not supposed to," he said and then saw her helplessness. "OK, I understand, you want it for protection. We all need one, don't we? Just promise you will not tell anyone I did this for you," Martine said as he filled the chambers. "That will be three dollars and twenty-five cents."

Kate handed him a $20 gold piece and Martine gave her $16.75 in change. He handed her the gun and the remaining cartridges and she placed them in her dress pocket.

"See, I gave it to you and you wrapped it up," he said with a big smile and a wink.

As she turned to leave, she could see that the stranger was still in the store. She turned her face away and slowly made her way out.

Kate headed south on Fifth Street. Before she reached the corner she saw a sign over a store displaying The Combination. The Combination was a building with multiple indoor stores found under one roof (similar to today's mall but on a much smaller scale). It would be an enticing place for any woman to spend time at, but for Kate, she simply stepped in for a moment or two before she left to cross the street toward Schiller and Murtha's. She loved emporiums and would have loved to step in for a look, but instead, she continued north on the walk. Maybe Kate realized she still needed to get another set of round-trip tickets. Maybe she needed to get something else. Kate headed north up Fifth and stepped into the Ship's Chandlery.

The Chandlery sold ferry tickets and if Kate hadn't already purchased a new set, she could have done so here. While she was there, she stepped towards Frank Heath to ask him a question.

"Can I help you?" Frank asked.

Kate looked around and then in a low voice asked, "Do you sell cartridges here?"

Frank couldn't quite hear her, though. The rain was beginning to fall. Kate repeated her question but she did not want to speak up, either. She was avoiding attention.

"Do you sell cartridges here?" she asked again.

"No, we don't have that here. Chick's across the street carries those," Frank answered, as if she had just wasted his valuable time.

Kate decided for now the cartridges she had would have to be enough. She headed back towards Schiller and Murtha's to wait for the trolley. She wondered what to expect when she returned to the hotel. *Gomer is going to be annoyed when he is told that G.L. Allen is out of town but at least he will start believing me*, she thought.

The weather was rolling in and the rain was falling a little steadier. She thought of the trip back on the ferry and the trolley and dreaded that in the weather. The Coronado Belt Line would be a better choice as she could ride and stay dry, but she didn't want to wait that long. She reluctantly decided to go by ferry again.

Kate might have been glad she had a coat while shopping in town but was she still wearing it on her trip back to the hotel? That coat would not be written in the description of her by the reporter who witnessed her body on that fateful morning. Instead, he would describe that she only wore a lace shawl.

When Kate stepped off the ferry towards the Orange Street trolley, the same trolley conductor was there to meet her. He gave her a smile. When they reached the stop close to the Hotel del Coronado, he graciously helped her down again. She was very tired and hungry and lightheaded and was grateful for his kindness.

Kate had her usual dinner in the children's dining room that evening. She took the stairs that led to the hall closest to her room. As she made her way, she might have felt a new weight in her dress pocket.

When she reached the second floor she took a short break. She stepped out to the veranda for a view of the courtyard and caught her breath. The rain was falling softly and steadily. She had been dealing with body aches all day and the stairs were not helping. Harry saw her across the courtyard and waved. Kate didn't see him, though.

Back in her room Kate turned the knob which illuminated her room. She always looked forward to turning that knob. It fascinated her to see how the electric lights worked. She sat carefully down at her desk. She picked up the phone and rang the front desk. "Hello, this is Lottie in room 302."

"I know who you are. What do you want?" Gomer snapped.

Kate was caught off guard, "Did you hear back from Mr. Allen?"

"No, but you knew that didn't you?" Gomer said, as if he was done hearing her lies and deceit.

"I don't understand, he should have responded. Did I get anything else, mail or any telegrams?" she asked in a very concerned way.

"No." Gomer said and then hung up on her.

Kate pulled a piece of paper out of the desk. Holding a pen, she began to write elegantly in cursive. She wrote feverishly at first and then began to take her time and make sure it was clear. It was a long letter in which she spilled a long, drawn out story detailing all she has endured since she has been at the hotel. When she finished, she sat that letter aside. She was concerned about George, too. She needed to set the record straight. "I merely heard of that man; I do not know him." Holding the pen as she thought of her next sentence, she became startled at a noise outside of her door. She quietly placed the letters inside the satchel. She sat still listening. It was quiet and she breathed a sigh of relief.

Kate feared Gomer was going to come to speak with her again and it distracted her. She couldn't believe nobody in Hamburg had responded to the telegram on George's behalf. She wasn't sure how much longer she could hold out at the hotel before she would be kicked out.

Kate was tired but she was far too nervous to sleep. Something disturbed her. Something put her on guard after her trip to San Diego. Kate was nervous, so nervous that no amount of steel concealed behind a thin layer of fabric could have been enough to quell her fears. She didn't feel safe. She couldn't remove her dress and crawl into bed. She needed to be ready.

TUESDAY, NOVEMBER 29

"CORONADO NOTES: A hunting party composed of Messrs. Cram, Weyburn, Arnie Babcock and Dr. Lorini spent yesterday below the line with the quail, bringing back with them their usual heavy bags."
-San Diego Union and Daily Bee, **Tuesday, 29 November**

Tuesday morning was gray and the rain had slowed significantly, down to a light trickle. A full inch of rain was recorded for San Diego County overnight. W.H. Jackson was transcribing a message he had just received that morning in the Western Union office of the hotel when he noticed there was a lot of chatter coming from the bar area, more than usual, especially so early in the morning. Jackson strained to hear what was being said when suddenly, in stepped Mr. Gomer.

Gomer looked at Jackson and ordered him to send a dispatch, "Please send a telegraph quickly to the coroner in San Diego. Tell him to come quickly, there has been a suicide here."

"What? A suicide? Where?"

"Out there, on the steps leading to the beach. We don't know much more. Just get the telegram sent!" Gomer said in a demanding voice.

"Yes, sir!" Jackson said. "Oh, here is a telegram we received for you, too." And he handed it to Gomer. Jackson noticed Gomer's forehead was glistening. *Was that rain or sweat?* Jackson wondered.

Gomer looked at it, reading every word. It was from the Farmers' and Merchants' Bank of Hamburg, Iowa. It was a response to the telegraph to G.L. Allen. The bank had approved the draw of $25 on behalf of Lottie A. Bernard.

Gomer was already nervous but reading the telegram started his heart racing. An awkward silence came over him. He looked back at Mr. Jackson, who was busy tapping away at the dispatch. Gomer looked over his shoulder towards the light coming from the bar area, somewhat distracted by the talk of the men coming from the hall. Gomer suddenly felt a sense of urgency. He had things to do, and little time to get them done before the coroner would arrive and he quickly darted from the Western Union office!

AFTER BURIAL

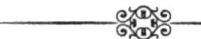

On Thursday, the 15th of December, two days after Kate was buried at Mount Hope Cemetery, P.M. Johnson, of Johnson & Co. Undertaking, made a special trip to Los Angeles. He visited with Los Angeles Chief of Police Glass. Mr. Johnson took a look at the photograph found in the trunk that the police had confiscated from the Grant home. A trunk marked Kate Morgan. Mr. Johnson said, without a doubt, that the woman from the Coronado suicide matched the woman in the photo. With that final identification, Chief of Police Glass prepared to have the trunk and contents shipped to the deceased's grandfather, Joe Chandler.

Up until this time, no family member from Hamburg, Iowa ever came forward on Kate's behalf, except for her grandfather, who merely took responsibility to pay for the burial. Why?

It is a difficult question to answer. The Fremont County Historical Society has a limited number of newspaper publications preserved for the year 1892. The *Fremont County Herald* and the Sidney paper had little coverage on the Coronado suicide. Would it be possible that the people of that town and area were not aware of the story other than what could be read from a major newspaper? Those publications would not be available for days after they were published. Is that why the local people were behind on that news?

The *Fremont County Herald* published a front-page story of W.T. Farmer (Billy's) letter to Chief of Police Glass. It was in their December 22nd edition, a week after it was first published in Los Angeles. Did that delay really cause the locals of Hamburg to not know more about the incident at the hotel?

J.P. Beach (president of Farmers' and Merchants' Bank) had had ties to the Morgan family ever since he had worked as a farmhand on the Finnell farm more than 20 years earlier. He was only 18 at that time and the 16-year-old boy John Finnell would later marry Sarah Morgan, the oldest daughter of the wealthy Tom O. Morgan.

J.P. Beach must have been very close friends with George Allen. Mr. Beach stuck to the story of a man named "Bernard," in defense of his friend George. Those communications slowed the investigation to identify the woman found on the hotel steps. There is some speculation that J.P. Beach might have taken it upon himself to forward $25 on George's behalf before George's approval. Maybe he had become accustomed to receiving wires from George, who traveled often, asking for funds. The request, albeit coming from a woman and not George, might have simply given J.P. a smirk as he dispatched the authorization of funds. There is no proof of that, though. If J.P. had sent the funds in that manner and received an immediate response that the woman had taken her life, he probably would have panicked. That mistake would tie him to the woman and any investigation around her death. He could not reveal that he sent money without authorization, especially from a bank "president."

J.P tried first to avoid any more communication with San Diego. Maybe he believed it would all die down, or maybe he was using that time to reach George.

After four days' delay, J.P. finally responded. This would be the first of what would eventually be three dispatches coming from Hamburg related to "Bernard."

On the third of December, J.P. Beach wrote:

"Johnson & Co., Undertakers, San Diego
Neither Allen nor myself know of the relatives of Mrs. Bernard. Her husband is supposed to be in Wichita, Kan. — J.P. Beach"

J.P. may have hoped this response would end his involvement. However, the detail of "her husband" possibly being in "Wichita" only added certainty to investigators' thoughts that a "Bernard" existed and it legitimized Lottie's name, too. They would not find

Mr. Bernard; instead, they would keep hounding J.P. and Mr. Allen for more information and each story on Bernard would become more elaborate in detail.

How unaware could the townspeople of Hamburg have been about the news of the suicide, considering that their town was a big part of that breaking news? Mr. Beach was telegraphing back and forth with the coroner in San Diego and San Diego was reaching out to Hamburg and the city Marshall hounding for answers on G.L. Allen.

What is remarkable and telling is that Emily Morgan, Kate's mother-in-law and a past schoolmate and stepmother of George, would also be aware if there were ever another schoolmate by the name of Bernard. She also attended the same school back in Old Berlin, Illinois. Why didn't she speak up? Did Emily talk with J.P. Beach or George to understand why they were perpetrating this story? Did she learn it was Kate before the investigators knew? Her silence, or support of the Bernard story would not be questioned by the townspeople of Hamburg, Iowa. They had no means of verifying its legitimacy. What was Emily's motivation for either support or silence in this matter?

In the length of time that the California authorities took to discover who the woman from the suicide was, the Hamburg townsfolk must have been following along. They must have wondered how close George Allen was with the woman and Mr. Bernard, his gambling schoolmate. They waited patiently to see how the story would finish. When the news reported that the suicide was actually Kate Morgan, the Hamburg townsfolk should have put it all together, that George must have known all along. Instead, an article was written in the Hamburg paper claiming they were simply surprised, and it left out George and any possible involvement he might have had.

The *Los Angeles Herald* received a message from the folks of Hamburg, Iowa. It read:

"Hamburg, Ia., December 16. - This town was much surprised on learning that the woman who committed suicide

a few weeks ago at San Diego, Cal., and was supposed to have been a Detroit lady, proved to be Mrs. Kate Morgan of this place. Mrs. Morgan has not been living with her husband for several months."

Did the townspeople hound George for answers? Was George even in town? These are legitimate questions since George never personally responded to any dispatches. George couldn't make responses without raising questions from anywhere other than a Western Union in Hamburg.

George had solid friends in Hamburg who covered for him. Peter Paul Wikoff was one of them. Peter was also the Hamburg, Iowa justice of the peace at this time. He proved his close relationship to George when he wrote to the *San Diego Union* newspaper on George's behalf.

"It Was for Charity

Peter Wikoff of Hamburg, Ia., writes to *THE UNION* that the connection of G.L. Allen's name with that of Mrs. Kate Morgan, alias Lottie Bernard, the Coronado suicide, was unjust to him, and conveyed a wrong impression. Mr. Wikoff says that Mr. Allen is an unassuming and honorable gentleman, and that through charity he sent the unfortunate woman $25, not knowing her personally, but being acquainted with her husband, who was his schoolmate. The highest references are named with which to prove Mr. Allen's standing, and Mr. Wikoff adds that 'the San Diego man who says that Mr. Allen is a sport and a lady-killer, is a coward and is afraid to make the statement over his own signature.'"

-San Diego Union and Daily Bee, December 24, 1892."

Peter came to Hamburg from Old Berlin, Illinois, too. Peter, George, Emily and Marcena all lived in that small farming community for years together. Peter was well aware that there was no Bernard from the Old Berlin area.

What was the purpose for this letter? It has to be questioned. Under the guise of a friend looking out for his fellow friend's honor by calling the person who claimed George was a sport and a lady killer a coward, Peter does something more. Peter perpetuates the Bernard lie and says George never knew Kate personally. Could Peter have had another agenda? Could there have been concerns that the police might have found evidence in Kate's effects that could implicate anyone close to or familiar with her? Evidence that might have been in either her trunk or the unclaimed trunks. Otherwise, what purpose was achieved in sending this after Kate had already been buried?

Billy Farmer did all he could to convince the police of Los Angeles to consider Kate's death as a possible murder, but that did not happen. There was little more Billy could do since Kate was already being buried when his letter was read.

Kate's cousin George of Hanford, California, must have found the news just as disturbing as his Uncle Billy, but George Farmer and his wife Gertrude were dealing with other problems at that time. According to the *Visalia Morning Delta*, the estate of his lynched brother-in-law, John Ruggles, was now in the courts being settled.

A.D. Swartz was a close friend of the family and he proved that when he took the time to write to the San Diego coroner, providing the names of Kate's relatives. That letter prompted them to send a dispatch to Kate's grandfather, and her grandfather quickly responded to have Kate buried.

On December 11, the news reported that the unclaimed trunks that sat at the D Street station were finally claimed by the owners. It was remarkable how long they sat there before they were claimed. It was equally remarkable that the police never examined them, at least as far as we are to believe. There is no means to discover if the police were the ones who collected those trunks, but it seems surprising that the police reported they had traced Kate's exact travel from Chicago to Omaha to Cheyenne to Ogden to Sacramento and to Hanford where she remained for a short time and then to Los Angeles. For them to discover this so quickly could mean that they found train tickets among her belongings and yet no tickets were listed as part of the contents of the trunk confiscated from the Grant family's home.

Mark Abbott had been making trips back and forth for several years from 1890 through 1895. His constant travel was remarkable. During the majority of his travels, he did not bring his wife along. In March of 1892, he checked into the Palace Hotel in Visalia. On September 23, he stayed at the Cosmopolitan Hotel of Los Angeles. Then on Sunday, November 27, the day before Kate purchased a gun at Chick's Gun Shop, Mark was in San Diego.

Mark left San Diego after his stay and was found on December 13 staying at the Arlington Hotel in Santa Barbara. He stayed there only one night and left the next morning, returning to San Francisco by way of San Luis Obispo and Monterey. On May 13 of 1893, Mark was in Tulare County checking into The Grand Hotel. Then on the eighth of June he was back in San Diego checking into the Hotel Brewster. Mark was listed as a hotel runner and he was certainly "running" from hotel to hotel.

Joe Chandler received Kate's trunk and effects that were sent from the chief of police of Los Angeles. We will never know what he or his wife Maria did with those precious memories of hers. Did they question the lock of blond hair marked "Elizabeth Morgan"? There is no Elizabeth Morgan, found within the Morgan family. There is only Sarah Elizabeth Morgan, Tom O. Morgan's oldest daughter, who was married to John Finnell, and she was not blonde. It is an unusual artifact Kate kept with her belongings. It begs the question of whether Kate might have given birth to a second child at some point in time. If so, what happened to her?

Kate's grandfather Joe revealed his true nature and character when he merely paid for her to be buried. He didn't even cover the cost of a grave marker for her eternal resting place. Did his wife Maria try to convince him to have her brought back and buried in Fremont County to have her placed by her mother or her first-born child? We will never know.

The *Fremont County Herald* published the following story on the 29th of December 1892:

"We are told Tuesday that Mrs. John Samuels would start to California in a short time to bring the body of Mrs. Kate

Morgan, nee Farmer, back to Fremont County for a final resting place."

Mary "Farmer" Samuels, Kate's cousin in Riverton, and the sister of George Farmer of Hanford, California, was deeply saddened by the news of Kate. Not only that, but she was also upset that Kate's body was buried in San Diego and was determined to bring her body back to be properly buried there in Fremont County.

Thursday, the 29th of December, was also the day before what would have been Kate and Thomas' 7th wedding anniversary.

No more news was published relating to Mary Samuels attempt to bring Kate's body back. Did she go? Did she make a stop to see her Uncle Billy and her brother George in Hanford, California where she would learn of the Ruggles brothers' lynching? If she did make it to San Diego, she might have learned that exhuming the body from its unmarked grave could prove difficult and the state of decay the body would be in would make it undesirable. We only know that Kate's body was never moved.

LIVES LIVED

After Kate was buried, there was no more thought about the unfortunate young twentysomething lying in a Southern California grave.

That was not true for room 302 at the Hotel del Coronado. Guests assigned to that room would make complaints about the lights flashing, or sounds of quiet talking. One woke to see a woman at the end of the bed who then pulled the covers off of him. The temperature in the room would change drastically for no known reason. Sometimes their belongings would move from one location to another. Some have experienced a sudden gust of wind or light scents of perfume. Yes, those odd and strange occurrences continued far beyond the life of Kate's immediate family and friends and all those who surrounded her last days and the investigation.

What happened to those characters that were a part of Kate's story? How did their lives turn out? Let's have a look.

Lizzie Wyllie: Many still believe it wasn't Kate that died on those steps. They believe instead it was Lizzie Wyllie. Lizzie had a number of remarkably similar features to Kate. All except the "pierced ears." That was the only physical difference preventing her from meeting the identity criteria. Once they dismissed her from being the woman found on the hotel steps, there was no more word from Detroit. There wasn't even any news related to the tin-type photo sent to Lizzie's mother by the undertaker for Elizabeth to either confirm or deny it was her daughter Lizzie.

We have tools today to find Lizzie's records. Evidence shows Lizzie was born on December 31, 1869. Lizzie married a man named

Wallace Cook in 1894 in Essex, Ontario, Canada. On the marriage registry, she wrote her age was 24, her father was John Wyllie and her mother was Elizabeth Donaldson. She listed her home as Detroit.

Her husband, Wallace, was from Ontario but he followed Lizzie to Wayne Michigan (suburb west of Detroit) and they lived there for years. They also never had any children.

Lizzie did have a sister, Jane, who had married a man named Jesse Anderson. They had three children (Maud, May and Myrtle) but no Louise. Jesse had no sisters or other women related on the Anderson side of his family with the names of Louise, Charlotte or Lottie, either.

On May 22, 1912, Lizzie passed away from heart disease. She was only 42 years old.

John G. Longfield: John was born in Cleveland, Ohio in 1859. He is found as a bookbinder in the 1880 Cleveland city directory. In the 1880 Cleveland Census, John Longfield, age 21, was listed as a bookbinder and married to a woman named Mary who was 4 years older than he.

He must have divorced her because John Longfield is found marrying Elizabeth Frazer in Detroit, Michigan in 1883 and it showed his occupation as bookbinder with a birthplace of Cleveland, Ohio.

He must have divorced her too, because John G. Longfield, a bookbinder at the age of 30, is found marrying 23-year-old Mary L. Dallas, a saleslady, on October 11, 1889, in Detroit, Michigan.

John is found once again in another marriage registry dated 9 July 1890 in Cleveland, Ohio, where he was marrying Mary J. Gresmuck. Mary was recorded as 4 years older than John. This was less than a year after marrying Mary Dallas. Could it be that Mary Gresmuck was the same woman listed with him in the 1880 census? Is it possible they were only living together back then when the census worker wrote her down as his wife?

Sometime in 1892, John was having an affair with Lizzie Wyllie while working as a bookbinder at Winn and Hammond in Detroit. John and Lizzie were fired because of it. Lizzie's sister May was also fired. The Wyllie family spoke of how close John was with the family and how often he dropped by. The newspapers wrote that he was a married man and he could not have been on the train with the unfortunate woman at that time because he said he was in Ohio looking for work. Longfield was also spoken of as a sport and a rounder of not the best reputation, even for one of his class.

There might be some truth that he was in Ohio. The question we might ask is who was his wife? Mary Gresmuck, who lived in Ohio, or Mary Dallas, who lived in Wayne Michigan?

Mary J. Gresmuck of Ohio remained a Longfield even to her death. She died in December of 1893 in Cleveland, Ohio. In the death register for Mary "Gresmuck" Longfield, she was listed as 40 and married!

Did John divorce Mary Dallas, less than a year into their marriage, and then go to Ohio and marry Mary Gresmuck? Or was he a polygamist? Records show that Mary Dallas bore two children with John Longfield. Their first daughter, Jessie, was born in 1895. Their second daughter, Catherine, came 4 years later in 1899. Maybe Mary Dallas had to pin him down with children to hold him accountable to her. Did that even work?

Mary L. Dallas held John Longfield in marriage until Mary passed away in 1933. Her death certificate showed her husband as John Longfield. Mary died of bronchial pneumonia at the age of 65, two weeks after she had a stroke.

On 23 August 1938, five years after the loss of his wife, John G. Longfield passed away. On his death certificate the doctor wrote the principal cause of death: hemorrhage following laceration of wrist. He was 78 years old.

The Lizzie and John Longfield story delayed the identity of Kate Morgan for nearly a week!

Thomas Edwin Morgan: It was never certain whether Thomas ever went to California but there are suspicions and vague evidence that he probably was there alongside Kate in the beginning. Had Thomas engaged in any nefarious activities with J.H. McDonough, Adolph Ottinger or Mark Leander Abbott? We will never know.

There is also some speculation that it could have been Thomas who rode with Kate on the train to San Diego. Could it be that he followed her trunks, that were sent to Los Angeles via Omaha, to find her? Was she arguing with him that she did not have an affair with George? Was she giving him news that she wanted a divorce or pleading with him to take her back? Was she begging him to hand over the trunk claim tickets during that ride? Whoever she rode with was angry enough to bolt at Orange. The man held on to those trunk's claim tickets, never considering sending them to her. Was that on purpose?

Thomas Morgan had his birthday on the third of December, just a few days after Kate was found dead. Was he unaware that the woman at the Hotel del Coronado was Kate? Kate and Thomas would have been celebrating their seventh wedding anniversary that December 30. Instead, Thomas was settling down in Burchard, Nebraska for the winter as a widower. The telegram he received of Kate's death was still in his possession, a telegram to which he chose not to respond. He would hold on to that telegram for the rest of his life and it would be passed down to his descendants.

The photo of Kate was also in his possession and he would hold on to it for the rest of his life, too. Whatever happened or he believed happened between Kate and George could not be remedied by her death. George was still family and George would still be coming and going in Hamburg of Fremont County.

Thomas would remain in Burchard, a distance that would keep him from running into George, and history shows he would never return to Fremont County again, at least not while he was alive.

Instead, he found a new love: a woman by the name Jennie Devor who grew up in that corner of Nebraska; just a few days after the one-year anniversary of Kate's death, Thomas married Jennie. Thomas and Jennie remained in Nebraska and based on Thomas' obituary, he wasn't much of a traveler outside of Nebraska during their lifetime.

Thomas worked various jobs in Burchard, including well digging during his early years of marriage with Jennie. When they finally left Burchard, the land and home were sold. The deed of transfer shows it had been owned by Jennie all that time. After he landed the job of rural mail carrier in 1898, he carried that role for eight years until he took the family to Hubbell, Nebraska in 1916. There he worked in the grain and lumber business and in 1922, he moved the family again to Ragan, Nebraska.

Thomas and his family didn't stay in Ragan, Nebraska for long; in 1928, he and the family moved again to Alma and here Thomas held the position of Sheriff of Harlan County. When he became too old for that work, he turned to traffic policeman until he retired.

In 1936, at the age of 75, Thomas Edwin Morgan passed away. In a very loving act, Thomas' sister Mollie Morgan Pauly had Thomas' body brought back to Hamburg for a burial. She held the local funeral services at her home. A part of his long obituary said "He was always of a cheerful disposition and made friends easily. He was liked by both young and old and being of peaceful disposition himself he always tried to bring peace and harmony out of chaos whenever possible." Thomas' body was laid to rest at Mount Zion Utterback Cemetery.

Joseph Wilson Chandler: Joe lost his school-age sweetheart and second wife, Maria Hand Chandler, on January 21, 1894, 14 months after Kate's death. Maria's children from her first marriage with Shadrack were living in Missouri, just south of Hamburg, at the time of her death. Her son, Allen Mode Chandler, filed in the Fremont court to be principal and executor of Maria's estate. It had Joe Chandler as sureties. It was filed on January 18, 1896, which was two years after Maria's death. The probate record book had a thick black cross marked over the page with the word "error" written boldly. This act or attempted act by Maria's son leaves some strange unanswered questions as to what he thought he could accomplish. Husbands were owners of their wives' properties at that time. When Maria's son Allen attempted this, Joe was already married again. Did that anger Allen Mode Chander?

In those early months after Joe lost Maria, he was seeing another woman. Her name was Rachel Lloyd. She was a Lloyd, but not by birth. She was actually a Swartzlander until she married John Lloyd. Rachel and John were married for 41 years until he passed away. Rachel had a daughter and four sons by him.

Her son Charles Lloyd was married to Frances Catlett, the sister of Emery Chandler's wife Mary. Charles and Frances Lloyd ran a saloon annex that was part of a billiard hall in downtown Hamburg at that time. Did Joe frequent the saloon and billiard hall, too? Did Emery frequent the saloon as well?

The tie of Mary Catlett Chandler to Francis Catlett Lloyd doesn't answer how Joe Chandler became familiar with Rachel Lloyd well enough to marry her shortly after he lost Maria. On March 7, 1895, 14 months after the loss of his wife Maria, Joe Chandler married Rachel Lloyd.

By 1900, Joe had sold his grain dealership and was living with his wife Rachael in downtown Hamburg on Park Street. Joe owned the house free and clear and he had his occupation as landlord. Joe lived there another four years and in January of 1904, at the age of 83. Joe Chandler passed away.

Joe was laid to rest at the Mount Olive Cemetery next to his first wife Matilda and his second wife Maria. They all had matching tombstones. When Rachael passed away five years later, she was not placed beside Joe; instead, she was buried in the Hamburg Cemetery in a plot of her own.

George L. Allen: George had lived the free life of a bachelor for many years. He also went through great measures to keep himself off the grid. Between the time his father passed away in 1870 until 1900, George is not found in either census records or agricultural records. He can be found in news articles, though, and that is where one can gain some idea of the type of man he was and the men he kept in his circles: mostly bankers, saloon owners and lawmen.

The newspapers of the nineteenth century often posted what the local people were doing. Someone had a birthday on Wednesday, someone traveled to see their aunt, someone sold cattle, someone was married. It is these simple, oftentimes one-liner news pieces through which one can follow a lot of what George was doing during the 1890s.

A news article posted in the *Los Angeles Herald* for November 26 has a G.L. Allen seen in Anaheim, California. He was listed as an Angelenos (the term for someone who resided in Los Angeles). If this is our George L. Allen, and he left Kate at Orange, California the day before, had he taken a trip to Anaheim, and if so, for what purpose?

In a Visalia news article dated Jan 12, 1893, a story was written on the marriage of Mr. and Mrs. Zumwalt. Mr. Zumwalt was a prominent businessman in Tulare County, California. The article said he had a host of friends who wished them joy in their new holy matrimony. Several intimate friends attended the after-ceremony party, and on that list was Mr. and Mrs. G.L. Allen of San Francisco. Coincidence? Or is there another G.L. Allen? The Zumwalt newlyweds left and went to the Hotel del Coronado for their honeymoon.

On January 19, 1893, the *Fremont County Herald* posted "George Allen, the Hamburg stock buyer, was in town today." Then on the fourth of April, the Palace Hotel in Fresno listed G.L. Allen as a guest. Then on April 9, the Hollenbeck Hotel in Los Angeles listed a G.L. Allen as one of their check-ins. When September of 1893 came along, George was attending the Chicago World's Fair. The others from Fremont that also went included Dr. Swiggart (the doctor who was an administrator of Mary Farmer's estate), his wife and daughter.

There is an article published on the front page of the *San Francisco Call* dated May of 1895. A man identified as George Allen was considered to be the mechanic for two other men caught in the production of counterfeiting. James C. Corbett and Charles Williams as well as George Allen were busted by Detectives Loomis and Burlew. It was reported this gang was manufacturing dollar pieces made of tin-plated silver. The two men (not Allen) came to Denver from Grant, Colorado and were married to sisters who were aware of their employment. Secret Service Agent Walker pronounced the dies and apparatus as the finest he has ever seen and their plant and facilities were of the best order. Was George Allen, who was arrested, the same man as G.L. Allen of Hamburg? Is it just coincidental that a man by the name of George Allen was involved in counterfeiting as J.H. McDonough would be busted doing later?

Between the article found in 1893 when George attended the World's Fair, until July of 1898, there is no more Fremont County news related to George Allen. Then, an article once again was found in July 1898. A one-liner that George Allen of Hamburg had shipped two loads of the Mart Dresher cattle to Chicago.

Through two preserved handwritten accounts– one on the back of an old photo of Kate kept by Thomas Morgan's descendants and a letter kept by Thomas Morgan's half-sister's descendants–a peek into that long-forgotten past was tucked away among so much other memorabilia the family kept. The story of a love affair Kate had with her husband's stepbrother. Was George in love with Kate? If he was, that answer went to the grave with him.

It is speculated that it could have been George on the train with Kate. If he had been, what angered him so much that he would bail on her? Could he have been so devious as to recognize he had her claim tickets to the trunks and not bothered to bring them to her, or at least send them via mail? What we do learn is that he wanted to distance himself from any perceived relationship with Kate once her identity was established. Was this because his affair with her was still unknown to all? Or was there something more? Did he fear the police had in their possession articles from her effects that could implicate him in a crime?

George remained a single bachelor for many years and was known as a lady killer. He stayed a single man until 1900, when at the age of 51 he finally succumbed to marriage. Maybe he was tired from all of the work and effort involved in chasing after women, something best left to younger men who had that kind of energy.

In early 1900, George had made the decision to marry. His fiancée was Frances Catlett Lloyd. Frances had been married for 20 years to George Lloyd but decided to divorce him sometime in 1899.

Frances was 18 years old when she married Charles Lloyd. Charles later became a saloon owner in downtown Hamburg. Charles and Frances never had children in their 20 years of marriage. In early 1899, both Charles and Frances Lloyd were being sued for injuries sustained by William Pierson after an altercation which took place in their saloon. On March 30' 1899, they lost the suit and had to pay William $187.50 in damages. Shortly after the lawsuit ended, so did their marriage.

Frances was the younger sister of Mary Catlett Chandler and that meant she was also the sister-in-law of Emery Chandler. Prior to her divorce from Charles, her step father-in-law was Joe Chandler. Frances was also a mere 4 years older than Kate.

In that same time frame, George L. Allen was busy traveling and handling his stock business. The *Fremont County Sun* posted a trip to Omaha he did in February of that year. Later, he shipped out eight cars of cattle. It was during this time that George and Frances were becoming more intimate. How did they keep their affair out of the eyes of the folks in Hamburg? How did George and Frances keep it from Kate's grandfather Joe who was now married to Frances' husband's mother, Rachel?

In May of 1900, just months after Frances divorced her husband Charles, George and Frances went to Lincoln, Nebraska and they married. In the *Nebraska City News Press*, Saturday, May 5, the following news was printed in the paper:

"George L. Allen and Mrs. F. Lloyd, of Hamburg, Ia., were married yesterday at Lincoln. Both are well known in this city."

How were George and Frances well known in Lincoln? Was that how they kept their secret from the prying eyes of the Hamburg social circles?

George and Frances Allen remained in Hamburg for a number of years after their marriage. Frances' ex, Charles, remained there, too. The news posted George's stock purchase and dealings regularly through those early years of the twentieth century. George bought the Elkhorn meat market on the east side of main street in Hamburg in January of 1906.

What is not known was how Frances' marriage to George may have impacted her relationship with her sister Mary. Mary's husband Emery Chandler might have learned over the past 8 years that the relationship George had with his niece Kate may have caused her death. Did he forgive and forget? Emery and George were now brothers-in-law, after all.

Around 1910, George and Frances made Southern Colorado their permanent home. They moved to the remote town of San Acasio, just west of San Luis, in Costilla County. Southern Colorado has a very barren landscape of flat plains filled with dust and desert vegetation. The town they lived in couldn't have had a population greater than a few hundred. It was an unusual place for anyone of wealth of that day to want to make their home. It was close to the rails, though, and made travel easy between California, Texas, or Hamburg, Iowa. They would continuously make visits to Hamburg at least once a year and nearly every time they would be found staying at the home of Mrs. Henry Clay Byars, a cousin of Frances on her mother's side. There was never news that they visited Mary and Emery Chandler.

In June of 1924, at the age of 75, and while on another train trip, this time without Frances, George Allen succumbed to a fatal attack of kidney trouble. He was assisted off of the train at Winfield, Kansas, where they immediately took him to a hospital, but upon arriving, he passed. The news in Hamburg had written he was in poor health for the last five years of his life. His body was shipped to Hamburg, where he was laid to rest at the Mount Olive Cemetery in Fremont County. He had no family other than his wife Francis. His stepmother Emily Dennison Morgan, who never remarried after the loss of Marcena, had passed away just 13 months earlier.

At the Mount Olive Cemetery, George's grave is marked by a large monument-sized grave-marker for which his wife Frances had made special for him.

In July of 1924, just a month after George Allen passed away, Emery and Mary Chandler celebrated their golden wedding anniversary. It was attended by 50 relatives and friends. Frances Catlett Allen was one of those attendees.

Emily Hope Morgan *nee* **Dennison**: There seemed to be no love between George Allen and Emily Morgan. When Emily lost her husband Marcena in 1886, she was only 42 years old and yet she remained single. Maybe her best years were behind her. George was 37 years old at that time and in his prime. He was also making a fortune for himself.

After Marcena's death, Emily left the large property she lived in for years and bought a modest home, which she owned free and clear of any mortgage, on Main Street in downtown Hamburg. Did she sell the farm and lands Marcena had amassed in McKissick's Grove? There seems to be no record of such. Did she work out something with Tom O. Morgan, her brother-in-law, who was working as co-administrator of the estate? Did he buy the farm and land from her? Did Emily's stepson Thomas inherit any portion of his father's estate?

Emily remained in the Hamburg home and stayed very close to her four children through her later years. After she lost her 40-year-old daughter, Gertrude, Emily took Gertrude's children into her own home.

It seems that Emily had lost touch with her younger brother William Dennison after he went to Ft. Buford in the Wyoming territory. Will had served under General Custer during those years. Will remained at the Wyoming Fort between 1871 to 1881 and then transferred to a regiment near Park City, Utah. His enlistment expired there, where he married a Norwegian woman by the name of Rachael. He and Rachael remained in Park City, Utah until he passed away in 1928. His obituary never mentioned his late sister Emily.

On the 29th of May 1923, Emily passed away while caring for her grandchildren, Pauline, Rita and Maxine Whisler. Emily was laid to rest at the Mount Zion Utterback Cemetery in a shared grave plot with her late husband Marcena Morgan.

James Plumb Beach: J.P. Beach had been living in Hamburg as early as 1862. He was a Canadian at birth before his family moved to Iowa. He was a farmhand on Simpson Finnell's farm for a year or more around 1870.

Simpson Finnell came to Iowa from California. Simpson's California family remained there. His brother John Finnell became very wealthy owning vast acres of land in northern California. John had a number of sons, one of which was James Stevenson Finnell.

James Stevenson Finnell had a farmhand by the name of Coleman Dalton, a brother to the men of the Dalton gang. This may be a coincidence but it is worthy to note. James Stevenson Finnell was as wealthy as his father John. The 1900 census showed James had four servants and 18 farm hands (Coleman listed as one) at his stockyard. On the 13th of December 1892, there was a check-in to The Hotel del Coronado for J. Finnell and his wife from Red Bluff. There is strong belief that this was James and his wife Isabel who were living in Red Bluff at this time. If they checked in on the 13th, they arrived the same day Kate was being buried. Was this also a coincidence?

James' Uncle Simpson Finnell had a level of wealth, too, even though he left California and moved to Iowa. Simpson's son John Finnell was close in age to J.P. Beach and it is reasonable to assume they had become acquainted with each other during J.P.'s employment at the Finnell farm back in 1870. John Finnell later married Sarah Elizabeth Morgan, the oldest daughter of Tom O. Morgan.

J.P. Beach was unwavering in his support to George L. Allen and the "Bernard" story.

James and his wife Eva stayed in Hamburg, Iowa until sometime after 1900. By 1910, he and his family had moved north to Council Bluffs, Iowa. He worked there in the real estate and loans business. By 1920, James and Eva were sharing a room in the home of their daughter and her family in Chicago. Sometime between 1920 and 1930, both James and Eva moved to Miami, Florida but that didn't last long. They returned to Council Bluffs and on 3rd of June 1939, James Plumb Beach passed away. He was 86 years old.

Abraham D. Swarts: If it were not for Abraham Swarts' letter sent to the coroner of San Diego, they would not have discovered the names of Kate's Hamburg-area relatives as quickly as they did.

Abraham D. Swarts had an unusual life. He was originally from Illinois and married a woman named Eunice in 1875. Sometime just before 1878, he brought his wife Eunice and their two boys to live in Locust Grove of Fremont County, Iowa. Locust Grove was a neighboring grove, east of McKissick's Grove, in Madison. He lived there for quite some time. Abraham then moved the family to Los Angeles in November of 1891. In 1900, Abraham was listed as a hotel clerk. He worked for several years in that capacity. Something happened, though. Sometime after 1914, Abraham moved into the Downey Poor Farm in Imperial, California.

The Downey Poor Farm rested on 124 acres of farmland. Los Angeles bought the land in 1887 with the idea of building an institution for housing the homeless. The first homeless "inmates" were moved to the farm in 1888, the same year of the grand opening of the Hotel del Coronado. The farm did very well during its first 20 years.

The *Los Angeles Times* wrote an article about the poor farm on Nov. 6, 1902:

"A poor farm sits in the midst of an orange grove. The delightful innovation of housing the homeless and unfortunates in such environments belongs exclusively to Southern California, for no other part of America bears record of having done likewise: Wrapped in sunbeams and wreathed with flower gardens, the Los Angeles County Poor Farm visibly resents the incongruity of its name, for it is rich in all the beauties of semi-tropical verdure, rich in productiveness of its orchards and fields, and rich in the great permeating joy of life, that trembles in every leaf and flower, transmitting the influence of its buoyancy into human hearts grown weary, dispirited and restless."

The farm grew during the following 12 years to be Los Angeles' most lauded of projects. Discovery that the farm's orange grove made $13,000 in 1909 gave it a moniker of the County Rich Farm. But shortly after 1910, dark stories were coming out about mistreatments of the inmates. Stories of one inmate drowning in a nearby river, and another who threw himself out of the window, caused concerns. It all went to the grand jury, who mandated reform.

It was during those terrible years between 1910 and 1920 that Abraham was found living at the Downey Poor Farm. Abraham's wife Eunice was living in Los Angeles with their youngest son. She marked herself married in the census just as Abraham did but they were living separate lives. Abraham lived out the rest of his days at that homeless farm and passed away in 1921.

Today the Downey Poor Farm is considered one of the nation's most haunted places. Many of the buildings were in great decay. As of this writing, Los Angeles is in the process of flattening and removing the remaining structures from this land. It is to wonder if the hauntings that took place on this ground will go away when the city permits new development on this ground.

Deputy Coroner H. J. Stetson: His full name was Herbert James Stetson but there are signs he preferred to be called Herbert. He was born in the area of Modesto, California the same year of Kate's birth. He had just turned 26 when he looked at her body for the first time.

When Stetson was charged in the Judge Dillar case, it was not the first time he had charges placed against him. In February of 1887, R.S.T. Lee filed a suit saying that Stetson had wickedly conspired and contrived to defraud him of a large sum of money. He said Stetson and his partner Hull had sold him a one-half interest in a patented invention of a gas-pressure regulator, for which he paid $1,500, but he charged that they didn't own the patent rights for that sale. Stetson was not notified of the charges because he had already left town and moved to San Diego. He had already used his portion of that money to buy land from F. Mertzmann (the same doctor who examined Kate for the inquest).

In November of that year, he married a young woman named Hattie Morris. Their ceremony was elaborate and Hattie wore a pale pink surah elaborately trimmed with cream white and pink ribbon. More than 60 friends and family joined the ceremony and the afterparty.

Mr. and Mrs. Stetson were enjoying their early marriage and building relationships in San Diego. In 1880, they attended a friend's birthday party that had a large number of guests. In attendance was C.W. Stevens (same man from Star Stables who said he had gone horseback riding with Kate).

In 1890, Stetson began buying and selling real estate, including a lot in Coronado which he bought from a man named John Bass for $600. Stetson would continue real estate purchases for many years.

In October of that year, 1890, Judge Wallace in Modesto dismissed the suit of R.S.T. Lee against H.W. Hull and H.J. Stetson on those defraud charges over the patent. It was dismissed for failure of plaintiff to prosecute.

In September of 1891, Hattie bore her first child, a daughter they named Pearl. Hattie was only 21, and Stetson, 25, when they became parents for the first time.

In 1892, Coroner Weller was under scrutiny for moving to Escondido. Men in San Diego were pressuring the mayor to have him fired because he couldn't do his job while living so far away. Weller maintained he continued to carry an office in San Diego but that wasn't enough. The city appointed H.J. Stetson as deputy coroner that February. By May, both Weller and Stetson were fighting various charges, Stetson for stealing from Judge Dillar, and Weller for conducting post-mortems and billing without first having an inquest. It appeared there were folks bent on having them both removed.

On December 24, 1892, just after Kate Morgan was buried, Stetson was sued again for $19.20, and this time, he didn't win. He had to pay damages, which forced him to sell some of his property at auction.

The following year, Stetson decided to leave his duties as deputy coroner. He took a book-keeping job for a newspaper called the *San Diego Vidette*. That job was short-lived and he changed jobs again to be a manager for the Paragon Oil and Gasoline Company. Even though he took on these other roles, Stetson never stopped buying and selling property, too.

In March of 1900, Stetson and Hattie left San Diego and moved to San Francisco. Here Stetson began a real estate company in partnership with a man named O. C. Baldwin.

In 1915, Hattie Stetson was on trial by her Methodist church for dissension and discord and she was on the edge of being removed. Whatever the argument she provided in her own defense, it led the church to acquit her of those charges. She was back in their good graces but it was too late. She did not wish to remain in that church. She was okay with her husband staying with the Methodist church, though. But was she? Shortly after this, the two divorced and she took her children with her.

H. J. Stetson remarried a few years afterwards to a woman named Lois Perry and they had three children of their own.

Herbert James Stetson lived a long life and on May 16th of 1951, in Mountain View California, Stetson passed away at the age of 85.

Kathleen Kate Morgan nee Farmer: Kate was about to turn 25 when she lost her life. After her death, her body laid on a slab for nearly two weeks, but she was not alone. She had visitors every day. Not from her family: No Chandler or Farmer or Morgan were there to say their last goodbyes. Instead, she was surrounded by the local women, women of prominence, women who may have understood the real cause of her tragedy.

Her Uncle Billy received his notification late; Kate was already being prepared for the burial. Her husband Thomas received a telegram at the same time as Kate's grandfather but there is no record of Thomas responding to his notification.

George Allen was the only one who could have come forward and set everyone straight. He knew the truth but he chose to remain silent. He distanced himself from the situation to protect himself from something he knew, a secret which he did not want anyone to be aware of, a secret he carried to his grave.

When Kate's grandfather Joe was notified, his response was swift, "Bury the body and send me the statement."

On the 13th of December, Kate received a beautiful service at the parlors of Johnson's Undertakers. Her casket was covered in a blanket of flowers that were arranged by the generosity of the prominent women of San Diego. Reverend Restarey of St. Paul's Church read several passages of scripture and offerings of prayers. In attendance were the members of the Brotherhood of St. Andrew and ladies of the Episcopal church. The Episcopal ladies took turns making responses during the service. When the service ended, the casket was placed in the hearse for conveyance to Mount Hope Cemetery but nobody followed.

The hearse driver rode east on Market Street, carrying Kate's casket for 10 miles, until he reached the Mount Hope Cemetery. He transferred the crude box containing her body to the grave digger, who lowered the casket deep below the excavated spot. He worked diligently to refill it and then took the blanket of flowers that once laid on her casket and placed it over the freshly-turned ground. Her body remains in this plot at the Mount Hope Cemetery, Lot 28, Row 6, Section 1, Division 5. It sits just feet from a set of rails where the sounds of trains ran by for many years. The plot remained unmarked for almost 100 years until Alan May, another author who wrote of Kate, had the grave properly marked.

Some are angry that Kate was buried in San Diego. Why wasn't she brought back to Fremont and laid to rest beside her son or her mother, or grandmother? Her dear cousin Mary Farmer Samuels had intended to go to San Diego to bring her body back but it never took place. Maybe a greater power had a hand in holding Kate to San Diego.

Kate may not have expected to die that November day. When her life ended, she found herself lying in the shadows of that mighty white fortress.

Kate had a weakness and tried to protect herself from it. She did not do well when she felt discarded. The Hotel del Coronado has not discarded her, though. They have embraced her. She is celebrated in their halls and shops and brochures. That is where Kate found solace. It was a great choice. It is one of California's greatest gems, a destination of luxury and beauty. A place where the wealthy, powerful, elite, and beautiful people choose to stay. It is a place anyone would wish to stay if given a chance to live forever.

Acknowledgements

Five years ago, I would never have conceived of publishing a book. I had no experience in book writing, publishing, or anything like that. What I had done was a short story of my husband's family using information extracted from an old bible and using Ancestry©. I found a certain level of pleasure digging up old documents and details of those who lived more than 100 years ago and turning it into a story. Honestly though, writing historical nonfiction is no simple task! I had no idea the amount of extra work involved in maintaining sources and keeping a story as accurate as possible. If it were not for a number of close friends and relatives pushing me along, I might have given up!

The first person I must thank is Donna Malmborg. Donna is also a writer, and has been published in American Paranormal Magazine, the New England Legends website as well as the second and seventh volume of The Feminine Macabre. Donna was the catalyst for my interest in Kate Morgan. Donna also stuck by me in those early pages of the book, always giving me encouragement and positive feedback. When I had serious doubts about being a writer or publishing a book, Donna would turn me around and keep me moving forward.

I must also thank Lilly Uva. I met Lilly nearly eight years ago in San Diego. Our husbands worked together and both were transferred to New Jersey. Lilly began reading the early versions of the book, marking pages up, and providing feedback to me all while in treatment for cancer. She spoke excitedly about certain chapters and hopes someday I will write a book on H.J. Stetson. We will see. When we talked about Kate, she would suddenly get goose bumps and it revealed to me that the story was more than mere words on paper. It pushed me through the last stages of completing the book and I will be forever grateful to her.

I must also thank my daughter Tina Hawkins who cheered me on from the beginning. She connected me with a close friend and book writer, Mariet Kay. Though historical non-fiction is not Mariet's genre of choice, she helped guide me through the self-publishing process. It is another daunting task required to get published. She guided me on how to get an ISBN, find alternative tools that format books for publication, and introduced me to Getcovers.com who I employed for the book cover. Mariet also shared some ideas for selling the product and a number of other behind-the-scenes requirements self-publishers should be in the know about.

During the second year of writing, I joined the South Jersey Writers Group. It is a unique group that brings local writers together in support of their craft. A special thanks to the group's president Amy Hollinger. The group holds a number of events in support of writers: virtual write-ins, book launches, book critiques and beta reads. Being a member of this group has given me a number of resources which all writers could use and the camaraderie amongst the members is immeasurable.

It takes a lot to take a story from concept to publishing. It is an absolute necessity to have a professional editor to clean up the work. I don't know how many times I have read a book and found a misspelled word or a confusing sentence that stopped me in my tracks. I didn't want my readers to be distracted by poor writing. My editor, Alicia Guide, has been invaluable not only for me but for this story! She was thorough, efficient and guided me through areas of the book that needed a deeper clarity. She scanned over the book not just once, but a few times and when I read the story now, I feel like I'm reading a professional manuscript. Thank you Alicia! I'm certain the readers will appreciate you, too!

I want to also thank my sister Jean McGovern, for helping me with the introductory piece on the Del. You really should consider writing yourself! I also want to thank my cousin, Lillian Ramirez for reading the book front to back and her positive feedback too!

Lastly, I must give a very special thanks to my husband Matt Malmborg. You put up with my late hours of writing. You patiently listened to my random rants as I excitedly talked about a new discovery related to Kate or some of the others written about in this story. I'll never forget how you showed me the goose bumps that rose on your arms after viewing the book cover! Kate seems to have that effect. Your encouragement and support will always mean so much to me! I'm very blessed to have you by my side!

BIBLIOGRAPHY

Most of the articles used in the creation of this story are from the online California Digital Newspaper Collection (CDNC) which is a project of the Center for Bibliographical Studies and Research at the University of California, Riverside.

News from Iowa publications were also referenced and are found in the digital collection of the Clarinda Library and through online access to the Historical Society of Fremont County (IAGenWeb).

Other research was obtained from numerous historical societies who work tirelessly to protect our past. Some of the key historical societies used for discovering records for this book are San Diego Historical Society, Fremont County Historical Society, Fulton County Historical Society and Sangamon County Historical Society.

The Internet Archive (archive.org) was also a valuable resource and was used for historical discoveries and references. It is a non-profit library of digital resources.

References to Find A Grave (http://www.findagrave.com: last accessed 24 April 2025) will simply be written as: Find a Grave

Maxwell's Directory of San Diego City using the "Internet Archive" shall be simply written as: San Diego Dir.

All references for US Census data will be from the "population schedules" unless otherwise noted.

All US Records such as Census data, Mortality Schedules, U.S. Death Records, U.S. Land office Records, Wills and Probate records, Civil War Pension records, Registries for Persons subject for Military duty, U.S. Civil records, and U.S. Marriage Index and records were obtained through Ancestry.com.

Stetson

1. *San Diego Union and Daily Bee,* "Local Intelligence." 6 February 1892, p. 4.

2. *San Diego Union and Daily Bee,* "He Shot Himself." 4 March 1892, p. 1.

3. *San Diego Union and Daily Bee,* "Another Suicide." 10 March 1892, p. 4.

4. *San Diego Union and Daily Bee,* "Death of Judge Dillar." 19 March 1892, p. 4.

5. *San Diego Union and Daily Bee,* "An Arrest Expected." 5 May 1892, p. 2.

6. *San Diego Union and Daily Bee,* "On a Serious Charge." 6 May 1892, p. 4.

7. *San Diego Union and Daily Bee,* "The Deputy Coroner Hearing." 12 May 1892, p. 4.

8. *San Diego Union and Daily Bee,* Stetson Discharged." 19 May 1892, p. 4.

9. *San Diego Union and Daily Bee,* "The Men Indicted." 17 June 1892, p. 4.

10. *San Diego Union and Daily Bee,* "Local Intelligence." 18 June 1892, p. 4.

11. *San Diego Union and Daily Bee,* "Would Not Plead." 23 June 1892, p. 4.

12. *San Diego Union and Daily Bee,* "To Go to the Jury Today." 9 July 1892, p. 4.

13. *San Diego Union and Daily Bee,* "The Stetson Trial." 10 July 1892, p. 4.

14. *San Diego Union and Daily Bee,* "An Ocean Mystery." 29 June 1892, p. 4.

15. *San Diego Union and Daily Bee,* "Buried Where Found." 30 June 1892, p. 4.

16. *San Diego Union and Daily Bee*, "It Was Curtis." 2 July 1892, p. 4.

17. *San Diego Union and Daily Bee*, "A Sad Accident." 15 July 1892, p. 4.

18. *San Diego Union and Daily Bee*, "Shot His Sister." 26 July 1892, p. 4.

19. *San Diego Union and Daily Bee*, "A Ghastly Murder." 18 October 1892, p. 2.

20. *San Diego Union and Daily Bee*, "An Unknown Suicide." 15 November 1892, p. 4.

Drenched in Black

21. *San Diego Union and Daily Bee*, "By Her Own Hand." 30 November 1892, p. 4.

Inquest Day

22. Terry Girardot, 2001, "The Coroner's Inquest." Fremont County, Iowa, last updated 2018 by Karyn Techau, IAGenWeb,

23. San Diego Dir. for 1889-1890, Internet Archive, p. 133, T.J. Fisher.

24. San Diego Dir. for 1889-1890, Internet Archive, p. 45, T.J. Fisher.

25. San Diego Dir. for 1892-1893, Internet Archive, p. 23, T.J. Fisher.

26. San Diego Dir. for 1892-1893, Internet Archive, p. 27, T.J. Fisher.

27. 1900 U.S. Census, San Diego County, California, San Diego, T.J. Fisher

28. *San Diego Union and Daily Bee*, "The Criterion." 10 September 1888, p 4.

29. *San Diego Union and Daily Bee*, "Across the Bay." 10 September 1888, p. 7.

30. *San Diego Union and Daily Bee*, "A Presentation." 3 Jan 1889, p. 4.

31. *San Diego Union and Daily Bee*, "IS CORONADO FREE?" 4 April 1889, p. 2.

32. *San Diego Union and Daily Bee*, "Coronado Cullings." 9 April 1889, p. 4.

33. *San Diego Union and Daily Bee*, "Judge Pierce Sustained." 29 October 1889, p. 7.

34. *San Diego Union and Daily Bee*, "Petitioners to be heard." 7 November 1889, p. 7.

35. *San Diego Union and Daily Bee*, "Fisher is City Trustee." 25 April 1891, p. 2.

36. *San Diego Union and Daily Bee*, "Coronado Notes." 9 October 1892, p. 7.

37. Find A Grave, mem ID 96253775, Thomas J. Fisher (1855–1936), by "Larry K."

38. San Diego Dir. 1889-1890, p. 132, Della Fisher, Hotel Housekeeper.

39. San Diego Dir. 1892-1893, p. 27, Della Fisher, Hotel Housekeeper.

40. *San Diego Union and Daily Bee*, "Across the Bay." 1 October 1888, p. 5.

41. *San Diego Union and Daily Bee*, "A Woman in a Hotel." 13 Jan 1892, p. 5.

42. *San Diego Union and Daily Bee,* "Coronado Beach." 15 February 1893, p. 2.

43. 1900 U.S. census, San Diego County, California, Coronado, Della Fisher.

44. Find A Grave, mem ID 222155845, Della C. Fisher (1858–1934), by "Pat McArron."

45. *San Diego Union and Daily Bee,* "Ad, Hotel del Coronado." 29 December 1892, p. 3.

46. Shrestha R, Kanchan T, Krishan K., "Methods of Estimation of Time Since Death." [Updated 2023 May 30]. In: StatPearls [Internet]. Treasure Island (FL): StatPearls Publishing; 2025 Jan-.

47. Denning DG, Conwell Y, King D, Cox C. "Method choice, intent, and gender in completed suicide. Suicide Life Threat Behav." 2000 Fall;30(3):282-8. PMID: 11079640.

48. *Daily Alta California*, "Morgue Statistics, One Year's Record of Murders and Other Sudden Deaths." 16 July 1889, p. 8.

49. *San Francisco Call*, "Morgue Statistics, A Plurality of Those Who Committed Suicide were German." 3 August 1894, p. 10.

50. *San Francisco Call*, "A Year of Death, Gruesome Morgue Statistics Compiled by the Coroner." 3 July 1898, p. 10.

News That Followed

51. *San Diego Union and Daily Bee*, "Still in Doubt." 1 December 1892, p. 2.

52. *San Diego Union and Daily Bee*, "A Probably Theory." 1 December 1892, p. 2.

53. *San Diego Union and Daily Bee*, "The Beautiful Stranger." 2 December 1892, p. 5.

54. *San Diego Union and Daily Bee*, "A Possible Clue." 3 December 1892, p. 5.

55. *San Diego Union and Daily Bee*, "Identified." 4 December 1892, p. 1.

56. *Los Angeles Herald*, "A Mystery Cleared Up." 4 December 1892, p. 1.

57. *San Francisco Call*, "Eloped from Detroit." 4 December 1892, p. 1.

58. *San Diego Union and Daily Bee*, "Not Yet Claimed." 5 December 1892, p. 4.

59. *San Diego Union and DailyBee*, "Further Evidence." 6December 1892, p. 2.

60. *San Diego Union and DailyBee*, "Not Yet Fully Determined." 7 December 1892, p. 4.

61. *Los Angeles Herald*, "Not Lizzie Wyllie." 7 December 1892, p. 4.

62. *San Diego Union and DailyBee*, "Darker Than Ever." 8 December 1892, p. 2.

63. *San Diego Union and DailyBee*, "The Gambler's Wife." 9 December 1892, p. 5.

64. *Los Angeles Herald*, "Not the Coronado Woman." 9 December 1892, p. 4.

65. *San Diego Union and DailyBee,* "No Longer A Mystery." 10 December 1892, p. 5.

66. *Los Angeles Herald*, "The Coronado Suicide." 10 December 1892, p. 5.

67. *San Diego Union and DailyBee,* "The Facts Unfolding." 11 December 1892, p. 5.

68. *San Diego Union and DailyBee*, "He Owns Her." 12 December 1892, p. 5.

69. *Los Angeles Herald*, "The Coronado Suicide." 12 December 1892, p. 14.

70. *San Diego Union and Daily Bee*, "Buried at Mount Hope." 14 December 1892, p. 2.

71. *San Diego Union and Daily Bee*, "Local Intelligence." 16 December 1892, p. 5.

72. *San Diego Union and DailyBee,* "The Town Surprised." 17 December 1892, p. 1

73. *Los Angeles Herald*, "The Hamburgers'." 17 December 1892, p. 5.

74. *The Fremont County Herald*, "The Coronado Suicide." 22 December 1892, p. 1.

75. *San Diego Union and Daily Bee*, "It was for Charity." 24 December 1892, p. 2.

76. *The Fremont County Herald*, "Riverton." 29 December 1892, p. 4.

Fremont County

77. History of Fremont County, Iowa: Internet Archive, 1881, Publisher Des Moines Iowa Historical Company, Collection: Brigham Young University Americana Contributor, Harold B. Lee Library, Added date 2017-06-13-22:57:34

78. Fremont County Historical Society, Community History Archive, "*The Fremont County Herald* (1887 – 1927), The Sidney Union (1875 – 1887), The Fremont Herald (1859-1859), The Fremont County Sun (1893 – 1909)," Fremont Historical Society, fremontcounty.advantage-preservation.com, accessed 2 March 2025.

79. The USGenWeb Project, Fremont County, IAGenWeb, last updated March 4 2025 by Karyn Techau, iagenweb.org/Fremont/, last accessed 2 April 2025.

80. USGenWeb Archives Project, Powered by mnoGoSearch 3.4.1, Search the Iowa Archives. Last accessed 12 December 2024.

81. Internet Archive WayBackMachine, 25 Oct 2004 – 3 Dec 2024, A.T. Andreas' Illustrated Historical Atlas of the State of Iowa, 1875, Transcribed by Pat O'Dell, iagenweb.org/fremont/history/andreas.htm, last read 28 April, 2025.

Joe and Matilda

82. Sharon Wick, Ohio Genealogy Express ©2008, "Welcome to Ashland County, Ohio History & Genealogy." ohiogenealogyexpress.com/Ashland/index.htm, A database of Ashland County. Last accessed in May 2024.

83. Farr's of Fulton County, Illinois, A History of the Farr Family in Central Illinois. "Fulton County, Illinois - What was it like in the 1800s?" farrfamilyhistory.com/landis/, website, last updated unknown, last accessed April 2025.

84. U.S. Marriage Index, 1860-1920, Fulton County, Illinois, 15 November 1843, Joseph W. Chandler and Matilda Savage.

85. 1850 U.S. Census, Grant County, Wisconsin, Cassville, Joseph W. Chandler.

86. 1860 U.S. Census, Grant County, Wisconsin, Cassville, Joseph W. Chandler.

87. 1870 U.S. Census, Fremont County, Iowa, Madison, Joseph W. Chandler.

88. 1880 U.S. Census, Fremont County, Iowa, Riverton, Joseph W. Chandler.

89. 1885 U.S. Census, Fremont County, Iowa, Riverton, Joseph W. Chandler.

90. 1900 U.S. Census, Fremont County, Iowa, Hamburg, Joseph W. Chandler.

91. U.S. General Land Office Records, 1776-2015, U.S. Preemptive Certificate, Document No. 12023, Issued 10 October

1859, Thomas Chandler Jr, Land purchase at the Council Bluffs Land Office. Ancestry.com

92. Potter, Lee Ann and Wynell Schamel. "The Homestead Act of 1862." Social Education 61, 6 (October 1997): 359-364.

93. Find A Grave, mem ID 8116154, Joseph W. Chandler (1820–1904), by "Christine Rogers Odell."

94. Find A Grave, mem ID 8116093, Matilda Savage Chandler (1816–1879), by "Christine Rogers Odell."

95. Find A Grave, mem ID 8116163, Thomas J. Chandler Sr. (1791–1881), by "Christine Rogers Odell."

George Washington Farmer

96. National Park Service, Living History, "Life on the Missouri: Adventure, Excitement, & Romance?" National Recreational River, SD, NE, Multimedia Presentations/ Living History Audio, last updated August 31, 2021.

97. Francis M. Wilson, Platte County Missouri, Historical and Genealogical Society, "The Kingdom of Platte." Last updated unknown.

98. Pat O'Dell, transcriber, A.T. Andreas' Illustrated Historical Atlas of the State of Iowa 1875. Internet Archive WayBackMachine, Last updated unknown.

99. National Archives Catalog, NAID: 78739544, Records of Appointments of Postmasters and the Establishment of Post Offices, 1870 Textual Records, G.W. Farmer, postmaster, p. 3.

100. *Fremont County Herald*, "Shooting of Wm. Neff and John Crosby." 3 April 1902, p. 2

101. *The Sidney Argus Herald*, "McKissick's Grove History." 3 June 1971, p. 4.

102. *The Sidney Argus Herald*, "Part Five, Early Frontier." 2 Jan 1986, p. 3.

103. U.S. General Land Office Records, 1776-2015, U.S. Preemptive Certificate, Document No. 17365, Issued 1 March 1850, Thomas Farmer, Land purchase at the Fairfield Land Office. Ancestry.com

104. U.S. General Land Office Records, 1776-2015, U.S. Preemptive Certificate, Document No. 320, Issued 15 June 1855, Thomas Farmer, Land purchase at the Kanesville Land Office. Ancestry.com

105. John Gregg, "Madison Township." Standard Historical Atlas of Mills & Fremont County, (J.T. Davis sets up Store, Tom Farmer's Stagecoach Station) last updated 20 April 2017 by Karyn Techau, last accessed 25 April 2025.

106. 1840 U.S. Census, Platte County, Missouri, Platte, Thomas Farmer.

107. 1850 U.S. Census, Fremont County, Iowa, District No. 22, Thomas Farmer.

108. 1860 U.S. Census, Fremont County, Iowa, Madison, Thomas Farmer.

109. 1870 U.S. Census, Fremont County, Iowa, Hamburg, Thomas Farmer.

110. Iowa, U.S. Records of Persons Subject to Military Duty, 1862-1910, Riverton Township for 1879, G.W. Farmer.

111. U.S. Civil War Draft Registrations Record, 1863-1865, 5th Congressional District, June 1863, George W. Farmer (Saddler), Unmarried man., age 23. Ancestry.com

A Time of Loss

112. Find A Grave, mem ID 8116096, Elizabeth Philamena Chandler Farmer (1844–1868), maintained by "Christine Rogers Odell."

113. Appointments of U.S. Postmasters, 1832-1971, Fremont County, Iowa, G.W. Farmer, 9 November 1870. Ancestry.com.

114. U.S., Register of Civil, Military, and Naval Service, 1863-1959, for Postmaster, G.W. Farmer, Hamburg P.O., 1871, (Salary 730.00), p. 575, Ancestry.com.

115. 1870 U.S. Census, Fremont County, Iowa, Hamburg, Lydia Burnett.

116. 1880 U.S. Census, McCulloch County, Texas, Brady, Henry and Lydia Eubanks.

117. Terry Girardot, "Lydia Jane Burnett." USGenWeb Archives, Pioneer Obituaries.

118. 1880 U.S. Census, Atchison County, Missouri, Lincoln Township, James Burnett.

Extended Family

119. 1870 U.S. Census 1870, Fremont County, Iowa, Madison, Baker.

120. 1880 U.S. Census 1880, Fremont County, Iowa, Madison, and Kate.

121. 1900 U.S. Census 1900, Logan County, Kansas, Russell Springs, Baker/ Salm.

122. 1910 U.S. Census, Fremont County, Iowa, Sidney, Baker / Salm.

123. Iowa, U.S., Marriage Records, 1880-1948, Record of Harriet Baker to Theo Salm, Vol 313, 1883, Ancestry.com.

124. Find A Grave, mem ID 8115102, Harriet M Chandler Sahm (1845–1924), created by "Graveaddiction."

125. Find A Grave (http://www.findagrave.com), mem ID 8116099, Theophilus Henry Tritle Sahm (1843–1910), created by "Graveaddiction."

126. 1870 U.S. Census 1870, Fremont County, Iowa, Madison, Thomas Chancler Jr., Lizzie Chandler, Emery Chandler.

127. 1870 U.S. Census 1870, Fremont County, Iowa, Madison, Joseph W. and Matilda Chandler, Emery Chandler, Kate Farmer.

Orphaned

128. Iowa, U.S., Wills and Probate Records, 1758-1997, for Mary Farmer Estate, Record No. 455, p. 39, 14 Jan 1878, Record of Administrator's Letters and Bond, Administrator: D.W. Swiggart.

129. 1880 U.S. Federal Census, Fremont County, Iowa, mortality schedule, Madison Township, Matilda Chandler, recorded 7 August 1879.

130. Iowa, U.S., Wills and Probate Records, 1758-1997 for G.W. Farmer Estate, Probate Date: 16 August 1879, Record of Guardian's Letters and Bond of minor Kate Farmer, by J.W. Chandler.

131. Iowa, U.S., Wills and Probate Records, 1758-1997, for G.W. Farmer Deceased, 14 June 1880, Record of Administrator's Letters and Bond, Administrator: H.F. Brumback.

132. 1850 U.S. Census, Congress County, Ohio, Morrow, Shadrack Chandler.

133. 1870 U.S. Census, Congress County, Ohio, Morrow, Shadrack Chandler.

134. 1880 U.S. Census, Mission County, Kansas, Brown, Maria Hand Chandler.

135. 1880 U.S. Census, Mission County, Kansas, Brown, Thomas Chandler Jr.

136. 1900 U.S. Census, Barada County, Nebraska, Richardson, Thomas Chandler Jr. and Emery Chandler.

137. 1880 U.S. Census, Fremont County, Iowa, Madison, Emery Chandler.

138. Iowa, U.S., Wills and Probate Records, 1758-1997, Fremont County, Iowa, for Thomas Chandler, Sr., Deceased, Date Filed:23 May 1882, Probate Combined Record, Vol 1-2, No. 346, Administrator: Thomas Chandler Jr.□□

139. *Fremont County Herald*, "Farragut (J.W. Chandler)." 26 April 1888, p. 10.

140. *Fremont County Herald*, "County Convention (J.W. Chandler)." 16 August 1888, p. 7.

The Morgans

141. 1830 U.S. Census, Sangamon County, Illinois, Old Berlin, Thomas Morgan.

142. 1840 U.S. Census, Sangamon County, Illinois, Old Berlin, Thomas Morgan.

143. 1850 U.S. Census, Sangamon County, Illinois, Old Berlin, Thomas and Marcena Morgan.

144. John Carroll Power, "Early Settlers of Sangamon County 1876." Biographical Sketch of Thomas Morgan, Ancestry contributor originally shared 11th March 2012, last accessed 24 April 2024, Ancestry.com.

145. U.S., General Land Office Records, 1776-2015, for Thomas Morgan at land office of Springfield, Illinois, 10 April 1824.

146. U.S., Civil War Pension Index: General Index to Pension Files, 1861-1934, for widow Elizabeth Morgan on Evan Morgan Filed April 23, 1889.

147. 1840 U.S. Census 1840, Sangamon County, Illinois, Old Berlin, Morgan/Skidmore.

148. 1850 U.S. Census 1850, Fremont County, Iowa, District No. 22, Jacob McKissick, M Skidmore, Elizabeth Morgan.

149. 1860 U.S. Census 1860, Fremont County, Iowa, Benton Township, Morgan/Skidmore.

150. Find A Grave, mem ID 69260053, Elizabeth Morgan Skidmore (1806–1879), created by "family history keeper."

151. Find A Grave, mem ID 69259862, Martin K. Skidmore (1814–1880), created by "family history keeper."

152. Mabel E. Richmond, "Centennial History of Decatur and Macon County." University of Illinois Library, Copyright 1930, Review Publishing Company, Decatur, Illinois, citations of Robert Benjamin Austin.

153. The Daily Review, Decatur Illinois, "Several Came." 20 March 1904, Benjamin R. Austin, Ancestry.com.

154. 1850 U.S. Census, Macon County, Illinois, Macon, Benjamin Austin.

155. 1855 U.S. Census, Macon County, Illinois, Shelby, Marcena and Purlina Morgan, Margaret and John Day.

156. 1855 Compiled Marriages, Film #1008065 – 1008066 and 1009139, Marriage to Marcena Morgan 14 June 1855, Ancestry.com.

157. 1860 U.S. Census, Sangamon County, Illinois, Old Berlin, Marcena Morgan.

158. 1870 U.S. Census, Sangamon County Illinois, Old Berlin, Marcena Morgan, Margaret Day, Emily and George Allen.

159. U.S., Federal Census Mortality Schedules, 1850-1885, for Purlina and John H Allen, 1870, Ancestry.com.

160. Find A Grave, mem ID 86768857, Purlina Morgan (1832–1870), by "By Grace."

161. Cay Merryman, "Fremont County, Iowa, Madison Township, Biographies." History of Fremont County, Iowa, Marcena Morgan, IAGenWeb, iagenweb.org/fremont/bios/madison_bios.htm.

162. 1880 U.S. Census, Fremont County Iowa, Madison Township, Marcena Morgan.

163. 1885 U.S. Census 1885, Fremont County Iowa, Madison Township, Marcena Morgan.

164. U.S., Indexed County Land Ownership Maps, 1860-1918, Fremont County, Iowa,1891 Plat of Madison Township, 67 North Ranges 41 and 42, Ancestry.com.

165. The Hamburg Reporter, 16 March, 1850, "Lyman Ditson Morgan." Obituary, p. 8.

166. 1850 U.S. Census, Fremont County, Iowa, Dist. 22, Thomas O. Morgan.

167. 1860 U.S. Census, Fremont County Iowa, Madison, Thomas O. Morgan.

168. 1870 U.S. Census, Fremont County Iowa, Madison, Thomas O. Morgan.

169. Fremont County, Iowa, "History of Fremont County, Iowa, Madison Township Biographies" Thomas O. Morgan, Elizabeth Ditson Morgan Skidmore and Melandus Kinner Skidmore, agenweb.org/fremont/bios/madison_bios.htm, last updated 2017 by Karyn Techau.

170. 1840 U.S. Census, Sangamon County, Illinois, Old Berlin, Morgan/Skidmore.

171. 1850 U.S. Census, Fremont County Iowa, District 11, Morgan/Skidmore.

172. 1860 U.S. Census, Fremont County Iowa, Benton, Morgan/Skidmore.

173. 1870 U.S. Census, Fremont County, Iowa, Madison, Morgan/Skidmore.

Thomas Edwin Morgan

174. Iowa, U.S., Marriage Records, 1880-1948, for Harriet M. Baker, September 22, 1883, p. 447, Ancestry.com

175. 1885 U.S. Census 1885, Fremont County, Iowa, Riverton, Kate Farmer.

176. 1880 U.S. Census, Fremont County, Iowa, Riverton, Mary Farmer Samuels.

177. *The Fremont County Herald*, "Riverton (Mrs. Samuels)." 29 December 1892

178. 1895 U.S. Census, Fremont County, Iowa, Riverton, Samuels.

179. 1885 U.S. Census, Fremont County, Iowa, Madison, Thomas E. Morgan, and Buck.

180. *Harlin County Journal*, "Thomas Edwin Morgan." Published April 9, 1936. Ancestry.com.

181. Iowa, U.S., Marriage Records, 1880-1948, Marriage Registry of Fremont County Iowa, June 21, 1885, Marcena Morgan and Lizzie Thompson.

182. Iowa, U.S., Marriage Records, 1880-1948, Marriage Registry of Fremont County Iowa, December 30, 1885, Thomas Morgan and Kate K Farmer.

183. Illinois, U.S., Compiled Marriages, 1851-1900, County Court Records, Springfield IL Marriage on 4 Apr. 1865, Emily Hope Dennison to John Allen.

A New Role

184. Iowa, U.S., Births (series) 1880-1904, Delayed Births, Birth Certificate for Nettie Gertrude Morgan, Born May 24th, 1886, Ancestry.com.

185. Find A Grave, mem ID 7398373, Marcena Morgan (1825–1886), by "Chris Tonn."

186. Iowa, U.S., Wills and Probate Records, 1758-1997, Record of Administrator's Letters and Bond, for Estate of Marcena Morgan, 26 September 1886, Administrator: Thomas O. Morgan.

187. Iowa, U.S., Wills and Probate Records, 1758-1997, Records of Guardian's Letters and Bond, for Mollie, Gertrude, Lulu and

Lyman, 23 December 1886, Principal/s: Emily Morgan and Thomas O. Morgan.

188. Iowa, U.S., Wills and Probate Records, 1758-1997, Record of Administrator's Letters and Bond, for Marcena Morgan, 27 April 1887, Administrators: T.O. Morgan and Emily Morgan.

189. Kristine S. Knaplund, "The Evolution of Women's Rights in Inheritance." Hastings Women's Law Journal, Vol 19, No. 1, Winter 2008, Article 2. UC Law SF Scholarship Repository.

190. Allgor, Catherine. "Coverture - the Word You Probably Don't Know but Should." National Women's History Museum, September 4, 2014.

191. Find A Grave, mem ID 7398364, Thomas Morgan Jr. (1886–1886), by "Chris Tonn."

George Allen

192. 1870 U.S. Census, Sangamon County, Illinois, Old Berlin, G.L. Allen.

193. U.S., Indexed County Land Ownership Maps, 1860-1918 for George L. Allen (160 acres), Plat of Madison, Fremont County, Township 67 North Ranges 41 and 42.

194. *Fremont County Herald*, "Real Estate Transfers." April 7, 1892, p. 10.

195. *Fremont County Herald*, "Local Matters." January 19, 1892, p. 5.

196. *Fremont County Herald*, "Hamburg." June 23, 1892, p. 4.

197. *Fremont County Herald*, "Hamburg." September 14, 1892, p. 7.

198. *Fremont County Herald*, "Farragut." July 19, 1898, p. 2.

199. *Fremont County Herald*, "Hamburg." February 16, 1899, p. 2.

200. *Fremont County Herald*, "Farragut." July 6, 1899, p. 2.

201. *Fremont County Herald*, "Riverton." December 3, 1903, p. 3.

202. *Fremont County Herald*, "Latest from Riverton." October 4, 1904, p. 6.

203. 1860 U.S. Census, Sangamon County, Illinois, New Berlin, Peter Wikoff.

204. 1870 U.S. Census, Sangamon County, Illinois, New Berlin, Peter Wikoff.

205. 1880 U.S. Census, Fremont County, Iowa, Farragut, Peter Wikoff.

206. 1885 U.S. Census, Fremont County, Iowa, Farragut, Peter Wikoff.

207. *The Opinion Tribune*, "Peter Wikoff." Glenwood, Iowa, 15 October 1892.

208. 1900 U.S. Census, Fremont County, Iowa, Hamburg, Peter Wikoff.

209. *San Diego Union and Daily Bee*, "It was for Charity." 24 December 1892, p. 2.

210. 1870 U.S. Census, Fremont County, Iowa, Madison, J.P. Beach.

211. 1880 U.S. Census, Fremont County, Iowa, Hamburg, J.P. Beach.

212. 1900 U.S. Census, Fremont County, Iowa, Hamburg, J.P. Beach.

213. 1880 U.S. Census, Holmwood County, Kansas, Jewell, Lloyd/Catlett.

San Francisco

214. *Los Angeles Herald*, "Not the Coronado Woman." 9 December 1892.

215. Corbett & Ballenger's 11th Annual Denver City Directory, 1883, p. 500, Ottinger, Ancestry.com.

216. Los Angeles, California, U.S., City Directory, 1888, Worth & Ottinger, Ancestry.com.

217. San Francisco Directory, 1891, Adolph Ottinger, Railroad Ticket Broker, and Wines, p. 1060, Ancestry.com.

218. *San Francisco Call*, "Ticket Peddler's Little Scheme." 20 November 1890, p. 7.

219. *San Francisco Call,* "Along the Rail." 11 December 1890, p. 7.

220. *San Francisco Call*, "Railroad Notes" 10 February 1891, p. 6.

221. *San Francisco Call*, "Along the Rail." 7 August 1891, p. 3.

222. *San Francisco Call*, "The Ticket-Broker's Cinch Bill." 30 September 1891, p. 1.

223. *San Francisco Call*, "Joseph G. M'Call." 15 November 1891, p. 6.

224. *San Francisco Call*, "Bruner is on Trial." 4 October 1892, p. 3.

225. *San Francisco Call*, "Beating out the Truth." 7 October 1892, p. 3.

226. *San Francisco Call*, "Bruner at the Grand." 11 October 1892, p. 3.

227. *San Francisco Call*, "Drawing to a Close." 18 October 1892, p. 3.

228. *The Morning Call*, "Wildwood Won Money." October 31, 1894, p. 12.

229. *San Francisco Call*, "How they Forged Tickets." 21 December 1894, p. 3.

230. *The Morning Call*, "Ticket Agents' Fight." 1 February 1895, p. 12.

231. *San Francisco Call*, "The Scalpers' Bill." 15 March 1895, p. 1.

232. *San Francisco Call*, "Around the Corridors." 16 July 1895, p. 5.

233. *San Francisco Call*, "Ottinger to be Investigate." 1 September 1895, p. 6.

234. *San Francisco Call*, "Ottinger Must Pay the Purse." 4 September 1896, p. 8.

235. *Daily Tulare Register*, "Conductor Massey Shot." 3 April 1888, p. 3.

236. *Oakland Tribune,* "A Conductor Shot." 3 April 1888, p. 1.

237. *Fresno Weekly Expositor*, "A Conductor Shot." 4 April 1888, p. 1.

238. *Fresno Weekly Expositor*, "The Courts." 11 April 1888, p. 10.

239. *Fresno Weekly Expositor*, "The Courts." 26 September 1888, p. 12

240. *Placer Argus*, Vol 17, "Last Saturday." 24 August 1889, p. 4.

241. *San Francisco Call*, "James McDonough." 8 October 1890, p. 7.

242. *San Diego Union and Daily Bee*, "Local Intelligence." 15 November 1892, p. 5.

243. *Marin County Tocsin*, "Real Estate." 6 Jan 1894, p. 3.

244. *Sausalito News*, "Real Estate." 2 February 1895, p. 3.

245. *Rawlins Republican*, "McDonough Not Guilty in Murder Trial." 8 June 1895, p. 2.

246. *San Francisco Call*, "Shot Himself in a Saloon." 15 June 15, 1895, p. 16.

247. *Sacramento Daily Record,* "Vagrants Sentenced." 16 October 1896, p. 4.

248. *San Francisco Call*, "Justice Was Swift." 12 November 1896. P. 12.

249. *San Francisco Call*, "Arrested on Suspicion." 28 October 1898, p. 12.

250. *San Francisco Call*, "Jim Meyers' Effects Disclosed." 22 February 1902, p. 7.

251. *San Francisco Call*, "McDonough Has Prison Record." 25 February 1902, p. 14.

252. *San Francisco Call*, "Prisoner McDonough Explains." 4 May 1902, p. 21.

253. *San Francisco Call*, "McDonough and Gray Guilty of Conspiracy." 16 May 1902, p. 9.

254. *Weekly Colusa Sun*, "Local Matters - The Grand (M.L. Abbott)" 29 August 1874, p. 3.

255. *Oakland Tribune*, "Police Court." 6 March 1876, p. 3

256. U.S., City Directories, 1822-1995, Bishop's San Francisco Directory, 1878, Mark L. Abbott, American Exchange Hotel agent, p. 8., Ancestry.com.

257. *Daily Alta California,* "The Hoin Inquest." 11 April 1880, pg. 1.

258. *Morning Press*, "The Hoin Homicide." 13 April 1880, p. 1.

259. *Oakland Tribune*, "Domestic Infelicity." 23 May 1883, p. 3.

260. *Oakland Tribune*, "New Divorce Suits." 31 May 1883, p. 3.

261. *Daily Alta California*, "Ella Abbott Complains." 15 October 1883, p. 2.

262. *San Diego Union and Daily Bee*, "City and Vicinity." 9 December 1886, p. 3.

263. *San Diego Union and Daily Bee*, "Wedding Bells." 9 June 1886, p. 2.

264. *Humboldt Times*, "Passengers Incoming." 17 December 1886, p. 3.

265. *Coronado Mercury*, "City Locals." 6 July 1887, p. 4.

266. *San Diego Union and Daily Bee*, "Real Estate Transfers." 11 April 1888.

267. *San Diego Union and Daily Bee*, "Pleasuring Pythians." 15 June 1888, p. 1.

268. *San Diego Union and Daily Bee*, "Wall Paper." 17 October 1888, p. 6.

269. *Daily Alta California*, "Petty Criminal." 9 May 1889, p. 1.

270. *San Diego Union and Daily Bee*, "Among the Lodges." 12 May 1889, p. 8.

271. *Los Angeles Herald*, "Santa Monica." 20 October 1889, p. 10.

272. *Los Angeles Herald*, "Personal." 15 September 1890, p. 8.

273. San Francisco Directory, May 1, 1891, M.L. Abbott, 911 Mission, Ancestry.com.

274. *San Francisco Call*, "One Ran North." 17 February 1892, p. 8.

275. *Visalia Times Delta*, "Palace Hotel Arrivals." 14 March 1892, p. 1.

276. *Red Bluff Daily News*, "Tremont Hotel Arrivals." 30 June 1892

277. *Daily Tulare Register*, "Hotel Arrivals-Grand Hotel." 15 August 1892, p. 2.

278. *San Luis Obispo Morning Tribune*, "Hotel Arrivals." 23 September 1892, p. 1.

279. *San Diego Union and Daily Bee*, "Personal Mention." 28 November 1892, p. 8.

280. *Morning Press*, Santa Barbara, "At the Hotels-Arlington" 13 December 1892.

281. *San Luis Obispo Morning Tribune*, "Hotel Arrivals-Ramona Hotel." 13 April 1893, p. 1.

282. *Daily Tulare Register,* "Hotel Arrivals-Grand Hotel." 29 May 1893, p. 3.

283. *San Diego Union and Daily Bee*, "Personal Mention." 8 June 1893, p. 8.

Tulare County

284. Thompson, Thomas H, Historic Map Works, LLC, Resident Genealogy, Historical Atlas Maps, Tulare County 1892, accessed last 25 April 2025, Illustrations.

285. Wikipedia, San Joaquin Valley Railroad, last updated 20 March 2025.

286. Wikipedia, Christopher Evans (Outlaw), last edited 6 February 2025 (UTC).

287. 1850 U.S. Census, Fremont County, Iowa, Dist. 22, W.T. Farmer.

288. 1860 U.S. Census 1860, Clear Lake County, California, Napa, W.T. Farmer

289. 1867, U.S., Voter Registration, Napa California, W.T. Farmer, Ancestry.com.

290. 1870, U.S. Voter Registration, Merced California, W.T. Farmer, Ancestry.com.

291. 1880, U.S. Census 1880, Tulare County, California, Mussel Slough, W.T. Farmer.

292. Tulare Advance Register, "Hanford News.", 5 March 1888, p. 3., Ancestry.com.

293. U.S., Indexed County Land Ownership Maps, 1860-1918, Tulare Land Ownership map, 1892, South Range 22 East, Quadrant 9, p. 49, W.T. Farmer, Ancestry.com.

294. *Los Angeles Times*, "The Coronado Suicide." 14 December 1892.

295. 1900 U.S. Census, Kings County, California, Lucerne, W.T. Farmer, Ancestry.com.

296. *Hanford Journal*, "Farmer Obituary." 9 July 1904, Ancestry.com.

297. 1860 U.S. Census, Fremont County, Iowa, Madison, George Farmer.

298. 1870 U.S. Census, Fremont County, Iowa, Madison, George Farmer.

299. 1870 U.S. Census, Yolo County, California, Woodland, Gertrude Ruggles.

300. 1880 U.S. Census, Tulare County, California, Mussel Slough, George Farmer/Gertrude Ruggles.

301. *Daily Alta*, California, "Republican County Committee." 9 May 1890, p. 1.

302. *Visalia Morning Delta*, "Redding Stage Robbers." 20 May 1892, p. 2.

303. *Expositor*, "The Ruggles Brothers of Tulare." 21 May 1892, p. 2.

304. *Sacramento Daily Union*, "Ruggles-Captured in Woodland." 20 June 1892, p. 1.

305. *San Jose Mercury*, "Desperate Fight with a Stage Robber." 20 June 1892, p. 8.

306. *San Jose Mercury*, "Ruggles Did Not Rob from Necessity." 27 June 1892, p. 4.

307. *Sacramento Daily Union*, "Big Fire at Woodland." 2 July 1892, p. 1.

308. *Fresno Weekly Expositor*, "Shasta County Mob Swings Them Up." 27 July 1892, p. 9.

309. *Sacramento Daily Union*, "Interview with the Father." 28 July 1892, p. 4.

310. *Chico Weekly Enterprise*, "Lynching at Redding." 29 July 1892, p. 1,

311. *Napa Register*, "No Excuses for It." 5 August 1892, p. 2.

312. *Visalia Times Delta*, "Wary Bandits." 13 August 1892, p. 1.

313. *Visalia Morning Delta*, "The Courts-Probate-Ruggles." 26 November 1892, p. 1.

314. 1900 U. S. Census, Kings County, California, Lucerne, George Farmer.

315. Menefee, Eugene L. and Dodge, Fred A, History of Tulare Kings County California with Biographical Sketches, George Farmer, CAGenWeb last updated 1/9/2024, last accessed 24 April 2025.

<u>Los Angeles</u>

316. Streissguth, Tom, "Nellie Bly (1864-1922) -The New York World - Trying to be a Servant." 30 October 1887, Historic Journalism, Website Builder, last accessed 24 April 2025.

317. 1880 U.S. Census, Los Angeles County, California, Los Angeles, Widney.

318. *Los Angeles Herald,* "Alameda Street Women." 15 June 1892, p. 3.

319. *Los Angeles Herald*, "His Sister Found." 2 February 1892, p. 8.

320. *Sacramento Daily Union*, "A Sectional Candidate." 5 September 1892, p. 2.

321. 1900 Federal Census, Los Angeles County, California, San Fernando, Widney.

322. *Los Angeles Times*, "Crazy Leopold." 30 September 1887, p. 3.

323. *Los Angeles Herald*, "In the Small Hours." 29 August 1890, p. 5.

324. *Los Angeles Herald*, "Russell's Fine Work." 18 February 1891, p. 7.

325. *Los Angeles Herald*, "Superior Courts." 25 February 1891, p. 4.

326. *Los Angeles Herald*, "News Notes." 11 June 1892, p. 8.

327. *Los Angeles Herald*, "Speedy Ones-Trotters." 20 Jan 1892, p. 3.

328. Census of Canada 1871, Charlottenburg, Glengarry, Ontario, L.A. Grant.

329. *San Diego Union and Daily Bee*, "Round About Town." 24 October 1887, p. 1.

330. Los Angeles City Directory, 1890, Contractor L.A. Grant, 808 South Fourth, Ancestry.com.

331. 1891 Census of Canada, Glengarry County, Ontario, Lancaster Village, L.A. Grant.

332. *The Kaleidoscope*, "Marriage Announcement." 4 July 4th, 1891, p. 1.

333. Wikipedia, "Grants, New Mexico." Page last updated 14 March 2025 (UTC).

334. Glengarry Historical Society, Dictionary of Glengarry Biography, "Grant, Lewis Alexander."

335. *Sacramento Daily Union*, "Improvements in Kern County." 11 February 1892, p. 2.

336. *San Francisco Call*, "The Railroads." 26 April 1892, p. 8.

337. *Morning Tribune*, "Locomotive Works at Los Angeles." 18 June 1892, p. 1.

338. *Enterprise Riverside*, "Latest Railroad News." 24 December 1892, p. 3.

339. *Los Angeles Times*, "L.A. Grant's Will." 16 December 1904, p. 14.

Those Last Days□

340. *San Diego Union and Daily Bee*, "Railroad Schedule." 24 November 1892.

341. *San Diego Union and Daily Bee*, "Waterfront News." 24 November 1892.

342. *San Diego Union and Daily Bee*, "Coronado Notes." 24 November 1892.

343. *San Diego Union and Daily Bee*, "Coronado Round Trip Rates." 24 November 1892.

344. *San Diego Union and Daily Bee*, "Coronado Belt Line Schedule." 24 November 1892.

345. Wikipedia, San Diego Electric Railway, en.wikipedia.org/wiki/San_Diego_Electric_Railway, last accessed 23 April 2025.

346. San Diego History Center, "San Diego Early Streetcars." last accessed 25 April 2025.

347. Reid, James William, 1852-1943, "Hotel del Coronado and electric railway." Calisphere, University of California, last accessed 25 April 2025.

348. Hennessey, Gregg R., "The Politics of Water in San Diego. 1895-1897." The Journal of San Diego History, San Diego Historical Society, Summer 1978, Vol 24., Num 3, last accessed 24 April 2025.

349. Olmsted, S.H., and Bynon, A.A., San Diego City Directory of 1892-93, E.S. Babcock, p. 276, Internet Archive, last accessed 24 April 2025.

350. Hoover, Gary, "Two Billion Passengers a Day: The Otis Story." American Business History Center, Articles, last accessed 25 April 2025.

351. M.U. Libraries, University of Missouri, "Prices and Wages by Decade: 1890-1899, last updated 29 April 2025, last accessed 30 April 2025.

352. Library of Congress, "First floor plan - Hotel del Coronado, 1500 Orange Ave, Coronado, San Diego County, CA Drawings from Survey HABS CA-1958." Last accessed 23 April 2025. (Link)

353. *San Diego Union and Daily Bee*, "Coronado Notes." 25 November 1892, p. 8.

354. *San Diego Union and Daily Bee*, "Coronado Notes." 26 November 1892, p. 8.

355. *San Diego Union and Daily Bee*, "Coronado Notes." 27 November 1892, p. 8.

356. Hanna, John Robert, "Arnold, Cheney & Co." Albumen Cabinet Card Company Photograph. Antipodean Books, Maps & Prints, David and Cathy Lilburne.

357. Moore, Ernst D., "89 20376, Weighing tusks inside the Arnold, Cheney & Co. warehouse in Aden, 1907-1908." National Museum of American History, Behring Center.

358. *San Diego Union and Daily Bee*, "Personal Mention," 28 November 1892, p. 4.

359. *San Diego Union and Daily Bee*, "Coronado Notes." 29 November 1892, p. 8.

360. Hibbard, Spencer, Bartlett & Co. General Catalog. Chicago, Ill.: Priv. Print, 1891." American Bulldog Revolvers." Catalog number 1544, p. 1084.

361. *Visalia Morning Delta*, "The Courts - Ruggles Estate Sale." 26 November 1892, p. 1.

Lives Lived

<u>Lizzie Wyllie</u>

362. 1881 Census of Canada, Durham West District, Ontario, Canada, Bowmanville, Elizabeth H. Wyllie.

363. Ontario, Canada, Marriages, 1826-1942, Schedule B-Marriages, Essex County, 1894, Lizzie Wyllie and Wallace Cook, p. 307, Ancestry.com.

364. 1900 Federal Census, Wayne County, Michigan, Detroit, Wallace and Elizabeth Cook.

365. U.S., Death Records 1867-1952, State of Michigan Death Certificate for Elizabeth Cook, Wayne Michigan, 5/22/1912, Heart Disease, Ancestry.com.

<u>John G. Longfield</u>

366. 1880 U.S. Census, Cuyahoga, Ohio, Cleveland, John Longfield.

367. Ohio, Cleveland City Directory, 1880, John Longfield, p. 174, Ancestry.com.

368. U.S., Marriage Records, 1867-1952, Wayne Michigan Marriage Record of 1883, Detroit, John G. Longfield to Elizabeth Frazer, record no. 3366, Ancestry.com.

369. Michigan, Detroit Michigan City Directory, 1889, John G. Longfield, p. 494, Ancestry.com.

370. U.S., County Marriage Records, 1822-1940, 11 October 1889h, Wayne Michigan, John G. Longfield to Mary L. Dallas, Film no. 001380375, Ancestry.com.

371. U.S., Marriage Records and Indexes, 1810-1973, 9 July 1890, Cuyahoga County, Ohio, John Longfield to Mary Gresmuck, p. 949, Ancestry.com.

372. U.S., Ohio, Select County Death Records, 1840-1908, Cleveland Ohio, Mary J. Longfield, 18 December 1893, p. 224, Ancestry.com.

373. Ohio, Cleveland City Directory, 1894, John Longfield, p. 328, Ancestry.com.

374. Michigan, Detroit City Directory,1895, John Longfield, p. 466, Ancestry.com.

375. 1900 U.S. Census, Wayne County, Michigan, Detroit, John G. Longfield.

376. 1910 U.S. Census, Wayne County, Michigan, Detroit, John G. Longfield.

377. 1920 U.S. Census, Wayne County, Michigan, Highland Park, John G. Longfield.

378. 1930 U.S. Census, Wayne County, Michigan, Highland Park, John G. Longfield.

379. Michigan, Detroit Michigan City Directory, 1932, John G. Longfield, p. 494, Ancestry.com.

380. Michigan, U.S., Death Records, 1867-1952, Highland Park, Mary L. Longfield, 21 February 1933, Ancestry.com.

381. Michigan, U.S., Death Records, 1867-1952, Highland Park, John G. Longfield, 23 August 1938, Hemorrhage following Laceration of Wrist, Ancestry.com.

Thomas Edwin Morgan

382. Rubio, J'aime, "Stories of the Forgotten: Infamous, Famous & Unremembered." (ISBN-13: 978-1523981175)

383. Western Union Telegraph, 12 December 1892, To Burchard Nebraska, Thos. Morgan, Photo Citation, Ancestry.com.

384. State of Nebraska, Pawnee County, Marriage Record, 12 December 1893, Thomas E. Morgan to Jennie Devor, Photo Citation shared 9/16/2021, Ancestry.com.

385. Girardot, Terry, "The Ghost of the Hotel del Coronado, The True Story of Kate Morgan."

386. 1900 U.S. Census, Pawnee County, Nebraska, Miles Precinct, Thomas E. Morgan.

387. U.S., Register of Civil, Military, and Naval Service, 1863-1959, Rural Free Delivery – Nebraska, 1903, Postmaster Salary, Thomas E. Morgan, Ancestry.com.

388. U.S., Register of Civil, Military, and Naval Service, 1863-1959, Rural Free Delivery – Nebraska, 1905, Postmaster Salary, Thomas E. Morgan, Ancestry.com.

389. 1910 U.S. Census, Pawnee County, Nebraska, Plum Creek, Thomas E. Morgan.

390. 1920 U.S. Census, Jefferson County, Nebraska, Pleasant, Thomas E. Morgan.

391. 1930 U.S. Census, Harlan County Nebraska, Alma, Thomas E. Morgan.

392. *Hamburg Reporter*, "Brought Back for Burial." Obituary, 2 Apr. 1936, Thomas E. Morgan, Photo Citation, Ancestry.com.

Joseph Wilson Chandler

393. Kansas, U.S., County Marriage Records, 1811-1911, State of Kansas, County of Brown, Marriage License, 21 September 1881, Joseph W. Chandler to Maria E. Chandler, Ancestry.com.

394. U.S., Indexed County Land Ownership Maps, 1860-1918, Plat of Riverton, Fremont County, Ranges 41-42, 1891, J.W. Chandler 160 acres, Ancestry.com.

395. Find A Grave, mem ID 8116094, Maria Elizabeth Hand Chandler (1819–1894), by "Graveaddiction."

396. Iowa, U.S., Select Marriages Index, 1758-1996, Fremont County, Iowa, marriage record of Hamburg, Joseph W. Chandler to Rachel A. Lloyd, 7 March 1895, Ancestry.com.

397. Iowa, U.S., Wills and Probate, Administrator's, Executor's, and Guardian's Bond Record. 18 January 1896, Allen M. Chandler administrator of Maria E. Chandler estate, p. 262, Ancestry.com.

398. 1900 U.S. Census, Fremont County, Hamburg, J.W. Chandler.

399. Find A Grave, mem ID 8116154, Joseph W. Chandler (1820–1904), maintained by "Christine Rogers Odell."

400. 1905 U.S. Census, Fremont County, Iowa, Hamburg, Rachel Chandler, Ancestry.com.

401. Find A Grave, mem ID 8116154, Rachael Schwartzlander Lloyd (1827–1909), maintained by "Graveaddiction."

George L. Allen

402. U.S., Indexed County Land Ownership Maps, 1860-1918, for George L. Allen, Madison, Fremont County, 1891, Ancestry.com.

403. *Daily Alta California*, "Hotel Arrivals-Grand Hotel." 11 January 1892.

404. *Fremont County Herald*, "Real Estate Transfer, 80 Acres." 7 April 1892, p. 10.

405. *Fremont County Herald*, "Hamburg." 23 June 1892, p. 4.

406. *Los Angeles Herald*, "Anaheim." Vol 39, Num 46, 26 November 1892, p. 6.

407. *Visalia Morning Delta*, "Wedding Bells." 12 January 1893, p. 2.

408. *Fremont County Herald*, "Local Matters." 19 January 1893, p. 5.

409. *Los Angeles Herald*, "Hotel Arrivals-Hollenbeck." 9 April 1893, p. 8.

410. *Fremont County Herald*, "Hamburg." 14 September 1893, p. 7.

411. *San Francisco Call*, "They Made Bad Money." 20 May 1895, p. 1.

412. *Fremont County Herald*, "Farragut – Shipped Cattle." 19 July 1898, p. 2.

413. *Fremont County Sun*, "Hamburg." 16 February 1899, p. 2.

414. *Fremont County Sun*, "Court Case – Charles Lloyd." 30 March 1899, p. 2.

415. Nebraska, U.S., Select County Marriage Records, 1855-1908, Lancaster County, G.L. Allen and Frances A. Lloyd, 2 May 1900, p 815, Ancestor.com.

416. *Nebraska City News Press*, "George and Frances married." 5 May 1900, p. 4.

417. 1900 U.S. Census, Fremont Iowa, Iowa, Hamburg, G.L. Allen and Frances.

418. *Fremont County Herald*, "The Local Grist." Vol XXIV, No 47, 29 October 1903, p. 4.

419. *Fremont County Herald*, "Local Notes." Vol XIII, No 24, 27 July 1905, p. 3.

420. 1910 U.S. Census, Costilla County Colorado, San Acacio, George and Frances.

421. *The Fremont County Herald*, "In the Local Field." 22 June 1916, p. 4.

422. *The Sidney Argus*, "Hamburg's Patriotic Day." May 1918, p. 6.

423. 1920 U.S. Census, Costilla County, Colorado, Mesita, G.L. Allen and Frances.

424. *Fremont County Herald*, "Hamburg." 11 March 1920, p. 1.

425. Find A Grave, mem ID 8311440, George L. Allen (1849–1924), by "Graveaddiction."

426. *The Sidney Argus*, "Riverton-Golden Wedding Anniversary." July 1924, p. 26.

427. Find A Grave, mem ID 8311441, Frances Allen (1862–unk), by "Graveaddiction."

428. Find A Grave, mem ID 92331994, Frances Catlett (1862–1936), by "kweaver."

Emily Hope Dennison Morgan

429. 1900 U.S. Census, Fremont County Iowa, Madison, Emily Morgan, Ancestry.com.

430. 1910 U.S. Census, Fremont County Iowa, Hamburg, Emily Morgan, Ancestry.com.

431. 1920 U.S. Census, Fremont County Iowa, Hamburg, Emily Morgan and Whistler children, Ancestry.com.

432. Find A Grave, mem ID 7398375, Emily Dennison Morgan (1843–1923), by "Graveaddiction."

James Plumb Beach

433. 1870 U.S. Census, Fremont County, Madison, J.P. Beach,

434. 1870 U.S. Census, Fremont County, Madison, Finnell and J.P. Beach.

435. 1880 U.S. Census, Fremont County, Hamburg, J.P. Beach.

436. *San Diego Union and Daily Bee*, December 1892, J.P. Beach.

437. 1900 U.S. Census, Fremont County, Iowa, Hamburg, J.P. Beach.

438. 1900 U.S. Census, Glenn County, California, Township 2, James Finnell/Coleman Dalton.

439. *San Diego Union and Daily Bee*, "Hotel Arrivals." 14 December 1892, p. 7.

440. 1910 U.S. Census, Pottawattamie County, Iowa, Council Bluffs, J.P. Beach.

441. Find A Grave, mem ID 26955704, James P. Beach (1852–1939), by "Warren Cupples."

Abraham D. Swarts

442. 1880 U.S. Census, Locust Grove, Fremont County, Abraham Swarts.

443. 1885 U.S. Census, Locust Grove, Fremont County, Abraham Swarts.

444. 1900 U.S. Census, Los Angeles County, California, Los Angeles, Abraham Swarts.

445. 1910 U.S. Census, Los Angeles County, California, Imperial California, Abraham Swarts.

446. U.S., California, Santa Monica City Directory 1914, Abraham Swarts, Ancestry.com.

447. Meares, Hadley, "Ranch of Friends: The Extraordinary Evolution of the L.A. County Poor Farm, March 30, 2015, PBS SoCal, 2014, Last accessed 24 April 2025.

448. 1920 U.S. Census, Los Angeles County, California, Downey, Abraham Swarts.

449. 1920 U.S. Census, Los Angeles County, California, Los Angeles, Eunice Swarts.

450. California, U.S., Death Index 1905-1939, 19 August 1921, Abraham Swarts, Ancestry.com.

Deputy Coroner H. J. Stetson

451. *Daily Alta California,* "Another Half Interest Case." 31 March 1888.

452. *Daily Alta California*, "Superior Court Cases." 14 October 1890.

453. *San Diego Union and Daily Bee*, "Constable's Sale." 4 Jan 1893, p. 7.

454. 1900 U.S. Census, San Francisco County, California, San Francisco, Herbert J. Stetson.

455. 1910 U.S. Census, San Francisco County, California, San Francisco, Herbert J. Stetson.

456. *San Francisco Call*, "Tried by Church Woman Quits Fold." 12 February 1915, p. 17.

457. California, U.S. County Birth, Marriage, and Death Records, 1849-1980, Santa Rosa California, Herbert J. Stetson marriage to Lois Perry, 12 May 1919, Ancestry.com.

458. 1920 U.S. Census, Contra Costa County, California, Rodeo, Herbert Stetson.

459. 1930 U.S. Census, Placer County, California, Auburn, H.J. Stetson.

460. Find A Grave, mem ID 228549116, Herbert James Stetson (1866–1951), by "Michael Elaine Calvin-Salsbury."

Kathleen Kate Morgan nee Farmer

461. *The Fremont County Herald*, "Mrs. Samuels to go to California." 29 Dec. 1892, p. 4.

462. Hotel del Coronado Heritage Department, "Beautiful Stranger: The Ghost of Kate Morgan and the Hotel del Coronado" Coronado California, first printed and copyright 2002.

463. Find A Grave, mem ID 7966, Kate Kathleen "Katie" Farmer Morgan (1868–1892), by "Johnny History."

www.ingramcontent.com/pod-product-compliance
Lightning Source LLC
Chambersburg PA
CBHW060414130626
46555CB00005B/2067